Occasion, Chance
and Change

To Jane
With gratitude and love
from

Henry

Occasion, Chance and Change

A MEMOIR 1902-1946

Henry Colyton

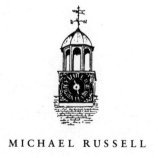

MICHAEL RUSSELL

© Henry Colyton 1993

First published in Great Britain 1993
by Michael Russell (Publishing) Ltd
Wilby Hall, Wilby, Norwich NR16 2JP

Typeset by The Typesetting Bureau
6 Church Street, Wimborne, Dorset
Printed and bound in Great Britain
by Biddles Ltd, Guildford and King's Lynn

ISBN 0 85955 198 9

For my beloved Barbara

Contents

I
Edwardian Dawn

My earliest recollection is of my brother Francis on the day of his christening. He was lying in his cot, an elaborate affair with a high pointed canopy at one end, all cream lace and satin. The room was bright, with a big window, and the sun was pouring in. The year was 1904, I was not quite three years old. At that time my father still owned the large and rather gloomy house at 78 Holland Park that my grandfather, General Henry Hopkinson, had bought on his return from India in the 1870s. He had had a distinguished career in the Indian Political Department, mostly in Burma and then the North East Frontier.

The house was crammed with nineteenth-century oil paintings, many of the Barbizon School. My grandfather had started collecting on his retirement with little knowledge of nineteenth-century art. This, reinforced by poor advice, led to his acquiring, at some expense, a collection of paintings of which many were not what they were supposed to be and even more of such slight interest that their authenticity or otherwise didn't matter anyway.

In our day the house had an Edwardian well-being about it, with a pleasant garden and a croquet lawn, but subsequently it fell on harder times, including a period as a shabby boarding-house. Then it was bought by King Fahd of Saudi Arabia. It has since been acquired by another rich Arab and has a formidable indoor heated swimming pool.

My father and mother were married at the close of Queen Victoria's reign. My mother was just twenty-two, more than twenty years younger than my father, very beautiful, with light brown hair, grey-blue eyes and an eighteen-inch waist. She was half-American, having been born in Waterbury, Connecticut, of a British father. For their honeymoon my parents first took the Orient Express to Constantinople, then returned by sea along the Mediterranean, with stops at Algiers, Biskra and Morocco. From there they crossed to

Spain, where they visited Madrid, and finally came down by rail to Gibraltar, where they hunted with the Spanish Royal Calpe foxhounds. Then they and the whole population of the little colony were thrown into the deepest black by the death of Queen Victoria.

I was born on 3 January 1902. My parents were keen to take me to the coronation of King Edward VII as a prelude to life. We had seats in the old Westminster Hospital stand at the west end of the Abbey, but we were thwarted by the inconvenient bursting of the King's appendix. Worse, when the coronation was eventually held I had just gone down with pneumonia. Not that I should have remembered anything of the ceremony, but nowadays merely as a non-memory it would be getting hard to match.

As a little boy my father had been brought up in Mandalay with the afterwards notorious King Thibau of Burma. At the age of six, as was usual, he was hustled home and deposited with a Montgomerie aunt on the Isle of Islay. There he learnt Gaelic and acquired a love of Scotland that he never lost. He had been destined for the Army but when his elder brother fatally broke his neck in Jamaica diving off another officer's shoulders into the sea, his parents deflected him into the law. It always struck me that it was an odd reason for suddenly supposing the Army, of all things, was too dangerous. There was in any case always a slightly military Anglo-Indian atmosphere at home with my father's love of spicy dishes and Worcester sauce and visits by relations old and young who could talk of their service in India. The 'Great Mutiny', when my great-aunt and her husband and children were all murdered at Cawnpore, still lingered in many memories. Later on, when we were settled down in the country, there would be visits from relations in the Army in India or in the Indian Civil Service. We three boys would be wide-eyed at our cousin's stories of pig-sticking near Meerut; then another showing us his sky-blue Bengal Lancer frock-coat with the blue and white turban, all ready for King George's coronation.

Soon after his marriage my father bought Duntisbourne House, near Cirencester. It was a solid eighteenth-century neo-Gothic house of Cotswold stone, built by the Pleydell family round the medieval shell of a summer retreat for the monks of Cirencester Abbey. Many of the older walls were five feet thick. It had big high rooms with long pointed windows. The rough stone circular stairway was said to date from the original monastic building. But the house's main attraction was its situation – on a Cotswold hilltop overlooking the Golden Valley which winds down to Stroud.

The small stream at the bottom, where we learned to tickle trout, was the boundary between my father's land and Lord Bathurst's extensive estate. The woods on either side were mostly beech and oak and in autumn the valley earned its name. Further along and oposite us, at about the same height, lay the village of Edgeworth with the woods running down to the stream on both sides. To Duntisbourne I owe the deep love of the countryside which has never deserted me.

My mother had very advanced ideas for that period about bringing up children and eventually wrote a book on the subject. Unlike most people of the day she actually believed that children should be with their parents as much as possible. So we had tea in the drawing room every day when they were at home and lunch in the dining room as soon as we learnt table manners. There was more to this than a mere way with the cutlery. It was forbidden, for instance, to talk about money at table or to comment on the food.

We were dressed in blue sailor suits and caps, with short trousers, and for special occasions a white linen outfit with a silver bosun's whistle and a black silk scarf in memory of Lord Nelson. But there were fewer restrictions on our activities, because my mother believed we should be allowed to develop our own tastes and interests. Consequently, though still under the watchful eyes of a nanny or governess, we were free to wander as we wished in the park and the adjoining beechwoods. Eventually we knew every inch.

Running a country property in those days – even a fairly modest one like my father's – was a considerable undertaking. There were ten servants living in the house, apart from nannies and later the governess: a butler and two footmen, a cook, a kitchen maid, a scullery maid, three housemaids and a French lady's maid for my mother. There was a coachman with two grooms in the stables, and further outside staff consisting of three gardeners, a gamekeeper, a cowman and a woodsman. They lived in cottages on the estate or in Duntisbourne village. In addition, there were seven farms, all let, with farmhouses and cottages. My father had no agent and liked to run everything himself. It was quite a task.

The servants were our great friends. We spent hours listening to their stories and interfering with their work. Camps, the butler, was our favourite. He loved children and he loved talking. He also liked being diverted from his main job. From him we learnt how to play cricket and to mend punctures on our bicycles. He initiated us into the elements of engineering and carpentry, and helped us in the construction of quite a solid house on the lower boughs of a tall chestnut tree.

One of the under-gardeners, Juggins, was also a special friend. He pandered to our relentless demands for help – warding off bumble bees, rescuing us from the stinging nettles, repairing the seesaw. Alas, he was taken very ill and we insisted on visiting him at his cottage on the outskirts of the village. Each time he looked thinner and thinner. We did not know it but he had terminal cancer. It was the first time we came face to face with death.

Rollins the cowman taught us how to milk the three Jersey cows that supplied the house and staff. He was also our authority on poultry. We collected the eggs and learnt all about broodies and incubators, buff Orpingtons, white Wyandottes and Indian game fowl. With Short the gamekeeper we inspected the hundreds of pheasant and partridge chicks being reared for the shoot. We also visited with suitable horror the keeper's larder where a long line of marauders – hawks, magpies, jays, weasels and stoats – were strung up on a wire with bleak severity on the path to Thick Wood as a warning to others. Here it was, too, that the carcase of a fox was found – shot and thrown over to our side of the boundary by the keeper of a neighbour, Mr Wills of Miserden Park. It infuriated Short and horrified my father.

We accompanied Butt the woodman at a safe distance when they were tree-felling, coming in to inspect the results when the trunks were down and the foliage and branches burning. About 1908 some timber had been felled in the back drive and there was a good bonfire going from the brushwood. We were taken there for a picnic lunch and supplied with potatoes to put in the hot ashes, unconscious of the fact that the fire had been built almost on top of a wasps' nest. Suddenly they swarmed into the attack and we were carried screaming to the nearby lodge. We had twenty stings between us. We were put in a darkened spare room and blue was applied. It was a good lesson.

Finally there was Budd the coachman. He was a tubby figure, but magnificent on the box of the brougham or the victoria in his dark green frock coat, top-boots, white breeches and top hat. In winter he wore a black bearskin cape which came down to his hips. He drove the two large bay carriage horses and generally supervised the stables, though the care of my father's hunters was left to the head groom. About the same time as our adventure with the wasps, my parents were making a croquet lawn just below a bank leading down from a gravel path to the little road down the valley. In the course of the work some human bones and a skull were turned up, which were left lying on a heap of earth. Shortly afterwards the household suffered a succession of mishaps: I went down with scarlet fever; then the kitchen chimney caught fire and someone had to ride into Cirencester to summon the fire brigade; finally my father developed serious pneumonia and was not expected to live. There was some old story that the path was haunted by the ghost of the builder of the house, Sir Mark Pleydell, who it was said frequented the path beside the new croquet lawn, carrying his head under his arm. The suggestion now was that the unearthed skull was one and the same as the detached item carried by Sir Mark's ghost. When it was reburied, things started immediately to improve. My mother was paying a visit in the village and when she got up to leave, her hostess said, 'Oh, Mrs Hopkinson, how glad we were to hear that all is going well at the manor now that Sir Mark's bones have been reburied.'

Several years later my brothers and I and our governess were walking down that same walk under the beech trees on our way to the stream to fish. To our astonishment an enormous bird with a wicked curling beak flew over just a few feet above our heads. We were much excited and reported back to our parents. Nobody knew what it was. The next week the local newspaper wrote that a white sea eagle had been seen in the valley and had later on been shot. It was a rare visitor to England. It may of course have been Sir Mark out to cause a little extra havoc in a different guise.

Later I became keen on farming and spent happy hours on the neighbouring farms haymaking or stooking corn sheaves at harvest time. We suffered from the attentions of the harvest bugs, minute red spiders which got under the skin and left a painful rash up arms and legs that was treated with sulphur ointment. The red wooden threshing machines were belt-operated by a traction engine with a tall brass-topped chimney, like the ones on the bigger estates that hauled the heavy ploughs back and forth. On Lord Bathurst's land next door, ploughing was also still done by teams of oxen – ten beautiful brown and white Herefords, a lovely sight.

Cirencester, still pronounced 'Ciceter', as spelt in Shakespeare, was our shopping town, and very attractive it was with the old parish church in the market place with its high tower, the classic mansion of the Bathurst family half in and half out of the town and the wonderful Roman museum. 'Corinium' had been the second largest town in Roman Britain and there is an old saying 'Scratch Gloucestershire and you will find Rome'.

Our shopping was comparatively simple. Sundries all came out from Cirencester by carrier twice a week. At the lodge he blew a hunting horn and someone walked up to fetch them. The butcher and the grocer delivered. Mr Knowlson the barber walked out the five miles once a month to cut our hair. The postman in his Victorian shako walked out every morning in winter and bicycled in summer. There was no electricity in the house and we depended for light on oil lamps and candles except for gas brackets downstairs with tubes running through some of the walls. They came from an acetylene plant with piles of white sour-smelling lime in some disused seventeenth-century stables down below the house. The system was rightly regarded as highly dangerous. There was only one bathroom and of course no central heating. The bedroom fires were lit at seven each morning by a little maid.

We boys were fiercely anti-social and resented all visits to or from our neighbours, although we were prised out for the big Christmas parties. But most of the year we lived in the woods in a fairy world of our own, ruled by its animal king and his consort and attended by the rest of the court. We were three chivalrous knights on chargers ready to defend them and their honour against all-comers. Since, in the privacy of our world, enemies were of our own invention they had little chance of getting the better of us.

Occasionally we were taken as a treat to Cheltenham, where we admired the Georgian terraces, or to Gloucester. Birdlip Hill was much too steep for either the horses or the car, so we had to descend to the sharp turn on the Cheltenham road at the Fire Balloon public house. In Gloucester Cathedral I came across one of my heroes, Robert of Normandy, lying on his tomb with legs crossed as a symbol of his part in the Crusades. We also went into Gloucester for the

Royal Show in 1908. We saw King Edward VII for the first and only time from the window of our rented room over a shop, driving in an open carriage to declare the proceedings open. We also ate the first bananas of our lives.

At Christmas came the usual celebrations. First we helped stir the plum pudding in October in the big kitchen. In those days it was still full of threepenny bits, silver bells, and other small objects equally easy for children to swallow. Then, at Christmas itself, there was first the hanging of the stockings beside the bedroom fireplace and the vain attempt to keep awake. Then the weight of the stockings across one's legs early in the morning, and later the church full of holly and the house the same. At teatime the moment of excitement when from the terrace outside the drawing room in came Camps, suitably robed and bearded and quite unrecognisable, to hand out the pile of presents from under the tree with its dangerous lighted candles. For years we were completely fooled. It may be one the tricks of nostalgia but a white Christmas seemed to be much more prevalent in those days. We built snowmen who lasted well into the New Year. We had no proper place to skate but occasionally ventured on to a filthy green frozen pond up by the cowsheds which at other times served to float my two-foot-long model of the new *Mauretania*. One day I filled it with a detachment of lead soldiers and it duly sank to the bottom like its real-life sister ship the *Lusitania*.

We had ponies at an early age and learned to ride. One was an iron-grey Dartmoor called Jerry who was inclined to shy, the other an Exmoor roan called Sammy whom we all liked. At the age of six I was taken out cub-hunting by a groom with a leading rein. It was at a met of the V.W.H., Lord Bathurst's, hounds at Overley Lodge in Cirencester Park, about a mile from my home. It was a beautiful, slightly frosty day, with every twig sparkling in the early morning sunshine. The scarlet coats of the hunt servants, the jostling of the big hunters and their riders; the occasional blast on the horn; and then at last a fox and everyone moving off together down a ride. It was a scene that stayed with me all my life.

Fox-hunting played a big part in our lives. My father kept four or five hunters and went out three or even four days a week, generally with a second horseman. Getting him ready for a day's hunting was quite a performance. The red coat almost always had to be thoroughly scrubbed; the white soft leather breeches were pipe-clayed by a footman and the Krupp leather boots made by Peal had pink soft leather tops which also had to be carefully pipe-clayed. The silk top hat had to be ironed.

To our children's eyes my father thus clad was a splendid sight. He was of medium height and though already fifty had a slim figure. He had good features and a short Roman nose. His eyes were blue, his hair had turned grey early – a feature I inherited in due course. He had a particularly sweet smile and a nice sense of the ridiculous. He was of gentle character but strong convictions. He was much loved in the village.

My mother also rode to hounds but she was always nervous and never really enjoyed it. She rode side-saddle and in her top hat and veil and her dark habit made by Busvine, with a small bunch of violets in her buttonhole, she was a sight for sore eyes. She made many conquests in the hunting field. Unfortunately one morning at home when she had just mounted, her horse, a tall black gelding called Blackamoor, took fright at something and to our horror reared up and went over backwards. If she had not managed to slide quickly out from behind the pommel he would have come down on her. She never rode again.

I have often thought that this was a turning point in her life. She lost her some of her zest for the country and entered a state which later bordered on melancholia and culminated in our leaving Duntisbourne for good in 1916, to the deep distress of my father, my brothers and myself. This is not to say that she was inactive. There was a regular programme of country social life, with its shooting parties, hunt balls, garden parties and outdoor games. She was a first class croquet player and later won tournaments at Ranelagh and Hurlingham. She taught me how to play and it became a game at which I have always done well.

She also embarked on building a stone balustrade terrace and steps to a new rose garden overlooking the valley. During the excavations they discovered a deep well and a small chamber with an underground passage leading out of it down towards the stream, where it became blocked. No one knew its origin but it was reputed to have led to Pimbury Park on the other side of the valley, which before the Reformation was the summer rest house of the nuns from the convent in Cirencester. Honi soit qui mal y pense!

[8]

My mother came from an old Huguenot family which after the Revocation of the Edict of Nantes had emigrated to Holland and thence to America. The first to arrive there was Dominie Gualterius Du Bois, a famous character, pastor of the First Dutch Reformed Church of New York from 1699 till his death in 1752. One son, John, had moved to North Carolina where he became a planter and a Tory. He fought on the British side in the Revolutionary War and his large properties were confiscated. He left the country and was duly compensated by Parliament; then, after a period of wandering about the world, he recrossed the Atlantic and became a sugar planter in Tortola in the British Virgin Islands.

My Du Bois grandfather was apparently a most attractive man, but very wild. As a youngster he had run away from home, by then in St Croix in the Danish Virgin Islands. After various adventures, including a spell in the American Navy, he married my grandmother, a girl from Waterbury, Connecticut. My mother's youth was unhappy. After their marriage her parents went to live in Montclair, New Jersey, where they led a comfortable country life. My grandfather, however, had a roving eye and soon became heavily involved elsewhere, later deserting my grandmother altogether. She died quite soon afterwards. My mother was adopted by her aunt whose husband, a keen sportsman, spent a good deal of time shooting in Europe, especially Austria and England.

With my mother's help I started to learn to read and write at the age of four. My textbook was, not surprisngly, *Reading without Tears* and by the end of the year I was sufficiently advanced to cope with *Strewelpeter* and other favourites of the period. From there we passed rapidly to *Our Island Story* and simplified editions of Spenser's *Faerie Queen* and the glories of Sir Walter Scott. Along the way I acquired my lifelong love of history. The English Civil War fascinated me. Though a Hopkinson ancestor was waggon master general of the Northern Association of the Parliamentary forces, Charles I became my hero. I remember at the age of nine insisting on going to our children's fancy dress ball in a magnificent Cavalier outfit copied from a Vandyck portrait.

My mother was determined that we should become fluent French speakers. She had a French maid called Louise who was with us for many years. It was laid down that nothing but French was to be spoken, first in the day nursery and later the school room. After a couple of years my brother John and I were bilingual, with my younger brother Francis not far behind. In due course we had a French governess who introduced us to our earliest studies of French literature, starting with *Les Malheurs de Sophie* and *Les Petites Filles Modèles*, whose trials and tribulations we followed with sympathy.

I can never be too grateful to my mother for her absolute insistence on our keeping strictly to this course. A good knowledge and practice of French followed by other foreign languages can open so many doors to enjoyment and friendship. That I had a knack with languages may have been something to do with genetics, for my Hopkinson grandfather, who was educated at the Collège de Ménars near Blois, afterwards spoke seven languages, four of them oriental. So French, the most beautiful of all, seemed to come very easily to me, though I had to work hard at it later on to pass the stiff dilomatic exam of those days.

Outside the school room my parents found my behaviour a little difficult. Undoubtedly a great nuisance, I was the ringleader in most of our escapades, always ready to take risks – sliding down a quarry, raiding a high bird's nest, duelling with my brother John on a sloping stable roof. I could hardly be surprised when at the age of seven I was informed that I was too old for a governess and was to go to a boarding school. It was about a hundred miles away, in Hove. It was called Belvedere.

In September I was driven there in the 'motor', as it was called, with my father and mother, a day's journey. On the luggage rack was my small trunk and an iron-bound playbox. I said a tearful farewell. On arrival my allowance – five golden sovereigns – was removed and held in a sort of bank from which we were doled out a few shillings on Saturdays.

We were about forty boys in all. We new boys were shown our dormitory, each with our own cubicle with varnished wood partitions. After a meagre supper we went to bed. I had a photograph of my mother in a leather frame. Clutching it to me, I cried myself to sleep.

I was homesick, but I gradually got used to a cold new world. It was not so bad. I managed the work and enjoyed the games. I was even plunged, a little improbably, into politics. It was 1909 and the Liberal government with Lloyd George in the van was launching fresh assaults on dukes, hand-reared pheasants and private incomes.

I suppose I was a ready-made Conservative, or Unionist as it was then called; but then, with one exception, so was the whole school. The boy who had the cubicle opposite mine. Michael Majolier, came from a Quaker Franco-Irish family living in Congenies in the Midi – a strange combination. He called himself a Radical, whether from conviction or perverseness I'm not sure; anyway he had a rotten time.

Things came to a head the following year with the rejection by the House of Lords of Lloyd George's budget and the 1910 General Election. We all had blue rosettes – except Majolier, who wore the purple and orange of the Liberals. On Guy Fawkes Day, with great enthusiasm, we burnt Lloyd George in effigy on a bonfire on the football ground. In spite of all our efforts the Liberals were returned to power, though with a reduced majority.

Each weekly letter home ended with a sentence giving the exact number of days remaining until the holidays. Once home I returned to the routine pleasures of life at Duntisbourne: hunting, ferreting rabbits, croquet, occasional shoots, and sometimes the meets of the Royal Agricultural College beagles. But there was a new joy – polo. Then, as now, polo was played regularly in Cirencester Park during the summer months, and as the ground was barely three miles away my father often took us there in the four-wheel dogcart. I don't think we quite understood all the niceties of the game, but at the end of each match there were always two or three white bamboo balls, bruised and a little out of shape, lying outside the boards for anyone to take. No wonder we and other small boys helped ourselves. By happy coincidence my brother John and I had just acquired our first bicycles, and in the oval forecourt at Duntisbourne, with its natural goalmouths at either end, we found the perfect bicycle polo ground. My parents were dismayed but decided to take a chance and let us play. It was a perfect distraction for several years.

Our visits to London were usually for such uninviting reasons as dentist's appointments. We generally stayed with our parents at the Coburg Hotel – this was before we acquired a long lease on a nice eighteenth-century house in Sloane Street which my mother redecorated and furnished beautifully.

When King Edward VII died in 1910 the whole country went into mourning and the newspapers came out with heavy black borders. For three days his body lay in state in Westminster Abbey;

thousands and thousands trailed past it. We were given a day off from Belvedere and my parents took us to watch the procession on its way to Paddington Station, en route for Windsor and the funeral in St George's Chapel. Nine monarchs rode in the procession, from the Kaiser (dressed as a British field-marshal) to the boy King Manuel of Portugal, soon to lose his throne through the revolution. The boy Emperor of China sent a prince to represent him. It was the last great state funeral of the old Europe. The Hotel Coburg would before too long be renamed the Connaught and the Kaiser would be talking about England's 'contemptible little army'.

It was Louis Blériot and his competitor Latham who first aroused my passion for aviation. In July 1909 Blériot had flown the Channel in a monoplane of his own design. There was a neck-and-neck contest between him and our favourite, the dashing Monsieur Latham in his Antoinette. Twice Latham got half way across and twice he finished up in the sea. He was rescued sitting calmly on one of the wings with a cigarette dangling from his lips.

So my pleasure can be imagined when the following year I heard that Gustav Hamel, the famous young aviator, was due to arrive in Brighton. He also flew a Blériot monoplane and he landed on a long strip of turf in Hove adjoining the Esplanade where the iron railings had been removed. I and several other boys went down with one of the masters to watch his arrival. There was a large crowd, but the master obviously had some trump up his sleeve because we were introduced to Hamel and allowed to inspect his machine. I was even permitted to sit in the pilot's seat, which was surprisingly lined with quilted scarlet leather. Hamel himself was lost, shortly before the outbreak of war, on a crossing from Paris to Hendon in a new Morane-Saulnier. Although he was by nationality a Swede, he had Teutonic connections and an unlikely rumour was started that he was a German spy.

Meanwhile the political battle continued with the Liberal government determined to cut down the power of the House of Lords to veto legislation. A second election was held on this specific issue and the government was returned with a much smaller majority; they were only kept in power by the Irish Nationalists and the few Labour members. The new king, George V, much troubled, had been persuaded by Asquith to agree to create if necessary enough peers to carry it through. The Parliament Bill wound its way through both

Houses and until the last moment the issue was still unresolved. Finally the diehards and last-ditch 'backwoodsmen' in the Lords, summoned from their country seats to oppose the bill, gave way and it became law. My parents, though staunch Conservatives, breathed again.

For George V's coronation we stayed at my American aunt's flat in South Street. Curiously, I have not much recollection of the procession other than the gold coach with its eight Hanover cream horses (which were given up during the Great War as too Germanic) and Queen Mary, very straight and tall in her crown, towering over King George at her side. However, I also clearly remember having my first boxed lunch in the stand at the old Westminster Hospital.

In 1908 my father had bought a 1908 20-30 h.p. Renault limousine, with the body painted in green and black vertical stripes in the French fashion. There were no doors in front and little protection of any kind for the chauffeur and the outside passenger. It had two large brass acetylene detachable lamps, each with its own leather cover, and there was a brass whistle at the end of the exhaust pipe which had not yet been declared illegal. It also had a big clanking gearbox, also brass, outside the driver's seat. I learnt to drive on it twelve years later.

We had been sent an open model of the car to try and my father had us driven down the steep hill to the stream at the bottom of the valley. There we turned round and prepared to climb back. No go. The petrol feed was at the back and not a trickle came through. The salesman promptly turned the car round again and we backed solemnly up for a quarter of a mile without mishap.

In January 1911 John joined me at Belvedere but, although we did not know it, plans were already afoot to send us somewhere else in the autumn where we would have more scope. This was Cheam School, and it was not a success. We hated it from the beginning and in every way. My parents agreed with us and we moved to Farnborough School in Hampshire. It had every sort of attraction, including a large piece of land, approached through a tunnel, that adjoined the Royal Aircraft Factory. We could see the great airship sheds beside the hangars of the newly formed Royal Flying Corps. The land also provided us with a nine-hole golf course and wonderful cover for camps and hiding places. I spent two happy years there and revelled in the aerial goings on next door. One day on the golf course a single-seater Army biplane crashed quite close by and I was able to pull the dazed pilot out of his seat. Then, when Colonel Cody, the famous American aviator, brought his new machine over from America, he came to give us a lecture on flying. Just a week later he was killed in a crash on Laffan's Plain.

My father had always taken an interest in different charities in London, which he kept up even after we had moved to Duntisbourne. As Master of the Merchant Taylors' Company he had to attend the state funeral in St Paul's Cathedral of the policemen who lost their lives in the Sidney Street siege in 1911 of Peter the Painter and his anarchists. He took me with him. It was my first such occasion and I was very moved by the three polished coffins in front of the altar. Afterwards we went across to Pym's Restaurant in Threadneedle Street and I was given my first oysters. They remained a more congenial memory than the solemn ceremony up the street.

In the same capacity my father also had to attend the coronation service in Westminster Abbey of King George V. He was also on the Council of the Royal Albert Hall, to which my grandfather had been an original subscriber. Later on he was asked to become honorary treasurer, which was a royal appointment and eventually no doubt led to his receiving a KCVO in the year of his death in 1936.

At school my brother and I were much preoccupied with entomology. We had a base in the rhododendrons, over which for some curious reason we flew the royal standard of Scotland, and from there we enlarged our butterfly collection. We also launched out into moths and captured numbers of great hawks, puss moths, death's heads and other species. We had killing bottles with lumps of raw cyanide capable of disposing of a dozen people. It seems amazingly hazardous equipment to be under the control of young boys but luckily we caused no casualties among the human population. We also bred silkworms, which we fed on mulberry leaves and in due course we produced some reels of lemon-coloured silk.

The teaching at Farnborough was good and when the time came for me to take the common entrance examination for Eton in the summer of 1914, I did quite well. I was also top of the school in French and according to custom was invited to take tea with the Empress Eugénie. The headmaster, who was a friend of hers, came too. The Empress lived nearby in the convent she had built to the memory of her husband, the Emperor Napoleon III. She was then very old and dressed all in black, but I remember her as being strikingly beautiful. When we had finished tea she asked one of the nuns to show us the chapel where the Emperor and his son, the Prince Imperial, were buried. The prince had been killed fighting with British troops in Zululand. I never saw her again, though she lived on until the 1920s having had the joy of seeing the honour and glory of France fully redeemed.

Europe was by now full of rumours of war with Germany. We had lectures about it, we read Lord Roberts's speeches, we all supported the Navy League. On 28 June came the news of the assassination at Sarajevo. Remembering the newspaper reports of the recent Balkan Wars, I fatuously observed to the headmaster as the crisis got worse that at least we should have a lot of exciting newspaper stories to read at breakfast time. He rounded on me furiously and said it could be the worst catastrophe the world had ever known. I was duly chastened.

Towards the end of July 1914 the Annual Military Review was held at Aldershot. Sitting at my bedroom window I could hear them marching off parade to the tune of Sousa's 'Stars and Stripes for Ever'. I supposed that was how they would be going into battle. I was very much mistaken.

2

Wartime Eton

The suspense did not last long. On 1 August the Imperial German Army invaded France and Belgium and three days later Great Britain declared war. We were at Duntisbourne for the summer holidays. There was no telephone and my father took up a scheme by *The Times* to send us bulletins of important war news by telegram. He also bought a machine called the 'Autowheel' for Camps to ride into Cirencester for news each day. This was a small wheel combining a little engine which was attached to the back axle of the bicycle. The Autowheel and Camps didn't take to each other and after a short time, to my delight, the machine was handed over to me for use in the grounds.

It was my first personal introduction to the internal combustion engine. Later on, at Eton, when I was about fourteen (then the minimum age for a motor-cycle licence), I saw an advertisement in the stationers' window for a motor-cycle for sale for £2. It seemed too good to be true. 'Apply Vickers at Brinton's', the advertisement said. He turned out to be a member of the famous engineering family. He took me to his housemaster's stables and there on the floor were the frame and – all in bits – the whole of the insides of a small four-stroke Belgian F. N. I decided to have a go, paid him the £2 and tackled my purchase on the stable floor. With no real mechanical knowledge I gradually put it together like a jigsaw puzzle. It worked. I painted it primrose yellow, opted for discretion and sold it. With the proceeds I bought a fairly battered but powerful Red Indian two-cylinder model, for which I built a self-designed sidecar of aeroplane wing material, doped and painted red with a copper nose. I was immensely proud of it.

For us life continued much as usual, though my father gave all his hunters to the Army remount service, followed by the carriage horses, leaving us with an old grey mare for the trap and my own pony. Along with the other younger members of the male staff, the chauffeur joined up, and his place was taken after a while by a bearded French civilian refugee who startled us and the villagers by trying to take corners on two wheels.

We followed the war news eagerly, but with increasing gloom as the initial advance was followed by retreat. When the wind was right we could hear the heavy guns in Flanders. I kept a war diary and pasted in photographs as they appeared. The British troops all wore khaki, but many French units were still in the dark blue coats and scarlet trousers of their peacetime uniforms. In one engagement the Cuirassiers were pictured in a charge wearing their heavy steel breastplates and silver helmets. But all was in vain. Little by little the line drew back until almost the whole of Belgium was occupied. Finally Paris was directly threatened, only saved by the miracle of the Marne when the Paris buses and taxis brought up the reinforcements which saved the day. Our great hero, however, was the Belgian burgomaster Max, who defied the Germans in Brussels.

In the third week of September I went to Eton. My parents accompanied me. My housemaster was A. B. Ramsay, a bachelor and distinguished classicist who was later to become Master of Magdalene College, Cambridge. He was a well-covered, pink-faced man with a silky grey moustache and a considerable knowledge of port. We had a brief talk, he introduced me to his sister, who kept house, and to his red and grey parrot.

After being shown my room, I went with my parents to have a cup of tea at one of the school's two 'sock-shops'. We found ourselves next to a family from Norfolk whose son, Bill Carr, was later to have a distinguished career in the 12th Lancers and commanded the 4th Armoured Brigade at Alamein. He was also at Ramsay's and we struck up a friendship that lasted both our lives.

Scholastically in those days Eton was divided vertically into forms, or 'divisions', for classics, and horizontally for other subjects. My favourite subjects were French and history, and I always had trouble with maths, not helped by the fact that the lower divisions had a tendency to get out of hand. One of the worst offenders in my maths division was the future Earl De La Warr, who years later become a close friend. Again and again he was on his feet with the unhappy master shouting, 'Buckhurst' – the De La Warr courtesy title and his name at the time – 'will you sit down!' He had good dissentient blood in his veins, his mother having been a prominent suffragette. When his time for call-up came in 1918, he joined the Navy but refused to serve in anything but a minesweeper as being against his principles. He had succeeded his father in 1915. When the General Election came in 1918 the voting age for the House of Commons was lowered to eighteen to cover servicemen. This right was not extended to members of the House of Lords, who could not sit before they were twenty-one. Buck, in his able-bodied seaman's uniform, rose in protest from the steps of the throne where he was sitting and started to harangue the House. He was soon bundled out. Later he became a Cabinet minister in both Labour and Conservative governments.

I was lucky with my division masters. One was C. H. K. Marten, historian and later Provost of Eton. Dr Gray, a chemist who had pioneered mustard gas, oversaw my disastrous endeavour, in my eagerness to get into the Royal Flying Corps, to become a science specialist. There was also a Frenchman called de Satgé who was credited with having swum the Rhine in the 1870 Franco-Prussian War with his dispatches in his mouth. Almost any school could devise such a delicious fiction, but only at Eton would it turn out to be true. M. de Satgé ran into slight problems of national supremacy when confronted with the obstreperous Prince Leopold of the Belgians, one of a group of refugee Belgians in the school, two of them in my house.

Life in wartime soon became very Spartan. Although in my first half (or term) the food was luxurious and at boys' dinner at midday we had the choice of beer, cider, ginger beer or lemonade, it soon came down to plain water. Thanks to the U-boat campaign we became desperately short of meat, eggs and butter. I remember in 1917 some dreadful stuff called 'potato butter', made up out of a little margarine and a lot of potato flour. We each had our own room but there was of course no central heating and we were allowed one scuttle of coal to last a week.

In 1915 I was taken acutely ill with appendicitis. An urgent operation was called for and my mother came down in a car to take me to London. At the Fitzroy Nursing Home, Sir John Bland Sutton, a leading surgeon, operated on me the next day. All went well and I left with my appendix in a bottle of alcohol which I proudly displayed on my return to Eton. I had also, incidentally, witnessed one of the first Zeppelin raids, wheeled over to my window by excited night nurses to see a long silver sausage picked out by the searchlights. But while Sir John had been sure of his target, he turned out to have been a little cavalier over the route. He had cut through my tummy muscle instead of pushing it aside. This left a weak spot which in a short time turned into a hernia, and I was forced to lay off games and wear a truss.

So unschoolboyish a situation in a world where games were all-important was doubly unfortunate. I was shy by nature, apallingly self-conscious, a bit of a loner. Though I enjoyed life, I was highly sensitive to the opinions of others. The gods must have kept me in mind, however, as towards the end of my school career I emerged, quite fortuitously, as a minor sporting hero.

In the summer you either played cricket or you rowed. Following my father's example at Cambridge I became a 'wetbob'. To do so one had first to 'pass' in swimming, which took place on a cold October day in a backwater of the Thames called Cuckoo Weir. Some fifteen small boys sat stripped and shivering on the sides of a punt moored in midstream. The temperature of the water was forty-seven degrees and it was like waiting for the guillotine.

Once I was over my abdominal setback I eventually got into the Boats, ending up as ninth man of the *Monarch*, an ancient clinker-built ten-oar boat reserved only for the Fourth of June celebrations. As such I was responsible for starting and supervising most of the races and entitled to use a bicycle – on the face of it hardly a luxury, but one of the pleasantly absurd nuances of school hierarchy.

I was at 'Rafts', about to coach a house four, when I saw a man in Air Force uniform photographing his wife and children as they prepared to go out in a skiff. He backed steadily away to bring his camera into focus until the moment came when he disappeared backwards into the river. His wife, in a state of consternation, called out that he couldn't swim, so I took off my coat and dived in. I soon found him and managed to get him to the surface. But the Thames flows strongly at Windsor and as I held him up we were carried rapidly down river as far as the bridge, with the weir looming ominously ahead on the other side. I was wondering in some alarm how to deal with this situation when a dinghy was rowed out just under the bridge and we managed to get him on board. For this I was given the Royal Humane Society award, which to my great embarrassment was presented to me by the Head Master at a ceremony of the school elite.

Life at Eton was heavily scored by the progress of the war. There was an intercession service held every Wednesday in College Chapel after supper. At the end of the service came the reading of the list of Old Etonians killed during the previous week – boys one had known and seen daily only a few months before. Then the national anthems of the Allies were played. We sang the 'Marseillaise', the Belgian 'Brabançonne', 'God Save Our Noble Tsar', and of course 'God Save the King'. In 1915 the 'Marcha Reale' of Italy was added and finally 'The Star-Spangled Banner'. Of the 4,852 Etonians who served overseas in the war, more than half were either killed (1,157) or wounded (1,467). These terrible statistics bore in on us week by week, a whole generation bleeding away. Yet the effect on most boys was to hope the time would soon come for their own call up.

I had a friend at Ramsay's called Tan Butt-Miller, a fellow Gloucestershire boy, from Kingscote near Tetbury. After the Somme we became more and more affected by the losses on the battlefields and wanted desperately to take an active part ourselves. We read in the papers that the new Royal Tank Corps with their headquarters at Bedford were taking volunteers at the age of sixteen. He already qualified in age and we thought that I, though a year younger, could pass muster. In the autumn we decided to run away and join up.

We made our plans carefully. We raised enough money for the journey, checked the ABC railway timetable, got together the right clothes and, sure that we looked the part, set out after supper one evening about ten o'clock. We carried two large kitbags and after climbing out of Tan's first-floor window into a yard and over a gate we started to walk to Slough. All went well until we got to the dimly lit station. We booked our tickets to Bedford via London and went on to the platform. It was practically empty and we waited for our train full of hope. Then fate intervened in the person of PC Pheasant of the Buckinghamshire Police. Strolling along the platform he passed us and then turned to take a second look. He came back towards us and asked us where we were going. We explained our purpose but he continued to question us and asked for written proof. Finally the truth came out. He was extremely nice but insisted we should return with him to Eton in a taxi to report to our housemaster. When we arrived back ignominiously, Mr Ramsay was aroused and we were sent to bed to await our fate the next day. We expected at least a flogging and possibly expulsion, but when we were summoned before the Head Master, Dr Alington, he said he was not going to punish us. He respected our motives but obviously the school could not allow such adventures. Not a word was ever heard of the incident either from official sources or from other boys.

I had another wartime adventure which was more successful. I had already developed a passion for aviation; I took in *The Aeroplane* and *Flight* weekly and was once severely tempted by an advertisement for an old Blériot monoplane for £65. Meanwhile the Australian Royal Flying Corps had taken over Rendcombe Park and built an aerodrome not far from Duntisbourne. I bicycled over in the summer holidays and, thanks to rather indifferent security, was able to get access to the flying field. There I met a young pilot called Needham who took a liking to me. He showed me his machine, a BE2C two-seater spotting plane. The next time I came over I persuaded him to take me for a flight. It was the highlight of my young life. I decided I must join the RFC as soon as I could and meanwhile kept in touch with my new friend. Early the following year I went over again and he agreed to give me another flight, this time in the new RU8 reconnaissance plane. I was well strapped in and we had another marvellous flight, finally looping the loop, then a fairly new manoeuvre and most exhilarating. Very soon his squadron went to the front and later I was distressed to hear that he had been shot down and killed in action.

Of course we all joined the Eton Officers' Training Corps. We wore uniforms of a peculiar pinkish-grey called Elcho tweed, which made us unpopular with other schools on field days or at camp in the summer. We were indifferent, for our own tight collars and Fox's Spiral Puttees were equally uncomfortable whatever the colour. We paraded one afternoon a week in all weathers under the lashing tongue of a Guards sergeant-major. Despite our heavy service boots and white string gloves we were purple with chilblains all the winter months.

When peace came we lined the route in Piccadilly just above the Ritz for the Victory Parade. Later on, but only as spectators, my brothers and I watched from my father's club when President Woodrow Wilson made his state drive through London in an open carriage. Opposite us in Cockspur Street there was a mounted statue of George III and we were delighted to find an American sailor in his white cap sitting behind with his arms round the old 'tyrant's' waist.

My father had sold Duntisbourne unbeknown to us and in the spring of 1916 we learned we were going to move to the new house in Sloane Street. It was what my mother wanted. For us boys, and I think especially for me, it was sheer tragedy. I never quite got over it; I felt lost – my roots gone. London was so very different from the city of today. Many of the streets were paved with wooden bricks. Hyde Park was full of sheep, and there were still many hansom cabs and four-wheelers with straw on the floor. The taxis were landaulettes with a hood that opened over the back seat. Buses were still privately owned and you had the blue Union, the White Steam Car and several others besides the scarlet General. The seats on top were always open to the air.

We went to plays, museums, galleries; we walked or rode in Hyde Park. One Sunday, in 1916, I was walking along Rotten Row with my parents, watching the riders, when we saw a tall figure in a white tunic and crimson breeches and a high gold and white cap. He was a Russian Chevalier Garde officer and he was having trouble with his horse. Suddenly it took control and jumped the railing into the crowd. People collapsed, screaming, all around us.

In the winter holidays we went to see Ethel Levy in *Hello Tango* at the Metropole; George Robey with Leslie Henson in *The Bing Boys*. Basil Hallam, the music hall dancer, was 'Gilbert the Filbert, the Kernel of the Knuts' at the Palace. He left soon after to join the Balloon Section of the Royal Flying Corps as an observer and met with a macabre death. His balloon was shot down and fell in the mule-lines where, so it was said, he was kicked to death by the frightened animals.

Most of us had very small allowances at school and lived on tick. There were some boys, however, who were financially rather more flamboyant. One was Jock Buchanan-Jardine. He was the head of a small group of us who loved animals and kept a selection of them at the Science Schools, looked after by the devoted attendant Mr Pendry. We gathered there after 'twelve'; there were rabbits, guinea pigs, rats and mice, a few ferrets and the occasional snake. Jock had a large polecat with an abominable smell which had been found wild as a baby at his home at Castle Milk in Dumfriesshire. I had a small stud of mice – white, silver, gold, cinnamon, and Dutch black and white. I was very proud of them and kept a stud book. It was good and prolific instruction, in cameo, of the facts of life. I also had a pet white rat which I kept in my leather top-hat case in my room. It seemed very happy there and was never discovered. I took it out in an inside pocket of my tailcoat from time to time and on one alarming occasion it got loose in College Chapel during the service. There was a lot of anxious whispering along the row but eventually it found its way back to me.

I made many friends both inside and outside my house, though never really intimate ones. There was a custom for the housemaster to go round the house each evening after prayers and have a few words with every boy in turn. 'The Ram' often brought an old boy or another of his dinner guests with him. I well remember one night a young Grenadier officer back wounded from the trenches in 1916. His name was Harold Macmillan and our paths were often to cross in future years. Much later we became good friends even though I was not to see eye to eye with him over the 'winds of change' in Africa. I thought the whole performance was far too rapid for the good of the inhabitants and democracy – and so indeed it proved to be.

On Sundays we had a long 'lie in' – at least it seemed so to us with our rather Spartan programme – until eight o'clock, with chapel morning and evening but otherwise a free day. No games were allowed and so we often walked up to Windsor Castle in the afternoons. Once at least I climbed the seemingly endless steps to the battlements. The State Apartments were closed in wartime, but the North Terrace was a beautiful place from which to survey the surrounding country. On the right of the little street leading to the Castle main gates there were a few small shops. One of them sold delicious chocolates with rose or violet interiors. They were made by two sweet old French ladies whose parents had actually fled from Paris as émigrés during the Revolution.

Sometimes we would walk up to the Copper Horse in Windsor Park, where George III sits on his horse in Roman attire with bare legs dangling without stirrups. The park in those days was still full of wild red deer. On a cold autumn afternoon it was wonderful to watch the rutting stags charging each other, darting and clashing their antlers, while the female deer, in groups, watched the proceedings discreetly through the mist.

I had developed a passionate interest in arms and armour. Collecting was way beyond my means, so I contented myself with visits to the Tower of London, the Wallace Collection and, later, the great arms collections of France and Germany. I also had the luck to find three early spurs in an antique shop in Windsor for a few shillings each. This led to the start of a spurs collection which was pretty comprehensive – from a Norman prick-spur down through the fierce long-necked rowel spurs of the tournaments to little Regency racing spurs and a pair of swan-necked Household Cavalry spurs worn at Waterloo. I was much indebted to the classic reference book on the subject by de Lacey-Lacey. I mounted my collection in a glass-framed cabinet and much later lent it for some years to the Museum of Fine Arts in Birmingham. I was told it was one of the best collectios in England. Later I sold it when I was short of cash.

My female acquaintances up till the war were limited to the rector's two daughters at home, with whom we played tennis. They were not conspicuously beautiful. At Eton after a year or so I was gradually more adventurous. Miss Lily Elsie, the star of *The Merry Widow*, was married to Ian Bullough, the half-brother of a boy at my house. She came down to see him several times. I became infatuated and carried a little photograph of her in my breast pocket for ages. There were also girls up from Gloucestershire from time to time and pretty sisters of other boys who came to tea with me. Later I acquired an actress friend, Nora Swinburne, who occasionally came down from London to make me feel grand. Then towards the end of my time I had a close friendship with a very pretty girl who worked in a shop in the town. As for homosexuality, of course it existed at Eton but not, at least in our house, to any very noticeable extent. I think it depended entirely on the housemaster's vigilance.

When the Armistice came I found myself in Sixth Form consisting of the first ten King's Scholars and the first ten Oppidans. Many of our classes were taken by Dr Alington himself, in classics and English literature, and very delightful they were. When the time came for me to leave in 1920 I had passed out well in my exams and had most of the necessary requirements to get into Cambridge. The recurring problem of my maths let me down again and I had to take an examination known as 'Little Go' in Cambridge itself. For some odd reason it included a knowledge of an intricate document called 'Paley's Evidences to Christianity', with a large genealogical tree of the Scriptures. This time I managed to get in.

3
Grand Tour – New Style

While I was still only six my mother had made up her mind that I should grow up to become an ambassador. This was based on a penchant for Lord Redesdale's memoirs and close friendship with several members of the Diplomatic Service. However, she never attempted to bring pressure on me in any way. Indeed at the end of my time at Eton, when I wanted to join the Foot Guards, she did not discourage me, even though her old idea remained firmly fixed in her mind.

Early in 1920 I took the first step in the travels which were to fill so much of my life. My father decided that we should visit the battlefields of Flanders. We were to concentrate on the area between Ypres and Loos, so heavily fought over by British troops over four terrible years. It took a full two days with a guide, by car.

We all arrived there on a lovely spring day and found it just as it had been left eighteen months before, familiar to us from the pages of the *Sphere* and the *Illustrated London News*. It was a total wilderness, with rusty barbed wire everywhere and dozens of battered tanks, both British and German. There were the deep dug-outs, looking habitable enough, the zig-zagging trenches, the sandbags, the high parapets. We were shown the long communication trenches, the miles of wooden duckboards for bad weather and the massive shell-craters. Naturally, as boys do, we sought eagerly for souvenirs and quickly found them – a spiked Prussian *pickelhaube,* an entrenching tool and a gruesome German steel helmet with a bullet hole through one side, all lying about to be collected by us and taken home. With our ex-service guide we followed by car as best we could the final front line right down from Passchendaele and the Ypres salient and so on to Festubert and Loos. Two things stand out grimly in my mind. First, the tattered shreds of the woods with what was left of the trunks shorn down into sharp spikes about eight to fifteen feet high. Second, the remains of the famous Cloth Hall of

Ypres, the tower almost all gone with just small battered sections of walls left. It was all peaceful now but desperately sad. In Buck's Club in London (itself founded by the Household Cavalry at Poperinghe in 1918), there hangs a coloured drawing by Snaffles, the horse painter. It is of two or three British soldiers with their horses and harness, evidently part of a gun team, with what was left of the Cloth Hall on one side. The caption below runs: 'This was a city once. Women lived here.'

My next visit abroad was further afield. My American aunt, Sally d'Aubigné, took a house at North East Harbour on Mount Desert Island in Maine for a couple of months in the summer. We arrived to find the whole place full of young people motoring back and forth between North East and Bar Harbour and Seal Harbour and having a wonderful time. They gave us a warm welcome. We must have looked quite extraordinary as we all turned up in pearl grey, stiff-brimmed Homburg hats with black bands in imitation of my father. However we became popular enough, even though we remained firmly aloof from the petting or 'necking' which was already the vogue among the boys and girls. No one swam in the sea, which is even colder than in Sweden, but in lovely swimming pools, particularly the fashionable Bar Harbour Club where the smart weekly dances also took place. The American boys and girls were astounded by our black bathing suits which had sleeves and came down almost to our knees, in marked contrast to the gaily coloured suits they all wore. We learnt about ice cream soda parlours, then unknown at home; we ate the fat Maine lobsters at dinner parties in the little restaurant at Jordan's Pond back in the hills; we rode with the Rockefeller children before breakfast on Green Mountain. We thoroughly enjoyed ourselves.

All too soon it ended and my brothers had to return to Eton while my mother and I went to stay with my aunt in her Park Avenue apartment. New York was New York and unforgettable with its sleek Pierce-Arrows and Cadillacs and the September air in those days like champagne, clear and dry. I saw all the sights and made a few friends. One day I had to go down to the British consulate general, then in the Cunard Building by the Battery, to obtain a tax certificate required by all aliens on leaving. Walking from the underground station I found a large crowd collected round the building. The Lord Mayor of Cork was on hunger strike and was slowly dying. His Irish supporters were marching up and down outside the consulate and handing out pamphlets to all and sundry. When I saw the consul general, Harry Armstrong, he told me of a curious incident which had just occurred. A young former Irish Guards officer, coming to the consulate for the same purpose as I, was handed one of the pamphlets. He asked for more, then proceeded to tear them up. He was down in a second, swallowed up by the angry crowd and fearing the worst when a bulky blue figure loomed above his head. 'Captain,' a voice said, 'I think you had better be taking it a bit quietly for a while.' It was his old company sergeant-major, now in the New York City Police. The young officer was Alec Koch de Gooreynd, the father of Peregrine Worsthorne.

There was a little song going the rounds when I was in New York:

'Cocaine Bill and Morphine Sue,
Strolling down the Avenue;
Oh, m'honey, have a little sniff on me,
Have a little sniff on me.'

In fact there was no appreciable drug problem among the young Americans. Serious drinking among the young was also negligible. The Volstead Act to enforce Prohibition had been passed that year but the evil effects had hardly been felt. It took only a few short years to get it going and thus undermine the morals of most of the nation where enforcement of the law was concerned.

I returned to England to make my first appearance at Trinity College, Cambridge. My mother still hoped I would go into diplomacy and I felt that unless something else more attractive turned up I should proceed on that basis. Consequently I arranged my studies so that I should read for the history Tripos for the first two years, leaving the modern language Tripos to be dealt with in one year instead of two. In between times I should pay visits during the long and shorter vacations to families abroad. The competition for the Diplomatic Service was very stiff – when the time came for my examinations four years later, there were only two vacancies. Total possible marks were two thousand with some nineteen papers and an interview. In the event, there were fewer than a dozen marks between the first five candidates. English, French and German in various forms were obligatory together with a fourth language. A fifth was optional but in the circumstances could not possibly be avoided; extra marks were vital.

Up at Cambridge I had no idea what I was in for and as the Tripos was not taken for two years I was tempted to take things fairly easily. As was the rule, I spent my first three terms in lodgings, only moving at the end of the first year into some beautiful rooms in Great Court with a painted heraldic ceiling in my bedroom. I joined the Pitt Club as soon as I could and found many old friends. Apart from putting in an appearance in Hall at dinner from time to time, we had most of our meals at the Pitt. Alas, in spite of a fervent appeal for funds by Rab Butler some years ago, the club's survival became shaky. With its contemporary Regency stone portico now painted a shade of pink, the lovely building in Jesus Lane has become a restaurant in which the club apparently retains one room on the top floor.

At that time however the Pitt was immensely popular. Though one ate very simply, the food was excellent. Prices were low. Even the Veuve Clicquot 1911, said to have been the best champagne of the century and regarded by us as a rare luxury, was only ten shillings a bottle. We mostly drank draught beer but a glass of vintage port was popular after meals. Cocktails were still almost unheard of in provincial England and the favourite apéritif at the Pitt was a sweet, very dark sherry. The thought of it today makes me feel a little ill. The copious newspapers, the comfortable armchairs and the excellent writing facilities and stationery with free postage all made life perhaps too agreeable. It was hard to get down to the essentials.

The move into rooms in college also had its advantages; no internal curfew at midnight, and if one wanted to give a small lunch party with ladies or hold a birthday celebration one could order a first-rate meal sent in from the Trinity kitchen. (We were always led to believe that they had been the inventors of crème brûlée.) In college we had a 'bed-maker', a lady who for a small sum kept your rooms in order. You also had a 'gyp', shared with several friends, who brought you your breakfast, looked after your clothes, and came in to wait at the occasional luncheon or dinner. Mine was a famous character named Reynolds who knew more about us than we did ourselves. The contrast to this comfort and indeed luxury was the early morning foray in dressing-gown, pyjamas and bedroom slippers to one's bath in an adjoining court.

I had a delightful and legendary history tutor in Trinity, Gilliard Lapsley, an American former Harvard don and a member of the intellectual circle which surrounded Edith Wharton at Hyères. He was a great gourmet and loved a good vintage port. Being well-off, he entertained generously in his own panelled rooms in Neville's Court. He was an excellent lecturer but he did not approve of the lady students from Girton and Newnham, then not members of the university. After the awful long-drawn out, catarrhal, hawking sound with which he began most of his sentences, he started with 'Gentlemen' and a fierce glare through his pince-nez at the poor girls sitting nervously in the front row. A famous professor of economics down through the ages and another of classical history completed my lecturers. It was mostly interesting but I admit that it seemed too early some mornings and one found it impossible to attend. The result was that at the intermediate examination at the end of the year I did rather poorly.

I had taken up rowing again and had joined the Third Trinity Boat Club shared by Eton with Westminster, the two original 'wetbob' schools. I found the training too time-consuming and, having done my share as a less than expert oar in a low-calibre boat in the May races, frankly rather boring. I decided in future to spend my spare time more profitably. I was given a Territorial commission in the University OTC; I played a lot of tennis, a little golf and in the autumn took a share, with four or five friends, in a syndicate in a small partridge shoot. I also hunted extensively in the fen country with the Trinity Foot Beagles, of which Billy Whitbread was master. One of my keen beagling companions was Alfred Gilbey of the gin family, who later as Monsignor Gilbey become well known as the Roman Catholic chaplain of Cambridge University. I often dine with him at Pratt's Club when I am in London. There was also a shy young undergraduate from Pembroke College named R. A. Butler who came out with the T.F.B.

At Trinity I made a number of new friends as well as meeting many old ones. Among the latter was Arthur Duckworth with whom I shared a birthday though he was one year older. We had also shared a pram at one time when his parents were living in Cirencester and we were waiting to move into Duntisbourne. He was later MP for Shrewsbury. Then there were the Gault brothers, also Old Etonians. Jimmy became a brigadier and Sir James and was personal assistant to General Eisenhower both in the war and again later at SHAPE. Another, also later an MP, was Spencer Summers of Outward Bound. Finally there was my friend and banker Rennie Hoare.

When I went up, Cambridge was further enlivened by the presence of several hundred wartime young naval officers who were distributed among the different colleges. To begin with they wore uniform so that they tended to move about in fairly self-conscious but sometimes trouble-seeking little bands, much enjoying their freedom from naval discipline. At the request of the authorities they were put into civvies and soon lost their identity; as I remember, they disappeared for good at the end of my first year. There were a few real veterans of thirty who were seeking specialised degrees such as agriculture or medicine and brought a little pre-war decorum to some of the more headstrong young members of the Pitt. The sporting community of racing, hunting and shooting enthusiasts, though all Pitt Club members, tended to congregate in the evening in their own horsy Athenaeum Club, the counterpart to the Bullingdon at Oxford. It had about twenty members and some small but attractive eighteenth-century rooms on the first floor of the tobacconist shop immediately opposite Great Gate. My brother John and I became members in my last year. We had a celebration each term known at the Athenaeum tea, originally so called as being the necessary refreshment after a hard day's hunting. It eventually became a full-blown dinner and a bit of an orgy. We also played a cricket match each year against the Bullingdon Club, alternately in Oxford and in Cambridge. During my year of membership it was held at Fenner's in Cambridge where the donkey which pulled the big lawn-mower was allowed to graze tethered in one corner. A bottle of champagne was kept behind the stumps and the fall of a wicket was duly celebrated. Towards the end of the match the donkey, which had also been given half a bucketful, was released and went careering and braying joyously around the field.

Finally there were the two select little eighteenth-century dining clubs, the True Blue and the Beefsteak, with four members apiece, the former attending their once-a-term dinners dressed in the white wigs and blue tailcoats of the Tories, while the others wore the blue and buff attire of Charles James Fox and his Whigs. Each member had to consume a whole bottle of claret, with its pro-French connotations, or, more challengingly, a whole bottle of port for the old Portuguese alliance and liberty, in the case of the Whigs. I was never invited to one of these affairs, but it must have been a bit of a shambles.

My parents had given me a small car, an open Calthorpe two-seater with a dicky which, as cars were something of a rarity then in Cambridge, was very convenient for our shoots, when we somehow managed to shoehorn in six people and a dog. It was also useful for occasional expeditions to London, though, with no windscreen wiper, in a heavy storm one had to put the screen flat down and arrive frozen, drenched and almost blind. It was also used for weekends away. Occasionally we also went to Newmarket, though I never became an ardent racegoer.

Such seductive diversions meant that I had to work very hard towards the end of my second year in order to get a respectable place in the Tripos examination. By working late into the night and getting up at dawn I managed to achieve a good second. In my third year I took the first and second parts of the modern language Tripos in the same year, which was tough and involved giving up practically all outside activities during the last two terms. In the event I got a second 'A' with which I was satisfied. When I left, at the end of the third year, first one brother of mine and then a second inherited the rooms at P3 Great Court. Years later, after the war, a painted glass window of my father's coat of arms was recovered from the bombed ruins of the Merchant Taylors' Hall in London. The Company kindly gave it to my brother Francis who, with the approval of the authorities at Trinity, had it installed in the mullion window of the sitting-room of P3, where it is today. We all three lived to be over eighty, faithful lovers of Trinity all our lives.

Apart from my studies at Cambridge, I was also putting in a lot of work abroad. From the Easter vacation of 1921 until July 1924 I spent almost all the holidays on the Continent with long months in the summer in Germany, France or Spain. I stayed with friends or families and worked regular hours, seeking to improve in these languages. I need hardly say I also managed to enjoy myself. My first expedition on my own was to Paris where I stayed with some friends of my family, the Loyson family in the rue de Bac. The father was the son of Paul Loyson, the famous ex-priest and preacher and later philosopher, Père Hyacinthe. The son, Jean, was about my own age and he and his pretty sister Marthe took me in hand. We did all the conventional things, including the ascent of the Eiffel Tower and the tower of Notre Dame, where my usual appalling vertigo reduced me to jelly. We went to the Place Pigalle at night and I was fascinated by the would-be Apaches dancing to the tune of 'C'est mon homme'. Mistinguett was displaying the most expensive legs in the world at the Moulin Rouge.

I made the acquaintance of Frank at the Ritz bar, then the great haunt of the young Englishmen and Americans about town. It was also on occasion patronised by a few of the foreign luminaries such as Ernest Hemingway, though they were mostly to be found in the Dôme or La Coupole. Both of the latter I also came to know well. Hemingway, incidentally, spent much of his time at the Closerie des Lilas in the avenue de Montparnasse, which subsequently became a favourite of mine. My formal lessons suffered but I formed a strong attachment to Paris, which excites me still.

In the succeeding years I stayed with other families – once at Sèvres, which provided a convenient base for visits to Paris. Returning half asleep in the metro about midnight, I recall the deep voice of the *chef de gare* or his acolyte calling 'Meudon, Meudon', waking me up just before we reached home. I spent three weeks at Christmas at the Château de la Mimerolle near Saumur, which belonged to André Turquet, the owner of Scoone's, the approved crammer for the Diplomatic Service immediately opposite the British Museum. The château itself was situated on the banks of the River Loire and, though comfortable, was no showpiece of plumbing. The only loo was a stone outdoor hut with a long seat fitted so as to take three occupants at the same time. Turquet told me that this had been put there for the benefit of his three maiden aunts who liked company. They had an *homme à tout faire* who had long moustaches and a liking for the bottle. One summer night he became very shaky after too much *vin rouge* and fell asleep in the loo. Unfortunately, one of the ladies chanced to pay it a visit and returned screaming for help – there was 'une bête' in the loo.

With Turquet's expert coaching I did quite well and was taken as a treat to watch the Cadre Noir of the French cavalry school at Saumur, with their black uniforms and cocked hats, going through their paces. They were a good second to the Spanish riding school in Vienna and in some movements perhaps even better. I also had the pleasure of following the entire process of fermentation and aging, with the addition of brandy and sugar at the appropriate moment, of the sparkling wines of the district, in the *caves* of Veuve Amiot. One January day I also attended my only wild-boar shoot. We were about twenty guns and formed a converging circle, at the centre of which we were supposed to find the boar at bay. After three abortive attempts we had seen no sign whatever of the quarry. It was decided to call it off, but not, however, before a number of the guests had started throwing their hats or caps into the air as targets to prove their marksmanship. As my cap was new from Lock's in St James's Street, I felt it best not to join in, even though I thought a hit was unlikely.

My longest stay in France, in 1923, was curiously enough in a convent immediately opposite the castle at Angers, also on the Loire. I was to be the pupil of the head of this female establishment, Monseigneur Pasquier. He was an old friend of my parents and a delightful and distinguished writer who helped me enormously. The main drawback was that breakfast with the nuns was served at five o'clock every morning and only consisted of a cup of coffee and bread and milk. After the succulent meals of porridge and cream followed by bacon and eggs or kippers brought in at anytime convenient to me by my 'gyp' at Trinity, it left much to be desired. But I loved my time at Angers. I met all sorts of agreeable people in the neighbourhood, bicycling out to their houses for tennis and *goûter,* and some of them remained friends for many years. I also attended my one and only mounted hunt of the boarhounds at the home of the Master, the Duc de Brissac, not very far away. The hunt servants carried – or rather wore, over head and shoulder – large round brass horns.

In my first visit to Germany from June till September 1922, I was to find a very different scene from the simple pleasure of Anjou or the more exhilarating goings-on of Montmartre. It took me straight to the hub of the great international problems of the day. For Germany, as so often in this anguished century, was once more the centre of anxiety of Europe. The trouble was that although defeated in battle and suffering humiliating conditions of peace, the Germans did not feel themselves a beaten people. In this respect conditions were quite different from 1945 which I suppose was an argument for unconditional surrender. For them, except for the Rhineland and the Saar, the country had not been occupied by victorious Allies. The disappearance of Imperial rule and its trappings had been brought about by their own people. The Weimar Republic was their own solution to their political future but it had no solid foundations. For no logical reason this was all attributed by its enemies in Germany not to the defeat of their armies in the field, but to a never-explained 'Dolchstoss', the famous 'stab in the back'. This position was made worse by the impossible and unforceable financial and economic conditions of peace. Finally, America had washed its hands of the whole matter.

Still, none of this was in my mind as I crossed the frontier at Osanabrück in a comfortable second-class German railway carriage, nor indeed when I reached the busy and of course quite undamaged city of Hanover. For the budding diplomat this former appanage of the British Crown was the natural place to go to study the language. The local accent, like that of Tours in France, was generally considered to be the best in the country, and indeed was identical with the 'official' pronunciation of the stage. With the old dislike of the Prussians there also went a sentimental attachment to Great Britain. I was bound for Hohenzollern Strasse 13, a rather sinister address in those days. It was a block of flats overlooking the Eilenriede, the large heavily wooded park in the centre of the town. My host and teacher was Dr Rudolf Münch, the headmaster of the big Realgymnasium, the leading boys' high school. He had been a reserve officer in the artillery and had served throughout the war. He and his family made me very comfortable. I persuaded him to ride with me early every morning in the Eilenriede. I had all my meals at home and chattered away with the family. I had fixed hours for lessons in his free time and much written work. In addition I did several hours every morning with an old professor, a 'geheimrat' who had fought in the Franco-Prussian War in 1870. Technically this stood for 'privy counsellor' but in fact was a purely honorary title. He wore an old green velvet smoking jacket and had a long curved pipe with a painted china tulip-shaped bowl which he puffed incessantly. About a month later I was joined by another pupil, Arthur Yates, who had been in my house at Eton. We also talked German together, except when we were not being overheard.

Hanover, largely destroyed by bombing in the Second World War was a beautiful town on the River Leine with a fascinating medieval quarter. It had a royal palace and a miniature Versailles called Herrenhausen a little way out of the town which was the preferred home of the early Georges. Occasionally I went to do some jumping at the Cavalry School, where I found a few young officers still wearing their brightly-coloured Imperial undress uniforms. There was also a fine opera to which we went almost every week. There were two night clubs, the Rote Mühle or Moulin Rouge and the Fledermaus, which Arthur and I often patronised after dinner. We found that listening to the haunting Berlin and Vienna love songs and melodies and chatting with the pretty girls over a drink well into the night was as good a way of improving our German as any other.

I had a few letters of introduction from friends at home but only one which I was able to present. It was to Baron von Cramm at Brüggen, not far from Hanover, and I was asked to come for a weekend and to bring a tennis racket. I found the Baron and Baroness in a charming eighteenth-century cream manor house with a classical front. They had no less than seven sons. The Baron, it seemed, had become a tennis enthusiast at Oxford early in the century and had taught all the boys himself. They had four or five pre-war rackets with sagging strings and a much-darned tennis net. They were electrified by my new Slazenger from Lilywhites. To my horror I found myself being asked to do the coaching and exhibiting my serves which were, to say the least, highly undependable. My consolation was to know that in due course the eldest son, Gottfried von Cramm, became a world champion – though no thanks I fear to me.

In Germany on the surface all was tranquil politically but beneath the surface there were sinister rumblings. Ever since the Kapp putsch in 1920, the failed monarchist coup of former soldiers belonging to the so-called 'Frei-corps', there had been small bands of right-wing malcontents carrying out secret training with the aim of overthrowing the Republic. This was aggravated by the constant pressure from the French to keep up the payment of the inordinate reparations. Then came the assassination of the distinguished and brilliant finance minister, Walter Rathenau, a Jew, by right-wing elements. My host Dr Mümch, though I believed him to be a moderate monarchist, was appalled and forecast trouble.

There were no immediate drastic results but the general nervousness undermined financial confidence and this began to be reflected in a collapse in the value of the currency. By the time I left in

September it was really serious. From time to time when I finished work in the morning I would take a stroll down to Kasten's, a smart hotel near the station where there was a small American bar. On the way down I passed a men's shop where raincoats and other items of clothing were displayed. I often noticed that a coat marked, say, 200 marks on the way down had become labelled 250 as I walked back. Later, on a short visit I paid to Berlin just before going back to England, I found in my first-class compartment that the cost of pulling the emergency chain, originally the equivalent of £5, would have been just one shilling. I myself stayed in luxury at the Adlon Hotel for a few shillings a night.

At this time General von Seeckt, the commander-in-chief of the Reichswehr, came to Hanover to inspect the regional troops at a review. Münch and I were able to get seats and it was an impressive performance, with all arms of the service involved. Under the Treaty of Versailles the size of the Reichswehr was restricted to 100,000 men and the old Imperial General Staff was abolished. The limitation on numbers was to some extent overcome by short-term commissions and short periods of service for the men. The general was a firm monarchist and many believed that it was only a question of time before he carried out a coup d'état in Berlin. I suspect that he finally abandoned any such plans because of the rapidly deteriorating financial position and its attendant uncertainties. Even law and order was not everywhere very secure for there were still sizeable pockets of Communism in Saxony and parts of Thuringia as well as in Berlin, a hangover from the defeated Spartacists. I have often wondered whether the abortive Munich coup of Hitler and Ludenforff in July 1923 was not precipitated by the failure of von Seeckt to take action the previous year.

When the schools all closed in August, the Münch family prepared to leave for their holidays which they were to spend with Frau Münch's parents, a well-to-do couple who owned a toy business at Ordruf in Thuringia, the centre of the German toy industry. Münch had also arranged to take me to stay for a few weeks at the Golf Hotel at Oberhof, one of the few courses in Germany. We worked steadily and on occasion I played a round of golf with the pro. Then it was arranged that I should do a short tour of the unspoilt medieval towns of northern Bavaria – Bamberg, Rothenburg and Nuremberg where I saw the original machine of torture, the 'Iron Lady', with its horrific spikes all pointing inwards from the metal shell. I ended up in Munich where Frau Münch's brother, a lanky young Reichswehr officer, was a *Rittmeister*, or captain, in some cavalry regiment. We went for a ride on two nice thoroughbreds in the Englischer Garten and he also showed me the museums and picture galleries, including the Glyptotek Galleries. Later they were all to be obliterated by bombing, though the contents were safe. Finally I visited a beer museum, where I saw some of the awesome exhibits of the effects of a lifetime of steady beer-swilling, including a painted scale model of a human heart about the size of a football.

I wound up with a brief stay in Berlin which was much as I had expected. I had some English friends on the Control Comission who showed me the sights, including the night resorts. There I had several shocks, starting with the beautiful and quite undetectable transvestites and the circulation of various white powders for sniffing at adjoining tables – which I watched innocently. I was unimpressed by the city itself, though in autumn the avenue of trees in Unter-den-Linden was striking. I left Germany sad at heart. Whatever happened, it seemed to me that things could only grow worse and one could see little future for the Weimar Republic. I myself thought the country would have benefited from a constitutional monarchy.

However by January 1923 the exasperated French had invaded and taken over the Ruhr with its mines and metallurgical industry and the fat was in the fire. The currency leakage in Germany had turned into a galloping inflation. I had ordered the Conservative newspaper *Kreutz-zeitung* to be sent to me regularly in England. By the spring the stamps on each issue had gone up steadily in value to some two billion marks a copy and then it abruptly stopped. When I returned to Hanover for a final brush-up of my German at Easter 1924, the financial collapse was complete. While fortunes were wiped out galore, the only people to survive intact were the landowners or owners of factories and mines, the value of which went up as the mark went down. Indeed by the wiping out of mortgages some were actually better off then they had been before. It took a full year with major American and British loans under the Dawes Plan to the virtual ending of reparations to put Germany on the way to recovery. No wonder the Bundesbank is determined that it should never happen again!

Finally in that summer I spent two months in Spain. I had only started learning Spanish towards the end of my time at Eton but with a fair knowledge of Latin I found it easy compared with the intricacies of German. I loved the language and the people. I have often thought that despite all our differences – race, and religion, history and social habits – there has always been an extraordinary rapport between the English and the Spaniards. I cannot account for it but I know that it affords great pleasure to both parties. We heard of a family in San Sebastian – the father incongruously French while his wife was Mexican. But he was a good teacher and they had a son and a bright daughter of about my age; it all worked quite well.

I arrived armed with a few letters of introduction, notably from an elderly Spanish princess, the Infanta Eulalia, whom I had met at a weekend party, to King Alfonso's private secretary, Emilio Torres. The Spanish court and government moved up to the Basque country every year for August and September. My friend James Bowker, later to be ambassador in Turkey and Austria, was also in San Sebastian and was very envious of me as his landladies were two elderly and unmarried countesses. We were both invited to join the Real Club Nautico where the youth and beauty of San Sebastian swam every morning. I had two special friends there, one a captain in the Tercio, the Spanish Foreign Legion, who was on leave from the war in Morocco, and the other Carmen Alonso, the sister of twin tennis-players of that name who had so distinguished themselves at Wimbledon. Later in England I met their uncle, who was chief justice of the Anglo-French Condominium of the New Hebrides in the Pacific. He was immensely fat and rejoiced in the name of the Conde de Cuerna de Vaca (Lord Cow's Horn). He spent little time in his bailiwick.

San Sebastian was beautiful with its vast shell-shaped Concha beach and Mount Urgell looming over it at one end. I also visited our summer embassy at Zarauz, the banking city of Bilbao and, further on, Santander, the yachting centre. Later in the day when it got cooler, we joined the evening parade of the young men and girls up and down the 'Paseo', the men ogling the girls and occasionally muttering 'Guapa, que guapa!' when they spied someone particularly delectable. Of course there were the more sedate married couples too and also the troopers of the Royal Horse Guards, specially selected for their height and resplendent in their undress uniforms almost identical with the Blues at home. We went to the races, both horse and automobile. There I became friends with the two sons of the Spanish ambassador in London, Antonio and Pablo Merry del Val, both very anglicised. Their uncle was the cardinal secretary of state at the Vatican in Rome. Antonio, who became a diplomat, I saw often over the years; Pablo was killed and hailed as a hero fighting in the forces of General Franco.

I went to the bullfights on a Sunday. To begin with I was horrified, especially as in those days the horses still wore no armour. Then little by little the magic overcame the cruelty and one watched the performance of the matadors with bated breath. It must be said that the pageantry and emotion of the spectacle greatly helped. Among my embassy friends who were keen *aficionados* were Andrew Holden and another honorary attaché, the fat and middle-aged (or so he seemed) George Bambridge who later married Kipling's daughter. Another was Gerald Agar-Robartes, the first secretary, who owned Wimpole Hall near Cambridge where I had often been asked to shoot.

At night my linguistic studies soon turned from Spanish to French. After dining with my hosts, I enjoyed going to the casino for an occasional gamble or for the little cabaret performances. There one day I met one of the act, a very pretty French girl whose professional name was Huguette de Neuville. To put it simply we became much attracted to one another and spent night after night dancing together after the show until the small hours. I learned much colloquial French and slang which I would never have encountered otherwise; but above all we had a very good time.

At one point Jim Bowker and I, with other young members of the Club Nautico, were invited to take part in a charity performance of *tableaux vivants* of paintings by Goya. The King and Queen attended and we were much complimented. In due course we were all asked to a tea party at the palace where we had a friendly afternoon. King Alfonso asked me about his aunt, Doña Eulalia, and I found him a most attractive personality and a good friend of Britain. There was a story going about San Sebastian that summer that one day he had driven himself alone over in his open Rolls to watch the polo at Biarritz. At the French frontier at Hendaye, he was asked for his name. 'Alphonse' he replied with a strong Spanish accent. 'Alphonse qui?' asked the French official with a very similar intonation. 'Alphonse, roi d' Espagne!' came the answer.

The government of the day under Count Romanones had been lax and ineffective and the long-drawn-out war against Abl-el-Krim was still going very badly; there was much discontent in the Army. As my future chief, Sir Esme Howard, then still ambassador in Spain, later recalled, Spanish politics were in a state of turmoil. Indeed for over four years there had been one government after another, ranging from the Liberals of Romanones to the extreme right. The strong man of a new Conservative Cabinet was Santiago Alba, the foreign minister. In addition there was a strongly Communist stream of thought with affiliations in Moscow. There was also much labour unrest fostered by the Socialists and many strikes. Finally, there were the rather sinister 'juntas militares', the officers' committees, which constantly interfered with government decisions in the interests of the officer corps with threats of direct action. The pot was on the boil.

On 13 September General Primo de Rivera, the Captain General of Barcelona who had often been mentioned as possible leader of a coup, declared martial law and asked the King to get rid of all politicians. We held our breath wondering what would happen next. In fact the government at once resigned and after a few days the King, now back in Madrid, accepted the coup as a temporary arrangement. It seems quite certain that he had been entirely ignorant of the plot, Primo, a staunch monarchist, having wished at all costs not to involve him. The new regime immediately went into action and reforms followed one another from one day to the next. Among other things the sinister juntas were dissolved. A month or so later *Punch* carried a cartoon showing the General saying 'Yes, we have no *mañanas.*'

In due course Primo arrived in San Sebastian. He was asked to be the president of a *corrida de beneficencia* or charity bullfight which I attended with some friends. I remember him, tall and heavily built, in khaki uniform in the presidential box watching the three top matadors of the day competing to be champion – Algabeño, Chicuelo and Nacional II. The former triumphed and at the end Primo stood up and threw into the ring a large gold cigarette case glittering with emeralds.

The time came for me to get back to London where Scoone's, the Foreign Office crammers, were starting our first term. Sadly I said goodbye to Huguette with promises to meet again and very soon I had my nose to the grindstone. We were about fifteen there in a poky little flat in Great Russell Street and spent our time going over old exam papers in the different languages, history, economics, everyday science and several others. Except for a stay in Paris at Christmas and a return to Hanover at Easter to rub up my spoken German, I was kept hard at it till the following July.

The examination covered a large field. In addition to the five languages we had to do papers on several aspects of history, simple economics, science and a general knowledge paper. There was also an oral held by four or five distinguished people including one senior Foreign Office man. The science paper gave you a choice, two subjects from six topics. One of them required the candidate to trace the course of a piece of food from the bill to the anus of a duck! One of those I actually faced the following year was 'Describe the sex life of the bee'. I wondered how useful this would all be to me in my new career. By the time we finished our three terms, interspersed between visits abroad, I must confess that we felt slightly overtrained.

The examinations were held at the old Civil Service premises in Burlington Gardens. There were about a hundred of us either for the Diplomatic or the Consular Service. I felt comparatively happy but knew the competition was so fierce that it would only be a matter of a few marks one way or the other. The interview went well. Indeed I later learnt to my amazement that I had got a hundred out of hundred. We separated with deep sighs of relief and I went up to join my family at the little moor on the River Tummel near Kinloch Rannock, which my father took every year.

There was a long delay and it was not until early October that the results were announced. I had come fourth and there were only two vacancies. I had failed. I ruefully began to make plans for another try, since being only twenty-two I was entitled to two more shots. Meanwhile I enjoyed myself as best I could. I was staying with friends in Ayrshire when to my surprise and delight a telegram came announcing that owing to one of the successful candidates backing out and another choosing the Consular Service, I had finally been accepted. I felt as if I had found the Holy Grail and gave thanks accordingly. My mother, to whom alone I owed the will to win, was in a seventh heaven. I fear that twenty-one years later, when I resigned to go into politics and had never become an ambassador, it almost broke her heart.

4
Washington, D.C.

Early in October 1924 I was summoned to the private secretaries' room at the Foreign Office. I was told that I had been appointed third secretary at the British embassy in Washington. Naturally I was delighted as I already had many ties with America, including my old aunt and godmother Mrs d'Aubigné, with the apartment on Park Avenue where I was always welcome. The United States was already the most powerful nation in the world although not yet fully aware of its strength. I had briefly made its acquaintance in 1920 and was overwhelmed by my luck in being posted there.

While I was still with the private secretaries, Gladwyn Jebb, another 'new boy', came in to discuss with them arrangements for his departure for Teheran where he had just been appointed. He was older and seemed very grand and full of talk about buying his camping kit, sporting rifles and a polo saddle. I was much impressed and a little envious but still very glad that I was going west rather than east. Our careers were not to overlap until over twenty years later, but I came to respect him greatly. His stinging ripostes at the Security Council meetings to the virulent attacks on America by the Soviet delegate, Joseph Malek, won him the admiration of the whole United States, watching on the brand new television service.

I was due to leave early in November and meanwhile I was assigned to the Communications Department to learn the elements of cyphering. Most of its members were also King's Messengers, ex-officers with their badges of silver greyhounds ready to set off in charge of the diplomatic bags all over the world. Eventually I sailed for New York in the Holland-America Line SS *Minetonka*. She was comfortable enough and I found myself at the captain's table. I was met in New York by my old friend Sir Harry Armstrong, the consul general, and the next day was deposited by the Congressional Limited in the palatial Union Station in Washington. There I was met by two secretaries of the embassy, Tommy Thompson, later ambassador in Brazil, and Jock Balfour, a future ambassador in Madrid who became a friend for life.

Washington in those days, though much enlarged during the First War, was still basically a Southern town. The population was about 450,000 of which just two thirds were black. It was to be my home for over four years and I loved it. I was lodged at the Racquet Club on 16th Street which in character rather resembled the London R.A.C. There I remained until I was able to find something a little more cosy.

I had met the ambassador, Sir Esme Howard, briefly at his summer embassy near San Sebastian in Spain the previous year. Now I was to be his private secretary. It was a challenging post for a complete novice of twenty-two and it was only thanks to his kindness and forbearance that I survived. As it was, there were many occurrences of what he called the 'henriades', in direct line from King Henri IV of France, when I totally forgot some important duty. He was the model of the perfect diplomat, tall, charming, of outstanding appearance, with the ability to make all feel equally at home and welcome. He had an unusual career. Having joined the service as a young man, he had resigned to fight a seat in Parliament as a Liberal; he had then joined the Imperial Light Horse in the Boer War and later had planted rubber in Louis d'Or, Tobago. He returned to the service as one of the high commissioners of the Great Powers to Crete in 1906. From then on his life lay along more conventional lines. As an ambassador in Washington he earned the respect of the American authorities and real affection in the many parts of the United States where he addressed so many diverse audiences.

His wife, Lady Isabella, came from a distinguished Roman family which happened also to be descended from a Scottish Jacobite earl, Lord Newburgh. She was serene, beautiful and outspoken, and a good friend. They were a devoted couple but living through deep sorrow. Shortly before my arrival they had learned from the Boston doctors that their eldest son Esmetto was suffering from Hodgkin's Disease and that there was no hope. He was a brilliant and charming boy just out of Oxford, whom they adored. I had briefly met him in Spain. Soon after I came to Washington he left with Lady Isabella for Switzerland hoping for a miracle which never came.

I was kept busy. My prime duty as private secretary was to plan and supervise every aspect of the ambassador's life – his daily engagements, the submission in proper order of the current office files, the collection of material for his speeches and in general the protection of his private life from invaders of all sorts. I estimated at the time that I answered about fifty telephone calls a day. I had to be available for duty on Sundays and holidays. I also had to read and mark three American newspapers a day. I had to meet all visitors and keep them in play until His Excellency ('H.E.') was ready to see them. I had to do my share of cyphering, in times of crisis often till two or three in the morning. Once a year I had to make a formal count of the valuable Georgian embassy silver, with services for a dinner of sixty people, with Fioravanti del'Agnese, the Howards' tall and handsome Italian major-domo. Finally I had to approve seating arrangements for official dinner parties proposed by Lady Isabella's secretary, Lady Bettie Feilding, a joyful companion who ultimately astonished official Washington by marrying the owner of three schooners on Rum Row, Colonel Sherbrook Walker. They moved to Kenya where he became the proprietor of the Nyeri Hotel and later built Treetops, the wooden tree-cabins overlooking the saltlick and water-hole for big game lit by artificial moonlight.

My embassy colleagues were few in number compared with the establishment today – just a counsellor and three other secretaries and a modest commercial branch under a remarkable man, Sir John Broderick, with a commercial secretary, based in New York. There were three service attachés with their staffs and also two or three honorary attachés. Then there was a vice-consul, an archivist, a small clerical staff and of course our chancery servants. We could never have managed without these embassy messengers, both black and white, and they became our close friends. One of them, a coloured man named Charlie Brown from one of our Caribbean islands, had been serving since 1884, in the days when the post was still only a legation. Afterwards he wrote a good book, a copy of which I still possess.

I had arrived at a time when Anglo-American relations were on an even keel. There were few major issues; indeed during the whole time I was there – over four years – there were only three serious problems. The first was a surprise request from the American government to pay certain claims from wartime shippers amounting to millions of dollars for the refund of contraband confiscated during the blockade of Germany. The dispute turned on which enemy and neutral goods were liable to seizure as contraband. The legal position was uncertain. We were fighting for our lives with only three weeks' supply of food and acted accordingly. The United States government, while helpful in many respects, took a different view (though once they came into the war themselves they acted in exactly the same way). It was in March 1925 that we learnt that the State Department was about to present this list of claims. The ambassador was authorised to see President Coolidge and point out what a shocking effect this would have in Great Britain on top of the already heavy War Debt Settlement. It was President Coolidge himself who found a solution, with these demands being set off against some corresponding obscure British claims. All was well.

The second issue arose from the attempt to put into practice the naval arrangements set up by the treaty of 1922 between Great Britain, the United States and Japan. The treaty had provided for parity between the United States and Great Britain for capital ships. In practice this was difficult to define. We on account of our large and scattered empire also needed large numbers of smaller ships. The American Big-Navy newspapers on the other hand were pressing for a large construction programme of capital ships. Violent attacks were made on Great Britain and its motives and American experts demanded exact parity in every type of ship. Matters were not made any easier by some of our own people not very tactfully voicing their private opinion that American did not need such a large navy at all. The issue was bitterly contested and so it went on for months and indeed for several years. In July 1927, while I was spending a lonely and searing hot month at the Washington embassy as duty secretary, a conference was called for which Sir Esme came back from the summer embassy in Massachusetts. I noted in a letter to my mother that the Admiralty, and particularly the First Lord, 'Willy' Bridgeman, had bungled things badly and the Americans had broken up the meetings. So the campaign rolled on. It was not until two years later, just after I had left, that at another meeting in Washington, this time attended by the Labour prime minister, Ramsay MacDonald, this prickly subject was finally put to rest.

Then there was Prohibition. It is difficult after this length of time and in a changed world to describe how this so-called 'reform' of 1920 had come to affect every aspect of private life in much of America. Every adult conversation in the long run seemed at one point to turn to this topic. It was perhaps over supplies of wine for their next dinner party; the excellence of one's bootlegger; the dangers of wood alcohol and the awful taste of bathtub gin; also the flasks that had to be smuggled into pocket or raccoon fur coats at football games. At official functions of course all alcohol was completely taboo. At the White House it was always just iced water. The former Governor of Pennsylvania, Gifford Pinchot, a dedicated 'dry', who later became a cousin of mine by marriage, at the dinner parties in his house on Dupont Circle used to serve big bottles of two different sorts of iced mineral water, each wrapped up in a napkin.

Rum-runners had perfected their techniques, and a large fleet of schooners was anchored on Rum Row just outside the three-mile limit. In response to the American revenue men's doctrine of 'hot pursuit', the rum-runners no longer sought to come in close themselves but used fast motor boats which could land at every suitable little cove. There was continuous scrapping and later hijacking both at sea and on land. Then the rum-runners turned their attention to the Bahamas where Nassau became a well-stocked centre of smuggling. Just as in the Civil War fortunes were made in Nassau in running the Union blockade, so in the Twenties there was a fresh boom. The 'Bay Street Boys' grew rich.

Many of the vessels lying off New York and again in the Bahamas cays were British or flew the Red Ensign, including numerous Canadians. The British government tried to be accommodating and agreed to certain steps to ease the task of the revenue men but again and again we had complaints and there were continuous serious incidents and even loss of life.

The hijacking of a cargo of liquor on a truck belonging to a Latin-American legation gave rise to much alarm. From then on when our consignments arrived in Baltimore our head office messenger, Bob Williams, was in the cab armed with a double-barrelled shotgun. The surprising fact was that the Washington diplomatic corps, by agreement with the US government, had the right to import as much liquor duty free as they liked. This was certainly agreeable to us and made our parties very popular. The prices helped too, for Scotch whisky cost us four shillings a bottle and gin half a crown, while a bottle of Veuve Clicquot 1911 also cost just four shillings, or twenty pence in today's currency. If one went out dancing at the Chantecler, the smart night-club where Meyer Davis's orchestra played nightly, it was cheaper to take a bottle of champagne with one than order a bottle of Ice-Rock water, even after paying the price of corkage.

As time went on the demands for repeal became more vociferous and put the Prohibitionists still more on their mettle. A friend of mine, John Phillips Hill, a Republican Congressman from Maryland, a strongly 'wet' state, filled his wine cellar with bottles of grape juice, waited till it fermented and then invited in the revenue men. He got off unscathed. Similarly pre-Prohibition cellars were also immune provided the contents were drunk on the premises – and this was difficult to check. By the 1928 election Governor Al Smith of New York, with his brown Derby hat and immense Irish charm, was able to secure his adoption as the Democratic candidate as an open 'wet', though his party platform itself had no such plank. He was beaten by Hoover in the full flood of the Republican Wall Street boom and repeal had to wait for Roosevelt and 1933.

Immigration was another problem and gave us many headaches. At that time it was operated on a fixed quota system based on the national origin of the population of the country. Consequently Great Britain was by far the biggest with, as I remember, 56,000 permits a year, the Germans coming next with 34,000. With an open border with Canada, every conceivable trick was used to get round this, and the Ellis Island detention centre was always full to bursting point.

There were also political developments to be monitored both in the United States and elsewhere. In China the large American missionary establishment kept Congress in a state of continual excitement and sinister events were building up. There was Haiti with a US Marines occupying force and a number of American advisers. There were Mexico and Nicaragua, itself soon to be occupied by Marines as well. There was also a mass of routine work, illegal immigration, deportations, lunatics and distressed British subjects.

One particular function which I much enjoyed entailed frequent visits to the White House. I went to present the lesser British visitors who came with introductions to President Coolidge. It seems astonishing today but in the 1920s it was still the custom for the president to receive all such visitors every weekday from noon to one o'clock in the Oval Room. First came any ambassadors bringing the VIPs. Then came myself or some other junior foreign diplomat with the lesser fry. In our case they came with letters from Canadian ministers, Anglican bishops, leading British businessmen, governors of Indian provinces – Australians, New Zealanders, South Africans and so on. This performance lasted till twelve-thirty when the flood-gates were opened and for half an hour the unhappy president was obliged to shake hands with any American citizen who had an introduction from his senator or his Congressman.

Over a period of doing this for four years I got to know Mr Coolidge quite well. He was always very nice to me. 'Good morning, Mr President,' I would say as I and the visitors were ushered in. 'Always pleased to see you, Mr Secretary,' he would reply. He often displayed a quite unexpected dry humour. Over the years I brought a fair variety of visitors, starting with the glamorous Hore-Ruthven twins, the daughters of the future Earl of Gowrie. They were identical and were dressed, as I remember, in tiger-skin bolero jackets and pale green skirts with large turquoise necklaces. After my introduction and one of his usual long silences the president said with his New England accent, 'Well I didn't quite get the names, but I guess you two must be sisters.' End of interview.

Sir Esme always said that whenever someone a bit out of the usual was presented to the president a parrot-like gleam came into his eye, which always meant that some humorous crack was coming. On one occasion an Indian in a saffron robe with long, rather oily locks arrived with an introduction from the governor of Bengal. He had a card on which was written 'The Swami Yogananda, Hindu Philosopher on a World Tour'. When I presented him to Mr Coolidge he handed the president his card. Mr Coolidge glanced at it, rolled it over in his fingers and after the statutory pause said, 'Say, Swami, how is the philosophy business doing in India anyway?'

On top of my private secretary's duties I was allotted a certain amount of official work to teach me my trade. Most of it was technical, being concerned with the deportation of illegal immigrants and many varied problems put to us by the Canadian government. Theirs in fact constituted one third of the whole embassy work. The first two files to cross my desk were 'The Claims of the Pottawatomee Indians' and 'The Case of the Sockeyed Salmon'. They had both been running for many years and I doubt whether either case has ever been settled. The embassy in those days was still responsible for representing the whole Empire, including the new Irish Free State. It was only in the summer of 1924 that the ambassador was instructed to raise with the secretary of state, Mr Hughes, the appointment of an Irish Free State minister to handle their affairs. The United States government agreed with alacrity and Professor Smiddy, smiling and kindly, arrived as the first Irish minister. He was soon afterwards followed by a Canadian minister, Vincent Massey, later to become high commissioner in London during the 1939 war and still later governor-general of Canada. From the word go we got on with him and his whole staff extremely well. It was incidentally a great relief to us for at that time a large number of the rum-running fleet were Canadian-owned and now passed out of our hands.

In the days before air-conditioning Washington became unbearable in summertime. In temperatures frequently well over a hundred the humidity from the reclaimed marshland and surrounding areas of the Potomac introduced a perpetual languor into office hours. So it was the custom of the White House and the principal embassies to move up to New England or elsewhere for the hot months. We ourselves had a permanent summer chancery overlooking the Singing Beach at Manchester-by-the-Sea a few miles north of Boston. The secretaries lived at the Essex County Club while our elders and betters took summer cottages in the neighbourhood. It was very pleasant and gave us the chance to meet some of the old families of Massachusetts on their home ground.

In mid-June Tommy Thompson and I set out in two cars, he driving the embassy Cadillac and I a new Chrysler Tourer which my aunt had given to me and which was my pride and joy. When we left Washington the temperature was 107 degrees. We stopped with friends in Philadelphia and Rheinbeck and on the way up we crossed the bridge across the Susquehanna River. There I noticed dozens of US wartime destroyers anchored in pairs stretching up and down as far as the eye could see. They were mothballed against future needs. Fifteen years later, in June 1940, as an assistant secretary in the War Cabinet office, I was working with Jean Monnet on the supply side of our American requirements It was during the first Battle of the Bulge in May 1940 when the German armies were sweeping through Belgium and Northern France to the Channel ports. We expected the worst. We talked one day of our utter dependence now and in the future on urgent help from the United States. I happened to mention the destroyers I had seen in the Susquehanna. After listening carefully he immediately took the idea first, I believe, to Sir Robert Vansittart at the Foreign Office and then to the new prime minister, Mr

Churchill. They were to become the basis for the 'memorable transaction', to quote Churchill, for the exchange of fifty US destroyers against the grant to America of naval and air bases in the Caribbean.

Those summer months on the North Shore passed quietly. We kept our regular office routine and were usually busy as one secretary was posted to Washington to hold the fort for a month at a time and at least one other was on leave. In the late afternoon we played golf or tennis. We had a standing invitation to a buffet lunch at the summer home of Mr and Mrs Leiter at Beverly Farms where they had a lovely sea-water pool. It was there a year or two later that I met 'Big Bill' Thompson, the mayor of Chicago, who for some reason never explained fulminated in Colonel McCormick's anti-British *Chicago Tribune* about 'keeping King George's snoot out of Chicago'. He was surprisingly mild and friendly.

Some American habits puzzled us. One hot day in Washington when I left for lunch I found a sticker on the windscreen of my Chrysler saying 'Hop in noble'. I could not imagine what it might mean. Then I noticed that other cars also carried it and the penny dropped. I remembered reading that the 'Nobles of the mystic shrine' – a distant offshoot of Freemasonry – were holding a national convention in Washington. The stickers were one of the ways their local branch sought to ensure that we were hospitable to the visitors.

A youngish Australian named Henderson and his wife who had a summer cottage introduced me to polo, which I had watched from early days at home. It was played at a nice old-fashioned country club called Myopia which also kept the local pack of foxhounds. I also got to know Freddy Prince whose father ran the foxhounds at Pau near Biarritz. Prince had his own polo ground and a large stable of ponies which were trained by an English ex-professional jockey called Harry East. The latter took me in charge and in the early mornings taught me to knock a polo ball about. In due course I bought a pony myself and played in a few modest games there and at Myopia. I took the pony back to Washington and had many early morning rides in Rock Creek Park.

In August my aunt herself took a cottage near Beverly Farms and my father, mother and brother Francis came out to visit her. I can remember few summers when I spent such an idyllic time of work and play. With the polo, tennis tournaments and small parties and our single visit to the great world of Newport, the summer passed all too quickly – though I was fortunately able to go to Newport again in 1927 and 1928. It was in 1927 that Mr Coolidge, then at the Summer White House in Black Hills, South Dakota, when questioned by the press as to his intentions about the presidency, made the Delphic statement, 'I do not choose to run.'

On our return to Washington in October we found ourselves on the eve of the signature of the Locarno Non-Aggression Pact, guaranteeing mutually the security of the frontiers of France, Belgium and Germany, which were further guaranteed by Great Britain and Italy. It was the outcome of a series of events starting with exorbitant Allied demands for reparations and the German financial collapse, down through the French occupation of the Ruhr and the Dawes Plan. It was the brainchild of Dr Stresemann, by then foreign minister of Germany, and it was followed by Germany's entry into the League of Nations. It was widely acclaimed. According to the foreign secretary, Sir Austin Chamberlain, Locarno was 'the real dividing line between the years of war and the years of peace'. That was certainly what we felt at the time but in the relative backwaters of Washington, where officialdom was pretty fed up with the eternal squabbling of the European Powers, it evoked little emotion.

On Locarno Day the German ambassador, the rather left-wing 'Rote Baron', von Maltzan, gave a reception at the embassy where with our French, German and Italian colleagues, including many youthful friends, we toasted Locarno till well into the night. Was Dr Stresemann sincere in his proclaimed aims of a peaceful future for Europe? Duff Cooper in his *Old Men Forget* saw it only as a step towards a war of revenge and quoted the ex-German Crown Prince as evidence of Stresemann's intentions. Significantly the treaty did not cover any of Germany's eastern frontiers. I prefer to believe that Stresemann's aims were honest and though no doubt, as a nationalist, in his heart he yearned for boundary revision in the East, he hoped to obtain this by peaceful negotiations. With Germany losing great chunks of territory to Poland and Russia, it is perhaps an abrupt and rather painful reminder of Central Europe today.

At that time there were only nine British ambassadors in all, the others being ministers or chargés d'affaires sometimes responsible for two or three small countries. Today there are 180 at least. Ambassadors were then very grand people, all automatically privy counsellors and all with direct access to the prime minister and

Buckingham Palace. It was not at all unusual for Sir Esme to write direct to the King on some topic which he thought might be of interest. There were a string of visitors who came with letters of introduction from all over the world, representing a whole variety of fields. They also generally wanted something. A few stand out in my mind. Early in 1925 Teddy and Kermit Roosevelt, the sons of President Teddy Roosevelt, arrived to ask for help in arranging an expedition to the Himalayas to hunt the *ovis poli,* the giant wild sheep of the Pamirs, named after Marco Polo. This was duly arranged and they got a fine specimen for a museum. Soon after there was a visit from Dr Chaim Weizmann, the head of the Zionist movement, who later became the first president of Israel. He was a charming man. We became friends and afterwards I often met him when I became a private secretary to Sir John Simon, the foreign secretary. Then one day there was one of the heads of the Bell Telephone Company which was anxious to take over the whole British telephone system. He got no encouragement from Sir Esme but in parting he assured me that if nevertheless a deal could be done it would be greatly to my advantage! It is the only time in my life that I was offered a discreet bribe.

There were also frequent visits from the Washington correspondents of *The Times* and *Morning Post,* Wilmot Lewis and Sir Maurice Low. We often chatted while they were waiting and I learnt a lot from them. One day when I was quite new Bill Lewis was talking about some violent clashes between the police and the Pennsylvanian coal miners. We were all very conscious of Communism in those days, so soon after the Russian Revolution and its horrors. I asked him whether he thought there was any danger of Marxism spreading to America. 'Henry,' he said, 'the danger over here is not Marxism but Hart, Schaffner and Marxism' – they were a well-known chain of ready-to-wear tailors.

Of the American correspondents perhaps the most outstanding was David Lawrence whose beautiful daughter, a friend of mine, later married Felipe Espil, the counsellor of the Argentine embassy. I was told years later that previously Espil had had a passionate love affair with Wallis Spencer (later Simpson) who had hoped to marry him. How history might have been changed! Lawrence himself had a distinguished career in journalism and eventually founded the *United States Daily.*

We lesser fry also had 'visiting firemen' arriving with introductions from overseas. One day one of them, Lord Elmley, the future Lord Beauchamp, arrived straight from a session of Aimée Semple Macpherson, the famous hot gospeller in Los Angeles. He described the black velvet background with the one spotlight on her, and her band of angels all in white behind. She began her address: 'You can say what you like about me and I will say what I like about you, but what I have to say about you I shall say on my knees.'

Closer to home there was the court martial of Colonel William Mitchell for his passionate advocacy of a separate American Air Force. Graham Christie, our air attaché, had asked me to get Mitchell a temporary flat in our apartment building; so each evening over a drink we had from him a full account of the day's proceedings up to his final conviction and dismissal from the Army. But when war came he went back to the newly created US Air Force and lived to become a general in it himself.

The British embassy which I knew was a large white Victorian building dating from 1874 at the corner of Connecticut Avenue and N Street. It had big rooms for entertaining and a vast ballroom. A small wing consisting of my office and three small rooms had housed the whole chancery in days gone by, but now the offices lay across a courtyard at the back and looked like a wartime camp with two long wooden army huts and a brick entrance. It was high time the whole thing came down and Sir Esme devoted many hours and much effort to producing the present handsome building. The site had been approved and Sir Edwin Lutyens chosen as architect. The ambassador decided to take a last look at it before finally signing the purchase deed. It lay alongside the already heavy traffic of Massachusetts Avenue below the Naval Observatory. Surprisingly the whole area was still covered with thick scrub and bushes. We found that the only way he and I could reach it comfortably was on horseback, pushing the branches out of our faces as we went up the narrow path. Even so, and though we had a detailed plan with us, it was difficult to work out exactly where the new building was to be.

Lutyens was full of charm but quite determined to stick to his own ideas of what the embassy should be – a grand English country house inside and out. It was to be a fine red brick stone-faced building in early Georgian style. The front was to look out in a straight line across the White House to the Capitol. He insisted that no bedroom should have direct access to a bathroom and the interior wall-heating on which he also insisted would make this impossible to change. The ambassador's loo was so built that his successor, Sir Ronald Lindsay, who was six foot seven, had the greatest difficulty in making use of it at all. The garage was long enough to house the old embassy Cadillac but not Sir Ronald's new Rolls-Royce. Presumably these and other little difficulties were later adjusted; certainly the building became one of the outstanding features of the Washington scene.

I was lucky in my embassy colleagues. There was first of all Billy Chilton, the counsellor, soon to be minister to the Vatican. Later on he was to become Sir Henry and ambassador to General Franco in Burgos during the Spanish Civil War. He and his wife Kitty practically adopted me. General Charlton, the military attaché, and his wife also gave me a second home and their son Wingate, then a small boy, was later to become a good friend when I met him again in Cairo as a young 8th Hussar. So he remains to this day. Of the others, two, Jock Balfour and Adrian Baillie, became my closest friends whom I saw constantly over the years.

Jock was a remarkable character. A cousin of the Conservative statesman Arthur Balfour, he had been at Oxford before the war and was studying in Germany when it broke out. He was interned with some 4,000 other British civilians on the racecourse at Ruhleben outside Berlin. He was striking-looking with deep-set eyes and an elegant turned-up moustache and he had a little habit of twisting up the right corner of his mouth when smiling which gave him the appearance of a slightly raffish French musketeer. He also bore a close resemblance to King Philip IV of Spain in the portraits by Velasquez, which cannot have passed unnoticed when he eventually concluded a successful diplomatic career with the embassy in Madrid. He was a fine linguist and could quote poetry fluently and at length in at least five languages. Brilliant and shrewd in diplomacy, in the more personal affairs of life he was often gloriously eccentric. From my windows in Connecticut Avenue I looked out on tramlines and once saw him mounting a tram on his way to the State Department. He wore his hat at an angle and carried his gold-knobbed cane. As he climbed up the cane shot down from between his fingers and on to the tramlines. He shouted and jumped off wildly as the tram moved on and was left waving the cane to show the conductor that he was safe. His widow kindly gave it to me last year as a memento of my old friend.

After he became first secretary and head of chancery I sometimes had to go across the courtyard to discuss some point. Once I found him sitting on the back of the chair with his feet on the seat, waving one arm while dictating some important dispatch. He also had a habit of nibbling bits of brass off the paper clips. He was not an easy companion to cater for when later I ran our Georgetown household, often announcing as we left in my car for the office in the morning 'Oh, by the way, I've asked six people to lunch today.'

Adrian Baillie joined us in the spring of 1925, also as second secretary. He was a dashing young baronet, ex-Scots Greys, who had been at Eton with me. He was very good-looking, a fine golfer and had a nice baritone voice which he had improved by training while learning Italian in Florence. He had great sweetness and *joie de vivre* and all the ladies fell for him. He was as uninhibited with his singing as with everything else. I can remember a supper party he gave in his flat for Chaliapin after his concert. After a few superb songs in which Chaliapin accompanied himself on the piano, the maestro was astonished to hear a light baritone voice joining in forcefully from the back with a rendering of 'The Bee'. Three years later Adrian left the Diplomatic to go into politics and in the 1931 crisis election was elected MP for Linlithgow. He did not repeat this feat but was later elected for Tonbridge which he held till 1945.

In the summer of 1925 Adrian and I attended an Old Etonian Fourth of June dinner at the New York Yacht Club where the America's Cup stood proudly on the sideboard. The temperature was over 100 degrees. We spent a pleasant evening and later left in our dinner jackets with a couple of friends for a tour of the town. We visited several speakeasies, starting with what became the famous Restaurant 21, which had a grille covering a sliding panel on the door like an ancient nunnery. Later we progressed to some more dubious night resorts where for five dollars one had a glass of doctored fruit juice labelled 'champagne' and a dance or two with a pretty girl. Dawn was breaking as we left and we managed to get a hansom cab to take us back to our hotel. Suddenly to my horror Adrian pulled the reins, which hung down over our heads, out of the driver's hands, gave them a shake, and off we went down Fifth Avenue at an easy canter with the cabby shouting abuse through the little trapdoor in the roof. There was nothing he could do but he was finally mollified by a good tip.

My other great friend on the embassy staff was Group Captain Graham Christie. He was a remarkable man who as a pilot in the Royal Flying Corps had won a DSO and MC. He had been educated at a German university and spoke the language perfectly. While in Washington he bought the first 2,000 parachutes the RAF ever had, as well as the Sperry bomb sight. In 1926 I had been able to look after him at a critical time on an Atlantic crossing when he had gone through a terrible operation and needed help. Later he was transferred to Berlin where he cultivated Goering, whom he already knew slightly. He became a personal friend of the Reichsmarshal and was so well informed on Nazi aeronautical and military affairs that after his retirement he decide to stay on 'in business' in Berlin. He was the main source of information on Nazi Germany which Churchill pressed in vain upon the reluctant Baldwin government.

We younger folk were invited out continually. There were private dances and we all also belonged to the Dancing Class, a club by invitation which gave periodical balls at the mansion of Mr and Mrs Leiter on Dupont Circle. Meyer Davis's band played and we learnt how to 'cut in' on the girls we fancied before being cut in on ourselves and retiring temporarily to the stag-line. We got stuck in corners practising the Charleston; we also found we had a duty to take our turn with the wallflowers.

A permanent feature of the Dancing Class and other Washington parties was one Arthur Bradley Campbell, a fattish young man equally unpopular with the men and the girls. His mother was a rich widow from Chicago determined to build a place in Washington society. It was said that in fact Arthur was the product of an affair with Sousa, the great band composer. I once mentioned this to a well-known wit in Washington whose comment was 'In that case Sousa waved his baton once too often.'

One New Year's Day soon after my arrival the president and Mrs Coolidge held a morning reception at the White House for the Diplomatic Corps which was attended in full uniform. At that time the Americans did not set much store by ceremonial and compared to Buckingham Palace functions it was a little flat. Iced water did not help much as the only beverage except for coffee but the warmth of Mrs Coolidge's welcome set everyone at their ease. The uniforms of the foreign guests, many of pre-war vintage, were sensational, including the national dress of the Hungarian minister, Count Lazlo Széczényi, who wore a long pelisse of leopard skin over one shoulder and a curved gold sword. He had married Gladys Vanderbilt and they later became friends of mine. There was also an immaculate Romanian who wore a monocle screwed into one eye and a brown uniform and was inevitably dubbed the 'Chocolate Soldier', a musical comedy still fresh in many memories. General Charlton, in his cocked hat with red and white feathers and his scarlet tunic, did not let us down.

We had a nice Canadian honorary attaché, Harold Sims, very rich and with close ties to the theatrical world. He liked to entertain his theatrical friends when they came to Washington and after each first night regularly gave a supper party with dancing at his house in R Street for the stars and selected members of the cast.

There were a few special American friends at those parties but almost no female socialites. Funnily enough the only local Washington girl I can remember there was Wallis Simpson – or Spencer as she then was. She became a good friend of mine although I though she was hard. She was also the only female invited to our weekly embassy poker parties. She was striking, with a nice figure, but not beautiful. She was also a 'good sort' and though by no means a flirt, was certainly much happier in the company of men than women. She had a certain wisecracking familiarity of manner which enabled her to talk to men on equal terms. I met her again in 1930 after she had married Ernest Simpson and come to London, but by the time she became involved so disastrously with the Prince of Wales we had left London for another post.

This was the period of the Prince's famous world tours to the principal countries of the Empire. History has dealt harshly with him in terms of character and behaviour and no doubt rightly. But there is no denying the universal feelings of admiration and devotion he inspired at that time. If affected us all, but more especially the young. It was totally different from the worship of the film star, the pop star or the football heroes of later years. One of the tours had just finished when I arrived in Washington and had ended in a happy visit by the Prince to New York for the International Polo Tournament on Long Island, though stories which reached us about the behaviour of some of his suite were not quite so glorious. Several years on I was chosen by the Foreign Office to accompany HRH on board the cruiser on his South American tour, perhaps because I spoke good Spanish. Unfortunately at the last minute my selection was cancelled and someone much senior went out. I was sorry to miss it.

After my initial stay at the Racquet Club I moved to the Anchorage, a building of a dozen brand new bachelor apartments on Dupont Circle where Jock was already installed and where Adrian later joined us. Then, after a year or so, Jock, Adrian and I decided to take a house in Georgetown, now the centre of Washington fashion. It had only slowly become popular and indeed many of the charming eighteenth-century houses were still boarding houses or even slums. However, by the time I was there it was regaining strength and many fashionable younger folk were moving in. By a lucky chance we found a house to be let furnished at the corner of 30th and P streets, with a nice walled garden. We took it with alacrity. We each had a bedroom and sitting room and we were also lucky to find an English couple, Mr and Mrs Kitchener, prepared to come as cook and butler. Our parties, though modest, became very popular and we had a happy year there.

In the autumn there was wonderful duck shooting on the River Potomac where the great prizes were the famous canvas-backs. I did not do much of this, but later my new uncle by marriage, Peter Labouisse, a remarkable shot, often took my wife and myself duck shooting at four in the morning on the Patuxent river. He was a delightful old-style sportsman from Louisiana who when young by all accounts fancied dry martinis. At the old Shoreham Hotel on F Street he was reputed to have won a bet by drinking fifty-six martinis in one evening – apparently with very little effect.

We had a number of friends among the younger members of the State Department. I always felt rather sorry for them. In a service where the best top posts were almost always filled by politicians, the career men were inclined to be sneered at by irreverent journalists like Drew Pearson as 'cookie pushers', with many references to 'cutaway coats' and 'white spats'. In fact the standard of the State Department officials, especially in the more senior ranks, was high. Many of them later served their country abroad with skill and distinction as ambassadors and ministers.

As might be expected, in Washington, with its small white

population, there were strong social and slightly snobbish diplomatic overtones. This led to marked competition between the leading society hostesses. Whatever bitterness may have existed among themselves, they were invariably charming and hospitable to their foreign guests, including the youthful element to which I belonged. The entertainment was on a lavish scale. It must be remembered that this was the height of the Coolidge prosperity boom and everyone was convinced that America had discovered the Philosophers' Stone or the Crock of Gold and that the good life would go on for ever. October 1929 proved them wrong. In the meantime the Beluga caviar, the diamond-baced terrapin (the delicious freshwater turtle of Eastern Maryland) and slabs of pâté de foie gras were the staples of Washington parties.

I was invited to stay in Philadelphia several times by my distant Hopkinson cousins. They were – and are – a most distinguished family in that city, the original immigrant in 1730 being Thomas, later judge of the Admiralty Court of the Province of Pennsylvania. He was a close personal friend of Benjamin Franklin and collaborator in his scientific experiments. His son, Francis, was a signatory of the Declaration of Independence and the first American poet and composer. Not to be outdone, Francis's son Joseph in due course wrote 'Hail Columbia'. Our two branches have remained in continual touch over 250 years and the father of James, the present head of the family, came to stay with my parents in the country while on his honeymoon in 1911, as did James himself with each of my two brothers in quite recent years.

In 1927 Sir Esme decided to make a full-scale tour of America, starting with New Orleans and visiting the Pacific Coast and the Canadian Rockies. Lady Isabella was to accompany him with her maid, the faithful Alda. I was included as there would be many speeches and official engagements. In addition the ambassador decided to take with him his Italian butler, Fioravanti. Perhaps fortunately the president of the Canadian Pacific Railway offered Sir Esme his private coach with its saloon, cabins and a full-length bath.

So in great style we set out for New Orleans. Our reception there was astonishing. All the notables of the city turned out to meet us and we found ourselves welcomed as heroes. We had read of unusually heavy flooding of the Mississippi but had no idea it had become so critical. In several places the levées, the high banks on either side, were expected to break at any moment. Whole sections of the city might be swept away and people were quickly evacuating the place. We had come at the crucial moment so it was not surprising that the ambassador, when he came to make his big speech, should have had what today would be called a standing ovation. We toured the danger areas on the river by motor boat. On our third day the waters began to subside.

Our coach was hitched on to another train and we left for the Grand Canyon. For two and a half days we rumbled through Texas, New Mexico and Arizona, with the train often stopping for passengers to get out for meals at little places like Freshwater. My chief recollection was the weird appearance of the Louisiana forests after Baton Rouge with the grey hanging beards of Spanish moss and then mile upon mile of near desert in New Mexico and Arizona. The Canyon when we arrived there was much what I had expected, a mile-deep cleft, thirteen miles across and two hundred miles long. Its peaks, precipices and buttes all looked like chemical crystals viewed through a microscope suffused with a blue film of air like the bloom on a grape. The ambassador decided that he and I should ride down on muleback and spend the night at the small hotel at the bottom. I have a bad head for heights and was advised by the guide who led the way to tie my reins round the high pommel of my saddle and, sitting with arms crossed, leave it to the good sense and deftness of the mule. I remember at one sharp turn in the precipitous path round a large rock finding my mule's head out of sight in front of me and his tail almost hidden behind. At the hotel by the bridge over the fast-running Colorado River the temperature was at least ten degrees hotter than up at the rim.

Two days later we left for Los Angeles where we spent two hectic days with the film community. I found myself sitting next to Mary Pickford at an English-Speaking Union dinner and we lunched with her and her husband, Douglas Fairbanks, the next day. She was 'nice but not very bright', as I described her in a letter to my mother, 'but he seems a nice fellow' I added, with the condescension of all my twenty-five years! We spent a whole day the Metro-Goldwyn-Meyer Studios, Louis Meyer being the only tycoon who was a British subject.

One day we spent a quieter but wonderful morning at the Hintington Collection near our hotel in Pasadena, with Gainsborough's *Blue Boy* and Sir Joshua Reynolds's painting of Mrs Siddons as the

'Tragic Muse' and so many fine works of eighteenth-century British painters. Then came the lovely train journey alongside the sea up to San Francisco, through Santa Barbara, Pebble Beach, and Monterrey. Once arrived, we did our usual official visit as well as attending a big function at the Country Club in Burlinghame, where we were treated to the intellectuals of the peninsula, including Gertrude Stein.

Next we visited Portland and Seattle, with a memorable drive up the Columbia River Highway with the river in full spate. Then by sea to Victoria, an old-fashioned, English-style provincial town, with scarlet letter-boxes and the famous Burchant gardens. Vancouver was to be our last official stop except for a short stay in Winnipeg. Then, after several engagements, the ambassador collapsed at a Ladies Canadian Club tea party. He had done far too much, for these continual speeches taxed him. I blamed myself for not having foreseen the danger but now the only question was how quickly we could get him back to Washington. The doctors had diagnosed a mild stroke and for the next five days he had no memory and we had to abandon Banff and Lake Louise which he had so longed to see. Sadly we returned in our comfortable coach through the Canadian Rockies, some of the most beautiful scenery in the world. I still managed to enjoy it, especially when the engine driver invited me to his cab over one of the highest points. Just before we came to the famous Kicking Horse Pass he asked if I would like to drive the locomotive. Very pleased with myself, I had the simple task of taking the brass control lever as we entered the tunnel and then, as we emerged, the satisfaction of seeing the last cars of the train entering way below us.

Fortunately the journey did Sir Esme no harm and by the time we reached Washington, after a short stop in Chicago, his memory had recovered. He was able to continue his work in America for another three years when he retired in high honour, having meanwhile become Lord Howard of Penrith, the Cumberland home he so adored.

Quite early on – at one of President Coolidge's Inauguration Day balls in 1925 to be precise – I had met a girl whom I had known briefly in Bar Harbour in 1920. She came from an old New England family in Saugatuck, Connecticut and her name was Alice Labouisse Eno. Her mother, from New Orleans, was dead and her father, Henry Eno, was now married to an English girl and was living at Montacute House in Somerset, which he rented from Lord Curzon.

Alice had a direct manner and never hesitated to say exactly what she thought or felt. She was golden-haired with large blue eyes, a high rounded forehead and a small but firm chin. She bore a faint resemblance to Bette Davis but without the chronic impression the latter gave of having some unpleasant object under her nose. She was a brilliant tennis-player and kept her end up playing singles with both Suzanne Lenglen and Helen Wills. She was also a fine driver who never allowed herself to get rattled and invariably showed complete courage and calm in moments of crisis. She had the courage of a lion.

She had a flat in New York where she was attending Barnard College but was often at her father's house at Princeton where she looked after her younger brother during his school holidays. I think that we had been taken with one another at once but we only met at intervals until she came down to visit a great-uncle in his home in Washington. Soon afterwards I was going to stay with her for occasional weekend parties with Jock or other Washington friends. By 1926 we were at the stage where I brought back from leave in England a Sealyham puppy which she wanted. By the following spring we were deeply in love but decided to postpone the final decision until I had returned from my tour to the Pacific Coast.

In the early autumn we announced our engagement and were married in November in the beautiful Bethlehem crypt chapel of St John's Cathedral. It was the only part of it which had yet been built. My parents came out with my brother Francis, who was my best man. We passed a rapturous honeymoon riding on three-gaited horses through the sugar plantations of Camaguey in Cuba and sunbathing on the beaches of the Bahamas and Bermuda. My marriage to Alice was one of rare happiness and enjoyment which ended with her early death in 1953. On the occasions when there were disagreements, I can only say that it was always my fault. Certainly such success as I later attained first in diplomacy and later as member of Parliament for Taunton I owed very largely to her help and comfort. She captured all hearts whether of friend or foe.

Although I had been promised a speedy transfer to the Foreign Office it was to be another twelve months before we left Washington. We found a nice furnished house with a large studio in R Street and spent a happy year there and up on the North Shore the next summer. The main feature of diplomatic interest was the signature of the Kellogg Pact in January 1929, named after the secretary of state. The signatories included the United States, Germany, Japan and Poland and it was agreed to renounce war as an instrument of policy and to settle all conceivable disputes by pacific means. It had absolutely no effect of any kind in the Far East, in Europe or anywhere else.

In the autumn of 1928 we lived through the excitement of the presidential election. All our sympathies lay with Al Smith, the governor of New York, and his 'East Side, West Side, all around the town' campaign song, rather than the slightly stuffy Mr Hoover, but we kept our views to ourselves. We led a fairly quiet life that year, going out a bit in Washington, with racing and point to points in the spring. About this time came the laying of the new embassy foundation stone by Sir Esme. There were some big tennis tournaments for Alice on the North Shore in the summer and some black duck shooting with Alice's uncle, Peter Labouisse, in September at his camp in Maine. There was tobogganing in Rock Creek Park when the snow came at Christmas time and of course there was the same steady grind of work at the office. It was not until after the New Year that we left Washington for London and the Foreign Office.

5
Civil Servant

It was good to be back in England again after four long years and especially to be arriving with a beautiful wife whom I was longing to show off to my friends. She knew England well and had a low-pitched mid-Atlantic voice which, apart from a few American mannerisms, made it difficult to tell her country of origin.

My first duty was to call on the private secretaries at the Foreign Office to learn my fate. I found I had been appointed to the Treaty Department. I had no idea what that meant but it was a disappointment; after four years as a private secretary I had hoped to go to a political and geographic department to learn a little more about my trade. It is true that by the end of my time in Washington I had become quite used to drafting many of the political dispatches to the Foreign Office, including the weekly accounts of the recent election campaign, but I really felt the need to concentrate fully on one country or area. As it turned out, during twenty-one years in the Service, including several spells at the Foreign Office. I never worked in a political department. For me, although I had many fascinating jobs, especially in wartime, it was a misfortune.

I discovered that the Treaty Department, apart from certain obvious duties such as the actual preparation and ceremonial signature of treaties, was basically concerned with all questions of citizenship – foreign marriages, dual nationality, extradition. The grant of passports, though not their actual issue, also came our way. It involved the most intricate technical problems in which I ultimately became fairly proficient. It also dealt with the issue by the Foreign Office of 'exequaturs' authorising foreign consuls to carry out their official functions. I recall the magnificent, brightly coloured commissions which all had to be examined by us before the 'exequaturs' could be granted. There were still many monarchies in the world and the commissions would list the full titles. I particularly remember one commission of King Alfonso XIII of Spain with its resplendent coat of arms and a long string of titles including 'King of Jerusalem'. It ended with the signature in the king's own handwriting 'Yo el Rey' – 'I the King'.

We were also to some extent concerned with low-level protocol – dealing with the appointment of foreign ambassadors – but when it came to the top stuff – the presentation of letters of credence by an ambassador to the Sovereign – it all passed out of our dusty office to that of the vice-marshal of the Diplomatic Corps, John Monck, next door to that of the foreign secretary. Eventually it ended with the marshal himself, with his plumed cocked-hat and scarlet tunic, in a state coach and, in those days, with an escort of the Household Cavalry for the occasion.

Once one had learnt the routine of the work from the two rather elderly but highly-skilled bureaucrats with whom my one diplomatic colleague and I shared a room, it was fairly straightforward and did not vary much from one week to another. However, I wrote reams of earnest minutes which worked their way up through the kindly head of our department to an assistant under-secretary where the buck always stopped. I cannot pretend that I was greatly interested or that our work had much to do with world affairs.

Having had no leave since our few weeks of honeymooning early the previous year, I was given a three-week holiday and we decided to go skiing. But first we had to find somewhere to live. As neither Alice nor I had much furniture of our own available we decided to take a furnished house. By a stroke of luck we learnt that Lord and Lady Willingdon had just what we wanted, a house which they always let while he was overseas, first as governor of Bengal and later governor-general of Canada. He was eventually to become viceroy of India. It was at No. 5 Lygon Place, a small row of nice Edwardian houses backing off from the end of Ebury Street near Victoria Station. It had all the rooms we needed including provision for a baby which was on its way.

Though the furniture had no special charm, consisting mostly of Edwardian satinwood, the house itself was in some ways remarkable. Lady Willingdon had a passion for the colour mauve, so all the sheets, pillowcases, towels and bathmats, as well as the drawing-room and bedroom curtains and carpets, were in the same colour. Even the loo paper was mauve. Our bedroom had a large double bed of gilded wood and cane with mauve damask hangings. It also had a sort of cupola from the centre of which hung a short chain with a gilt statuette of Eros shooting a little arrow into the centre of the mattress. We felt this to be unnecessary and had it taken down for as long as we were staying there. There was a well-kept garden at the back and of all things a full-size squash court, a game of which we were both keen players. It cost £1,000 a year, including the salary of a trusted housemaid who Lady Willingdon always insisted should remain in place.

About a year later Lady Willingdon, a tough and determined lady on leave in England, asked if she might come to tea. She examined the whole house with occasional tut-tutting over some item which was out of place. Coming down the stairs to leave she noticed a fine oil painting by, I think, Augustus John, of a distinguished-looking Indian in khaki uniform and turban. 'Heavens,' she said, 'Sir Pertab Singh, the first Indian VC of the war! I'm taking it.' Before we had time to protest, she had it off its hook and under her arm – to put straight into her waiting motor-car.

In late March we had two weeks skiing at St Moritz. We stayed at the Palace, which then as now was the fashionable centre. I had already learnt to ski passably at Semmering in Austria one Christmas holiday. Alice started from scratch. However, she was already a good skater and her extraordinary natural sense of balance quickly enabled her to leave the practice slopes for short runs. By the time we left she was accompanying me on longer expeditions, including one run down to the Italian frontier where we sat happily in the sunshine drinking 'Offener Asti'.

We returned to take up our abode in our new home. In those days even a medium-sized house entailed a full staff, which my mother had helped us to collect. There was no lack of candidates at the numerous domestic agencies. There was a butler with the surname of Ellen, which his small size and certain natural instincts fitted perfectly. He was high competent but even though we were young and entertained very modestly, he still required the help of a footman in livery before he thought he could do his job. There was a cook and a kitchenmaid and a second housemaid. The house had a front door step which had to be washed every morning. There was an argument between the kitchenmaid and the junior housemaid as to whose job it was. We frankly had no idea, so the step went dirty. The next day Alice, determined to put an end to the matter, took a pail of hot water and went and scrubbed it herself. The question did not arise again.

We did all the usual things of the youth of that day. We joined the Embassy Club in Bond Street which was the fashionable place to dine and dance to Harry Roy's band. This was the favourite resort of the Prince of Wales and Prince George. The other popular nightclub, the Gargoyle, belonged to my friend David Tennant and was more Bohemian in character. We went a lot to the theatre, which Alice loved. I had met Noël Coward in earlier days and we often went to his house in Gerald Road, which was not far from us. We also played a lot of bridge at friends' homes. It seems astonishing now that even if they just had a couple of tables after dinner, it was very probable that you would be told it was 'white tie' and full evening gowns for the ladies. So was it at my club, the Marlborough, where evening dress was obligatory in the Coffee Room, even if you were dining alone, while several older members still invariably put on a white tie.

Over weekends we rode in Richmond Park or played squash in our own court. But we also had another piece of luck. Sir Robert Vansittart, the head of the Foreign Office, was a keen and good tennis player. He had stayed out in Washington a couple of times during my years there and I had got to know him well. I had great admiration and affection for him. He and his lovely wife Sarita lived at Denham House, just out of London, and once he realised how good a player Alice was, we were asked down to play tennis there as an almost weekly event. We often stayed for a lovely cold supper and through him I became familiar not just with the Foreign Office but major world events far removed from the routine of the Treaty Department. He had a brilliant mind. I was told by one of my Washington colleagues that when second secretary at the Paris embassy in the early 1900s, Van, as he was known, had three of his own plays in French running in Paris simultaneously. He had an almost palpable charm and enthusiasm which set one aglow. But he was also a Cassandra, notably about the German threat. In the long run I suppose he was deemed a failure. Was it that he was too unorthodox for the Whitehall mind, even for the more free-thinking members of the Diplomatic Service? Or was it that the politicians could not think fast enough for him? I am afraid it was a bit of both.

Adrian Baillie was back in England looking for a seat in Parliament but also busy courting Olive Wilson-Filmer whom he married a year or so later. She was originally Olive Paget, the daughter of Lord Queenborough, a leading light in the Conservative Party. Her mother had been Pauline Whitney so she was not exactly short of cash. She had in fact at just about that time bought Leeds Castle in Kent, 'the loveliest castle in England'. Olive became one of my greatest friends and Leeds was a home from home for many years – indeed until her death in 1975. Adrian meanwhile persuaded me to join Buck's Club off Bond Street which was a little livelier than the Marlborough. It occupied a beautiful early eighteenth-century house off Bond Street and as well as a good chef it had an excellent oyster bar. The expert opener, Marks, was eventually suborned by Olaf Hambro, a Buck's member, when he bought Wilton's and together they turned it into the most famous oyster restaurant in the world.

Life began to settle down to a routine. We had moved into our new house and were happy there. I had met many old friends and we had made some new ones. We had acquired a chauffeur, ex-RAF, who enjoyed driving the open Lincoln we had brought from Washington. The baby was due in September and I had become if not satisfied at least resigned to my job in the Foreign Office. We decided the time had come to face the rigours of the London Season of which neither of us had any experience.

Admittedly in 1921, the only year in which I did not go straight abroad after Cambridge summer term, I had spent a hectic two months in London doing the ballroom circuit. Young bachelors were apparently much in demand and scarcely an evening passed when I was not asked by friends of my family or indeed sometimes total strangers to accompany some débutante first to a dinner party and then on to a private dance. There you sat out on the staircase and drank claret cup. Otherwise it was a big ball in some great mansion. So it was that I attended the last ball to be held at Devonshire House before it was pulled down and another at Lansdowne House, still with its large garden, the rented home of Gordon Selfridge, whose son was a friend of mine at Cambridge. Ticket affairs such as charity balls were rare, being roughly limited to the Caledonian and Rose Day balls.

In 1921 London had been still trying to pretend that everything would go back to what it was in 1914. Typical of this was the Sunday after-church parade in Hyde Park on that broad path running alongside Park Lane. We four males put on our top hats and morning coats and my mother and any girls with us wore their best. Up and down one went, bowing and tipping one's hat every few minutes. About half way up, at Grosvenor Gate, there was a fountain and around this were assembled on the grass a hundred or so of the little hard green folding chairs supplied by the park authorities for which you paid a penny. All in all it was a most extraodinary performance and by the time Alice and I came back to London it had, luckily, almost died out. We preferred a round of golf.

Another standard event of the Season was the Eton and Harrow match at Lord's. But in one way it had radically changed. I had last attended it in 1921 and I believe that was the last time when, in another pre-war revival, all the top-hatted brigade, aged from twelve to eighty, when stumps were drawn and whatever the result of the match, invaded the pitch and went for one another tooth and nail with sticks or umbrellas, bashing and shouting, to try to tear out the bright blue cornflowers of Harrow or the pale-blue dyed carnations of Eton from the others' buttonholes. It was a wretchedly undignified spectacle and the embarrassment it caused other onlookers was such that this last relic of Victorian boorishness was abandoned by agreement of all concerned.

Compulsory features of the Season were the Drawing Rooms at Buckingham Palace where the débutantes were formally presented at Court. They were held at eight o'clock at night. At least as awesome as any other part of the proceedings were the two to three hours' wait that one had to suffer on the way to the Palace. Cars assembled in Trafalgar Square and from the Admiralty Arch down the Mall there was a long line of limousines each with its chauffeur and footman. Their movement was at snail's pace, for as well as the formalities when you ultimately reached the gates, there was a crowd of eager onlookers leaving their Whitehall offices crowded round each vehicle, staring at the occupants. We felt like goldfish. The girls were in pale-coloured dresses, the three required ostrich feathers in their hair, long white gloves above the elbow, while we men were either in full dress uniform or black velvet court dress, all with swords. The lady who was doing the presenting, in our case my mother, could according to the rules introduce young friends as well as relations so that sometimes the little groups moving slowly down the corridors had a slight look of the barnyard.

Once they arrived at the Throne Room, the drill was for the ladies about to be presented to advance in line to the Lord Chamberlain. A footman adjusted their trains, their name was called out and then down they went in a full curtsy with the right leg stretched back and the plumes on the head almost touching the ground. It must have been a terrifying ordeal. That same year, our friend Alice Hammond of New York, married to my oldest friend Arthur Duckworth, to whom I was best man, was also having a baby. She fainted clean away on the steps of the throne.

The presentations took several hours and as far as I remember we were not given supper. As I had been there on duty I was entitled to the 'entrée' and so to use the Diplomatic Corps entrance to the left of the palace to leave. While we were waiting for our car, there was the sound of horses' hoofs and in the soft yellow lamplight a high red coach with coachman and footmen in powdered wigs and cocked hats came clattering into the small courtyard. It was the state coach of the Duke of Norfolk, the Earl Marshal, and you felt you were straight back in the eighteenth century.

Our next and, as it proved, disastrous engagement was Ascot Week. We went with my family and some American friends to our first experience of what in those days was considered the ultimate social occasion of the year. As a member of the Marlborough, which was the only club with a tent on the stand side of the course (a privilege stemming from its founder, King Edward VII), I was able to give them a suitable lunch. Unfortunately we decided to come back a second day with another long, long wait in the car under a boiling sun. It was too much for poor Alice. She felt desperately tired when we got home and the next day she lost her baby.

We were heartbroken. To begin with Alice had not wanted the baby but once reconciled had looked forward to it desperately. Parliament was due to rise in about a month so, once she was fit to travel, our leave, which in those days was two whole months a year, was brought forward. We decided on the South of France. That year, 1929, was the first time that the Riviera, always hitherto a winter resort, had taken the bold step of opening its hotels and beaches in the summer. It was an instant and overwhelming success and the famous hotels of Cannes, Nice and Monte Carlo were packed. They never looked back. We decided to stay at the rather more select Hôtel du Cap at Antibes. There was a lovely swimming pool at Eden Roc and the blue Mediterranean itself, still quite unpolluted. We felt we were back in the Caribbean and Alice slowly recovered her strength. There were rather too many old friends from London but we managed to keep to ourselves. One day, as we were walking back to our room after lunch, two large Rolls-Royces swept round the curved drive to pull up at the hotel. Out came two leading Socialist Cabinet ministers, Sir Oswald Mosley and John Strachey, with their wives, chauffeurs, governesses and children. We thought what an admirable photograph it would make in the *Daily Herald*.

Once home in London we soon got back to normal. The only break in my usual Foreign Office routine was the organisation of yet another Naval Conference, this time to ratify the results of the prime minister's visit to Washington. The conference was opened by the King and that evening the government gave a dinner party at the Savoy to welcome the guests. There was a long and select menu. The claret was a Château Lafite 1865. Willy Bridgeman, the former first lord of the Admiralty, whom I found opposite me, looking at the bottle remarked, 'Of course no Conservative government could afford to give a dinner like this.'

The event that year that burned itself into the minds of the whole world was the Wall Street Crash. It was destined to turn the politics of the United States inside out and to initiate the Great Depression. We ourselves were not at once directly affected. We had no investments in common stocks on margin, our incomes, apart from my meagre salary, stemming mainly from government securities or real estate. To begin with, once the first mad panic had subsided, the American public, ever optimistic, thought that it would soon right itself. It was not to be.

It had little effect on my own work or on our private lives. On the contrary, I had started to organise my affairs so that I could get an occasional day's hunting with a pack of hounds near London. I had also acquired from a friend a well-bred sixteen-hands hunter called Supercharger. He lived up to his name and took on some frightening obstacles. The first season I kept him at Harpenden, hunting with the Hertfordshire, and sometimes in the Garth country. Whitehall in those days always worked till lunchtime on Saturdays, so to get a free day one had to do a deal with a colleague in the department, and take on his work every other weekend. The next winter I rented a small house in our old village at Duntisbourne and stabled Supercharger at Andoversford so as to be able to go out from time to time with our old pack, the Cotswold. It was in every respect a breath of fresh air and I had some glorious days over the stone walls. To this day I can imagine nothing more wonderful than a fast run with the Cotswold on a cold dry December afternoon.

My family came down to stay with us for Christmas. Somehow we all managed to pile into the small Cotswold house. We brought no staff and thought it would be fun to handle the big turkey ourselves. Unfortunately there was nowhere big enough in the kitchen to take it so after church it had to be roasted in some fashion over an open stone fireplace in the drawing-room. It took three hours with my father anxiously basting it. To add to the confusion, I had given Alice a new type of cocktail shaker from Asprey. It was designed for places such as this with no ice available and it froze the cocktails with chemicals screwed into a little compartment at the bottom. With the long delay, we had first one dry martini and then another. it was only after a while that we realised that their evident potency was due to the fact that though ice-cold, no water had been mixed with them at all!

Soon after the New Year of 1931, when I became a second secretary, I learned that I was to be appointed to the legation in Stockholm in the early spring. It was a small post but had the merit, from my point of view, that as the only secretary I would occasionally be called upon to take charge of the mission when the minister was away on leave. We said our farewells and made our plans. Sadly I parted from Supercharger and we got our skis out of store.

6

Venice of the North

In April 1931 we left for Stockholm, travelling for some odd reason via Berlin with a short sea passage from the island of Rügen. We stayed at the Grand Hotel. Snow lay thick on the Skärgård, the archipelago surrounding the capital, and the innumerable canals and inland lakes were still frozen hard. The city was beautiful with its medieval centre contrasted and glorified by the spires of the modern churches and the Town Hall. Yet Stockholm still seemed only a big country town with the woods and cultivated land running straight into the outskirts on all sides. Our legation was newly built on one of the smaller pieces of water only a short walk from woods and open fields.

The minister, Sir Howard Kennard, brusque, outspoken but likeable, was about to leave on transfer to Poland. He was the only career diplomat on the staff apart from myself. There was an honorary attaché, Kenneth Harrington, a commercial secretary and a translator. Then there was Strandberg, the chancery servant, who had known generations of British diplomats and upon whom the whole edifice depended. Yet except for very rare occasions it would be fair to say that we were overstaffed. I estimated that I had about one hour's serious work a day and apart from reporting the squabbling of the local Conservative and Liberal politicians, the only important dispatch I had to write that spring was on a new scheme for increasing corn production. I did not feel I was earning my pay.

Despite the great industrial and banking achievements of Sweden, such as Swedish Match, her great steel industry and the SKF ball-bearing company, there was a Rip Van Winkle quality about life which differentiated the country from anywhere I had ever been. I suppose it was partly due to the fact that they had not been drawn into the Great War, nor indeed had they been engaged in war at all for 120 years. Except in international circles, six o'clock was the staple hour for dinner parties and woe betide you if you arrived one minute late or one minute early. Many were the times when we walked round the block to get it just right. White ties and decorations were generally *de rigueur* with formal toasting and speechifying by host and guest of honour. At ten o'clock a big silver tray with teapot and cups appeared in front of the hostess. It was known as the 'go to hell' tray! In their strictly personal affairs they were more up to date except for a fond belief among the youth that out in the woods on Midsummer's Night there was no need to resort to any form of contraceptive. We had a mooring alongside the legation which was most convenient. Unfortunately on normal days its rustic appearance was marred each morning by dozens of condoms floating in the water around the boat.

Not long before leaving England we had acquired a 1929 6¼ litre Bentley. Freddy March, later Duke of Richmond, who had a passionate and lifelong love of motor racing and all its adjuncts, was then working for W.O. and H.S. Bentley. He showed us a car which belonged to Babe Barnato, the millionaire racing driver; it was the machine in which he won a bet to beat the Blue Train from the Riviera to London (in the event he arrived there before the Blue Train got to Calais). It had been little used and he was letting it go cheap. The body was made of a fabric stretched over wooden struts and known as a 'Wayman' which was popular at the time. I cannot imagine, given a serious accident, any structure better calculated to lead to instant death. It was much admired in Stockholm and, we were told, led to a small-scale demand for Bentley products. Alas it was too late to save the Bentley brothers from bankruptcy – due, I fear, to more skill in engine and chassis design than in their financial methods. They were swallowed up by Rolls-Royce and for forty years lost all identity except for the name and radiator design. I foolishly sold my car three years later for £100 when I was appointed to a post in Cairo. I was told recently that it is now in the Automobile Museum of Southern California and its value is rather higher!

At the time of our arrival King Gustav V was seventy-three years old but was still playing tennis, which he loved, during his annual visits to the French Riviera. Above all he encouraged and helped finance the immaculate indoor courts in Stockholm. We joined the King's Tennis Club as it was called but soon afterwards Alice started another baby and she was too determined to avoid any risks to make much use of the club. But it was those same indoor courts which launched the epic story of Swedish professional tennis and the dominance of Borg and Edberg.

We took over the flat of my predecessor at Engelbrechts Gatan 25 in a nice square called the Hummlegärden – the Hop Garden. This time Alice had a welcome consignment of furniture from the Princeton house which had been left to her by her father and which we had picked out the previous year. It was mostly English eighteenth century though there were also a few nice French pieces. There was a medium-sized Chippendale four-poster bed and a lovely yellow Herat carpet of the early eighteenth century. We filled out with local Swedish kitchen furniture and for our spare room a style known there as '*funkis*', or functional, which was the latest fashion but did not stand up to the test of time or taste.

The building in which we lived belonged to Count and Countess Karl Bonde. He was the head of a famous Swedish family and she was a Wallenberg, the sister of two of the leading bankers of the country, Jacob and Marcus of the Stockholms Enskilda bank. The Bondes had the flat immediately above ours where they entertained lavishly. They also owned one of the splendid medieval or, more often, seventeenth-century castles, complete with moat and drawbridge, which adorned the Swedish countryside. We were later to be asked to stay in one or two of them and made many friends, including the von Rosen family of Katrineholm, to the south of Stockholm, where we later stayed frequently. The son, Klumpus, who became my closest friend there, was in the Horse Guards and he and I often rode together in Stockholm in the early mornings. Soon after I left he was killed looping the loop in a friend's private plane with the seat-belt left open. His sister Maud was a brilliant sculptor and pupil of Milès.

Life in the country was very simple and unpretentious with the usual naked swimming in the lake even when, as on one occasion, Prince Gustav Adolf and other young Bernadotte princes were also staying. The father, Count Clarence, was a famous horseman and chairman of the Swedish Olympic Committee. Later they introduced me to a club in Stockholm which ran a drag hunt, very fast over stiff post and rail fences, culminating rather tamely with a presentation of sprigs of fir all round. In the autumn I had a few days shooting the '*rep-hüne*', a type of grouse. At an open-air lunch we each ate half a cold bird and I was amazed to see my fellow guns

[75]

throwing the stripped carcases and bones to their pointers and other dogs. They explained that they had never any harmful results. I was also invited to hunt an elk, the Swedish name for its still bigger cousin, the Canadian moose. I had often come across them when driving through a forest, standing gaunt and aloof with their great flat antlers, and could not bring myself to shoot them.

When the minister left I had a few days in charge of the legation before his successor, Archibald Clark Kerr, arrived. He was of Australian origin but had come to Scotland as a boy. He had ability, charm and a quick wit, albeit with a tendency towards malice. He had a brilliant career and had particularly distinguished himself as second-in-command to Lord Lloyd, the high commissioner for Egypt, from 1926 till 1930. His liberal sympathies in political matters formed a useful brake on Lloyd's authoritarian views at a delicate moment when it was necessary to balance strength with understanding. We and our wives became close friends though with my set Conservative views he and I quite often found ourselves in disagreement. Needless to say, this hardly applied to events in Sweden where there was little room for differences of opinion.

His wife Tita was an enchanting young Chilean whom he had married while minister in Santiago. Curiously enough his best man had been the hard-line right-wing dictator of Chile, Senor Ibañez. Tita was very pretty, combining soft brown eyes with light hair and a fair complexion and nicely rounded figure. She always reminded me of a white kitten. On the liner back to England she had a fall on the companionway which led to a miscarriage. It was a crushing blow which led to misunderstandings with Archie and eventually to the break up of a marriage which in any case had always been full of pitfalls. The birth of an heir would have done much to obviate Archie's tendencies in other directions.

When I met him he had become an almost professional Scot with strong views on Scottish nationalism. He brought out two young footmen with him, one of whom almost caused a revolt in the neighbourhood by marching in kilted splendour round the legation on its little promontory every morning at eight, playing the pipes. They also waited at dinner parties in the rather small dining room, similarly attired and at the end almost deafening the guests with the bagpipes. The Swedes grumbled and put it down to eccentricity but I believe were secretly rather proud of it.

When the time came for the minister to present his letters of credence to King Gustav, I drove with him in the eighteenth-century state coach to the palace, an imposing building on another small island of its own. We were accompanied by a troop of the Horse Guards in their bright Swedish blue uniforms and pointed Germanic helmets. Inside, on the long stone staircase leading up to the Throne Room, there were tall guardsmen in the original buff leather surcoats of King Charles XII, one on every step alternately to right and left, with their three-cornered hats and thigh-length boots. Each held his sword at the present. The King was affable and talked about Wimbledon while the ladies of the court were attractive in their eighteenth-century court dress and puffed short sleeves. Oddly, at about this time someone had the idea of putting the whole Swedish conscript army in their greyish service dress into three-cornered hats the time of Charles XII, which looked most peculiar. It was unpopular and did not last long.

In Stockholm itself we also made many friends, including the other members of the Wallenberg family, one of whom had an attractive Scottish wife who later married Charles Hambro. Alas, almost all are gone, but I still have one great friend, Princess Ann-Mari von Bismarck (née Tengbom), whom we see whenever we can. We played a lot of bridge for low stakes, we skated, we rode, we danced and I hope at least did something to maintain good Anglo-Swedish relations if nothing much else. Among the younger group who used often to come to dine and play bridge was Alexandra Sjiernstedt, the attractive daughter of Baron Erik Sjiernstedt, the head of the Swedish Red Cross and a friend of the Bonde family. A year later a kindly fortune was to introduce her to my brother John whom she shortly afterwards married, to everyone's satisfaction.

In the summer there were visits by two British cruisers and a ball at the legation with 150 people for dinner. We ourselves somehow managed to give a dinner in the flat for forty people. My young brother-in-law, Amos Eno, had come over from Princeton University to stay with us and produced a very welcome present in the form of a 22-foot Cris-Craft. We found it very useful at the little island house in the archipelago off Dalaro which with the Clark Kerrs we had taken for a couple of months in the summer. From it one of us drove in to the legation every other day. We had a beach and sometimes swam in the sea but it was cold and we preferred to go from time to

[77]

time to the big swimming pool at Saltsjöbaden on the way to Stockholm.

August was the season for eating '*kräftor*', the delicious saltwater crayfish of the Gulf of Bothnia. With more taste even than the sweet *langostinas* of the North Spanish coast, they are only beaten in my opinion by the *camaroens,* the giant prawns of Mozambique, especially when cooked in *pili-pili* sauce. The sun set very late and *kräftor* picnic parties set out nightly for the Skärgard with only a few hours of twilight till dawn. There was skill involved in picking out the most luscious ones; the trick was to find the females, which could be recognised by their rounded behinds. Washed down with classic O.P. Andersen snapps, they take a lot of beating.

Meanwhile in our idyllic island life we read and heard the ominous rumblings of financial and economic events which were the signal for the Great Depression. In Great Britain unemployment, already very high, had risen to over two and a half million. Our exports had fallen dramatically. By September the Labour government was in dire distress and torn in two over the necessary steps to stop the rot. The gold standard was suspended and panic followed. The government resigned but Ramsay MacDonald was persuaded by King George V to form a national coalition government. We were about to go to England on leave and I remember going down to Thomas Cook to pick up the tickets for our journey from Gothenburg by sea. As usual I offered to pay in the crisp white Bank of England five pound notes of the day. I was told that they could not accept them. Having been brought up on the almost holy belief of the total solidity of the Bank of England, I was horrified. We managed to collect enough dollars to make do.

Once arrived in London, we found ourselves in a blaze of patriotic fervour. A powerful Cabinet team of Conservatives, Labour and Liberals was being formed. Noël Coward's *Cavalcade* opened at His Majesty's and we all sang 'Land of Hope and Glory'. We took a nice corner flat at No. 1 St James's Street where you could get meals. Alice consulted a gynaecologist and to our surprise and delight we found that she was to have twins. We had discussions as to whether she should not wait until January for them to be born in London, given the drastic severity of the Swedish hospital code under which no anaesthetic could be given. We were still doubtful when an urgent call came to me from the Foreign Office to become temporarily assistant private secretary to Sir John Simon, the new foreign secretary. When I explained our situation they offered to keep me in London until the birth of the babies in January, as little was likely to occur in Stockholm over Christmas. This was agreeable to Archie Clark Kerr and to all others concerned.

We lived very quietly. One Sunday afternoon we had asked two friends to come in for a game of bridge. We sat playing at a table in the semi-circular niche immediately overlooking the front of St James's Palace. Suddenly there was an overwhelming smell of ether. It hit us all and I threw open the windows. It was some time before the air in the room cleared. Finally we gave up and after a drink the other two left. Dinner was brought up and we went to bed early. Towards midnight Alice awoke in great pain and it was clear that the twins were on their way. I telephoned her gynaecologist and at once took her by taxi to the nursing home in Welbeck Street. By three o'clock it was all over and the babies, a boy and a girl, were both apparently doing well. The boy, who had had a difficult breach presentation delivery, was safe and well but the girl, who had given no trouble, proved to be a blue baby who lived only four days.

Afterwards we puzzled over the episode of the ether but finally let it drop from our minds. Here I must anticipate future events to describe a strange sequel. It was about a year later and we were staying for the weekend with the Sutherlands at Sutton Place near Guildford. The only other guests were the Duke of Alba, the future Spanish ambassador, and a niece of our hostess. I left early on the Monday by train to get to the Foreign Office. The Duchess had asked Alice to drive up with her later in the morning. It was an old Rolls-Royce with a partition. The day being cold, the windows were almost closed. Passing through Camberley there was suddenly an unbearable smell of ether which they both noticed simultaneously. They opened the windows and after a few minutes it disappeared. There was no way to account for it. When they reached London, Alice was dropped at my family's house in Hans Street where she was having lunch. She found the household in turmoil. It emerged that, an hour before, my mother had been taken to hospital by ambulance with a burst appendix and apparently with little hope of recovering.

Six years later in Egypt Alice's brother, Amos Eno, was staying with us for Christmas and had brought with him an American friend, Kate Davies Pulitzer. We had arranged a small desert expedition down the Red Sea coast, spending one night at a hot sulphur well called Ain Sukhna – now incredibly a thriving oil terminal – and going on next day to the fifth-century hermitage of St Anthony in the hills where the saint, tempted by the Devil, had taken him with hot pincers by the nose. At the last minute Alice heard of a big tennis tournament due to take place in Heliopolis and she and her brother, also a first-class player, decided to take part. We others, including two friends, Aziz Eloui Bey and his American wife Lee Miller, the surrealist photographer, left for the Suez desert in two cars soon after lunch. Though early in December it was still very hot and Lee and I drove in shirtsleeves in my old open Ford two-seater with balloon tyres, with the others following us closely. On arrival we were making a fire on the beach and preparing drinks and dinner when I felt suddenly very cold. I though nothing of it and we settled down in our bedding rolls to sleep under the stars. About midnight I was awakened by an excruciating pain in my chest. Feeling very sick and having difficulty in breathing, I thought it must be a heart attack. All they could do was to give me a few aspirins and I had a painful night. At dawn we set off in my car for the French hospital in Suez along the bumpy desert track. Lee was driving, I was still in anguish. It took about two hours. When they finally came to examine me it turned out to be a severe dry pleurisy, very painful but not immediately dangerous. They gave me a sedative and in the afternoon we set out for Cairo, arriving about six. When we rang the bell the door was thrown open and there was Alice white in the face. It appeared that on their way back from the tournament in the station-wagon with its windows wide open there had suddenly been an overpowering smell of ether which, given her past experience, had understandably terrified her.

After I had been at the Foreign Office for a while Sir John Simon asked me to stay on permanently and I did not return to Stockholm until February and then only temporarily. In the spring I was arranging for the furniture to be packed when there came a bombshell. Ivar Kreuger, the world-famous multi-millionaire financier, the head of the Swedish Match empire and the Kreuger and Toll finance house, had shot himself in his Paris flat. Something had happened in Sweden at last to force it into the headlines.

Stockholm immediately blossomed with American and English

bankers and chartered accountants, Brown Shipley, Lee Higginson among others. I had only once met Kreuger, at a cocktail party he had given at his penthouse the previous summer in a luxurious block of flats. There was a nice roof garden where we circulated in the summertime and someone pointed out to me a small but solid windowless brick block on the top. I was told that this was where the great man did his thinking, planning the international loans to governments and industries from which his fame and fortune were derived. When later they came to break in, it was found that the main piece of furniture was a printing press on which he himself had printed the scrip of these international loans. There was one still in the press – an Italian government loan worth £23,000,000. The effect of Kreuger's vast financial banditry was much the same at the time as the Maxwell scandal.

One of the young accountants selected by Price Waterhouse to go out for them was my brother John, to be left behind with a few others after the turmoil subsided to try to sort out the mess. He was there for several months and in the process got engaged. I finally arrived home in May after such a rough passage from Gothenburg that I and the famous General Lord Allenby, who had been staying at the legation, were the only two passengers to remain on deck – and that only thanks to copious refills of snapps.

7
Life with Simon

The private secretaries' room adjoining the secretary of state's room at the Foreign Office overlooked St James's Park. There were three large desks for the private secretary, Sir Walford Selby, and the two assistant private secretaries, Nigel Ronald and myself. In addition there was a small occasional desk for the Parliamentary private secretary, Edgar Granvill, National Liberal MP for Eye. Our own secretaries, headed by the indispensable Miss Evans, were known as 'the ladies next door'. Nothing except a few old Foreign Office lists and a *Who's Who* was kept in our room but the cupboards next door were brim full of top secret papers and there was a formidable safe with some material so secret that it was hidden even from our eyes. Selby was a senior Foreign Office man who had been one of my sponsors. He seemed to know everything but was nervous by temperament and frightened of our secretary of state which tended to make him splutter when he talked to him. Ronald was a former Grenadier from Dorset who had been badly gassed in the war and took the Foreign Secretary more philosophically.

Frock-coated office-keepers came in and out with the scarlet leather, gold-crested dispatch boxes which carried files from one department to another, while in a corner were half a dozen older snuff-coloured boxes with a special lock, to which only a select few had keys, for papers coming from No. 10 or MI6. The latter included telegram intercepts as well as records of telephone conversations with London-based foreign diplomats. Sometimes they also revealed astonishingly indiscreet remarks by some of our own people, even in the highest positions.

On a large round table lay the morning papers which were removed at four o'clock to make room for a casual tea-party to which I was duly made welcome. Beside ourselves it was attended by two or three assistant under-secretaries and from time to time by Vansittart himself and his private secretary, Clifford Norton. It was an opportunity for exchanging news and gossip which was often useful and always agreeable.

Sir John Simon himself was a remarkable man. His intellect was of the highest order as were his personal standards of conduct. He was alleged by the Nazis, notably Goebbels, to be of Jewish origin, presumably on account of his biblical name, but in fact his father was a Welsh Nonconformist minister. He was regarded as the most able lawyer of his day, his chief rival being F.E. Smith, later Lord Birkenhead, with whom he had been an undergraduate at Oxford. I remember my father in the Twenties telling me that Simon was earning over £70,000 a year at the Bar, an enormous sum in those days. He went early into politics as a Liberal and was soon appointed solicitor-general, to become once again an opponent of F.E., this time in the House of Commons. By the time the war came Simon was attorney-general and then, when the coalition government came in, home secretary. When Asquith brought in conscription in 1916, it was too much for Simon's Liberal principles and he resigned – but only to join the Royal Air Force. He came back to the Commons in 1922 and was to be out of office for another ten years. Meanwhile he made quite a nice fortune at the Bar.

Tall, grey-haired and distinguished, he had brown eyes that were just a shade too close together for him to be described as handsome. He could be witty and charming but in spite of his efforts had a rather chilly personality. Among his colleagues at the House of Commons he was not popular and when he reached high office it was unkindly said of him by some of my Tory MP friends that he had a habit of looking away when he shook hands. Still worse he was accused of slapping members on the back and calling them by the wrong Christian name. He was nervous and could be sarcastic. He had a little trick when irked by something one said of twisting his head down and to one side while he pointed out the idiocy of one's suggestion. But I always believed that by nature he was a kind man. He was certainly always remarkably good to me.

Our job was little different from that of all other private secretaries in Whitehall and included the collection of material for answers to Parliamentary questions and for speeches on public platforms or in the House. Like many good speakers the Foreign Secretary was desperately nervous beforehand. Twenty years later as a new MP myself I had been helping Mr Churchill, once more in opposition, with a major foreign affairs speech in the House of Commons. As Question Time ended and we walked together down the long corridor from his room to the Chamber he suddenly scowled and muttered to me through his teeth, 'By God, how I hate speaking.' As a complete neophyte I was much encouraged.

It was my special duty to accompany the foreign secretary to the House for questions each week and during all foreign affairs debates. I sat in the Official Gallery virtually on the floor of the House, ready, I hoped, to provide the answers sought from time to time by his PPS, Granvill, who came scurrying along the backbenches with little notes. It was there that the fascination of the House of Commons got into my blood and was to draw me in due course into politics myself.

When I arrived at the Foreign Office in October 1931 the gloomy and uncertain financial position in England and America was our main preoccupation. But Germany was also seething with troubles due to mass unemployment and continued resentment over the conditions of the Versailles Treaty. Even though the reparation clauses had faded out, the limitations on armaments were a constant source of popular anger. With the rising Nazi flood the scene was rapidly moving to fresh elections and Hitler. Poor Dr Brüning, the Catholic centre party chancellor, was now mainly governing by decree and with precious little help from the Allies. The only hopeful prospect lay in the Disarmament Conference due to meet at the League of Nations headquarters in Geneva in February 1932.

This had been laid down in the League Covenant and there had been years of work by a preparatory Commission. The delegations of sixty nations were to take part which did not help matters. Sir John Simon was the chief British delegate and made a great oration. There were many other speeches, long and time-consuming since all had to be translated, but the only immediate result was a hostile exchange between French and German delegations which seemed to be leading to an early breakdown. Simon was constantly being called upon to travel to Geneva which in those days was a exhausting process by ferry and rail. One or other of us always went with him. Later, when the work at Geneva became still heavier, he asked me to stay out there on a semi-permanent basis. Anthony Eden, the Parliamentary under-secretary at the Foreign Office, was also appointed a substitute delegate to stay more or less full-time in Geneva.

Though we knew from French sources that in addition to General von Seeckt's clever dodges for building up the numbers of trained men in the Reichswehr, a new chancellor, Herr von Papen, was clamouring for complete equal rights in weapons defence. British and French plans were drawn up to try to meet their complaints but they were never satisfied. In the autumn the German delegate withdrew from the conference altogether. Probably their refusal to get down to brass tacks was as much a manoeuvre to give more time to speed up their secret rearmament as anything else. Once more everything looked set for a total breakdown.

Meanwhile in January 1931 an event had occurred which later was to have a disastrous effect on future Conservative defence policy. Baldwin's 'Shadow Cabinet', as it would be called today, was busy preparing its policy on Indian self-government which had been generally accepted when Lord Irwin was appointed viceroy. But there were also a number of Conservatives who felt that Irwin had been going too fast in his attitude towards concessions and indeed to Gandhi himself. Churchill sympathised so strongly with these views that he felt himself obliged to resign from the Shadow Cabinet. This meant that when the National Government was formed later in the year Churchill was excluded and left alone to fight the forlorn battle for British rule in India just at the moment when his experience, personality and drive were most needed on matters of disarmament or, as it turned out, rearmament.

Churchill formed his own small group of Germany-watchers with the unstated blessing of Vansittart and the help of Desmond Morton formerly of MI6, who was to be one of his close personal advisers on many such matters in the war. My old friend Graham Christie, our former air attaché in Washington and Berlin who had won Goering's confidence, was able to supply him with many ominous statistics on German rearmament which he also passed to Van and sometimes myself.

It was obviously not my place as a junior private secretary to address memoranda to the Foreign Secretary but I did my best quietly to arouse his alarm by quoting from Christie's reports. Van himself put them over more forcefully to the Cabinet though due to his remarkable style not always in terms very intelligible to some of its members. He did so in a series of Cabinet papers which he called 'The Old Adam', setting out his doubts as to whether the Germans' warlike characteristics had in fact miraculously disappeared. This all fell largely on deaf ears. Time after time Simon came back to us from Cabinet meetings saying that his colleagues could not accept Van's doctrines. We sometimes wondered how much of it had received the support of the foreign secretary himself.

For six weeks or so I had settled down at the Beau-Rivage Hotel in Geneva which was the headquarters of the British delegation. Sir John Simon kindly suggested that as with other members of the delegation my wife should come out to join me. Geneva was a dull city with an unpleasant climate but we managed to enjoy ourselves playing a little golf at Divonne over the French border and seeing a few old friends. While at Geneva we got to know Anthony Eden with whom we used to lunch at the little restaurant with green shutters, La Perle du Lac. He admired Alice and we became close and so remained for nearly fifty years till his death. He was soon the leading light of the conference with the help of Alec Cadogan, later to be the wartime head of the Foreign Office. I remember a Fench journalist at the League once describing Eden after a press conference as 'ce jeune homme terrible qui aime tellement la paix' – a far cry from the attitude of the world press towards him at Suez.

In my view Eden is today a much-maligned man. Many seem to ignore his twenty years in the front line of world politics and diplomacy, concentrating only on the Suez debate. Yet in the Second World War Churchill scarcely made a single important decision on foreign, military or indeed domestic matters without consulting Eden, and this was even more noticeable in his peacetime premiership. Despite some faults he was an outstanding foreign secretary.

Another man I got to know in Geneva was the Italian Marchese Theodoli, for many years head of the Minorities Commission, who had several times asked me to attend their sessions. After a meeting on one difficult case, I asked him what was the possible solution. 'You can take it from me,' he said, 'after many years of bitter experience I have learnt that there is no solution to any minority problem.' It was a pessimistic view which shook me but which I fear over nearly sixty years has proved to be all too clearly correct.

Simon's first real test came in September 1931, when the Japanese launched an invasion of Manchuria, preceded by a massive aerial bombardment. The issue was immediately brought before the Council of the League of Nations. There were long debates and much talk of sanctions and indeed of the use of force; but the only positive

[86]

action was the dispatch of a League mission to Manchuria under the Earl of Lytton to investigate and report to the Council. Then there followed the occupation by the Japanese of the whole of Manchuria and later aggressive action against Shanghai.

The League of Nations Union in London and its supporters soon began to criticise what they regarded as inaction and blame fell mostly on Simon's shoulders. Yet I have no doubt that the one overriding desire of the British people was to stay out of war almost at any cost. Simon was bound to work for conciliation, at any rate until the report appeared. When it came out in the autumn of 1932 it recommended a compromise which, while accepting a temporary Japanese presence in Manchuria, would continue to recognise Chinese sovereignty. This half-hearted arrangement was adopted by the Council but it was Britain and particularly its foreign secretary who got the blame. A final call for an arms embargo also failed and Japan recognised an independent Manchuria under the former boy-Emperor of China.

Once we had heard that my appointment with Simon was permanent we started looking for a place to live in London. We were lucky to find just what we wanted, a small Queen Anne house for sale in a quiet street in Westminster. It had all the original panelling and open fireplaces. After our furniture from Stockholm was installed it was charming, with a bright nursery for our small son. We had found a nanny who was to stay with the family for forty years. We had also brought over a young Swedish maid and I managed to find a butler, Peachey, also a Gloucestershire man who afterwards accompanied us everywhere. He was a real character with a sang-froid and a special type of wit which could cope with any emergency. After the war he married our nanny and stayed with the family until his premature death.

Among our friends we naturally also had many young American couples living in London, including the former Wallis Spencer, now married to Ernest Simpson. We went to their house in Regent's Park where Wallis, sleek and imperturbable and now for the first time in her life with some money to spend, entertained beautifully.

In the spring we attended the wedding of Adrian Baillie to Olive Wilson-Filmer, at which I was an usher, and soon after went down to spend our first weekend at Leeds Castle. It was the first of many such visits over forty years. There they entertained every week on a lavish scale but fortunately with no publicity. Adrian was the new MP for Linlithgow and there were always a few of his colleagues and their wives staying too – for instance Captain David Margesson, the tough and brilliant chief whip of the Conservative Party, Brendan Bracken, Winston Churchill's faithful acolyte, and Geoffrey Lloyd, a Cambridge contemporary of mine and later wartime minister, all of whom I had come to know well through my work in the House.

Our minds often turned to the possibility of finding a house in the country for ourselves. This had been my dream since we left Duntisbourne all those years before. We started studying the tempting advertisements each week in *Country Life*. We wanted a small property in Gloucestershire where we could spend our leave and get Nicky used to life in the English countryside. We even considered the possibility of buying back Duntisbourne, changed as it was, without its wings, from a Gothic house to a very charming small Cotswold manor. Unfortunately when it came on the market in 1934, just after I had gone abroad, the agents in Cirencester forgot their promise to keep me informed and it went to someone else. It is now the home of Lord Richardson, the former Governor of the Bank of England.

By the spring of 1933 Eden and Cadogan were in despair at the lack of progress and had come to the conclusion that the only way to prevent a breakdown was to put forward a complete draft Convention with full details of numbers and categories of weapons to be allowed to each nation. With the help of General Temperley, the senior military adviser, a scheme was proposed and approved by the Cabinet. The prime minister agreed to present it himself and arrived in Geneva with Simon in time to speak on 16 March. Ramsay MacDonald excelled himself and had a warm reception. It was accepted as a basis for future work and was known as the MacDonald Plan. I was once again out in Geneva and remember well a dinner with the prime minister and Simon one night at which the only other guest was President de Valera of the Irish Free State. During the Irish troubles in the early Twenties I had regarded him as the devil incarnate. Now, contrary to my expectations, I found him both friendly and extremely good company.

There were immediate consultations in various capitals and while the Germans and Italians accepted the plan in principle, the French, by now deeply involved with domestic problems, hedged and spoke of a 'trial period'. The American delegate, Norman Davis, a kindly man, tried his best to be helpful. He talked a lot about 'locking horns' but in practice he achieved very little. It seemed, as Eden wrote in his memoirs, that 'the US wanted the highest degree of disarmament while contributing the least to security'. We ourselves, under pressure from the Air Ministry under Lord Londonderry, the air secretary, caused confusion by insisting on retaining the right of 'police bombing'. It was really a minor issue involving a method of policing and frontier control by air evolved by Lord Trenchard after the war for scattered and remote villages, employed originally in Iraq and Transjordan but by now mainly confined to the Aden Protectorate. It was said to be humane and was largely used on buildings; above all it was economical. But it was not indispensable, it did us much harm and it caused further delay. By the autumn it was the Germans who no longer seemed interested in the Convention. Talks between Simon and the German foreign minister, von Neurath, led to nothing. Simon, after an agony of preparation, addressed the Conference in a speech rejecting the proposal put forward by the Germans for their own immediate rearmament. He was supported by the French, the Italians and the Americans. That same afternoon Germany withdrew from the Conference and Hitler made a broadcast resigning from the League of Nations.

One is bound to speculate as to what was the reason for the timorous approach of the Cabinet to so many imaginative attempts put forward by Eden and the Foreign Office for breaking the deadlock. In Simon's presentation of proposals to Cabinet colleagues he seemed often to give only half-hearted support; sometimes he even sided with those who favoured inaction. This attitude was I believe due in large part to their awareness of the intense nationwide reluctance even to think about the possibility of another war. This led to many Conservative supporters shutting their eyes to the dangers ahead and eventually to that great sigh of relief when Munich seemed to have saved the situation. It affected policy both as it was deployed at Geneva and debated in Parliament. It led on the Labour side to their total opposition to any rearmament and the formation of such bodies as the Peace Pledge Union which in 1934 inundated our office with cards of support by the thousand, no doubt in preparation for the 1935 election.

It must be realised that at this early stage it was not a question of appeasement. That came later. To many in Britain the Germans were only making claims to what people thought was reasonable – the means to defend themselves. The strength of the Allies – or rather the French – was still overwhelming.

In the face of blatant German rearmament the only solution appeared to be to invoke the Treaty of Versailles; but that in the long run meant the use of force. The French with their internal political troubles were in no mood for that. It was made clear again by their refusal to act two years later when, far more provocatively, German troops swept into the demilitarised zone of the Rhineland against the strong protests of the German general staff. Nor had the French the necessary leader to impose drastic action. They were torn by inner troubles and constant changes of government which boded ill for resolute and unpopular decisions. In Great Britain it was little better, though with less excuse – for the National government faced no serious Labour threat, as was soon shown by the election results in 1935.

Eden by this time was lord privy seal and to all intents and purposes minister for League of Nations affairs which he later was called. In February he visited Berlin where according to his own account he found Hitler well-informed and restrained. There were promises of the scrupulous observation by Germany of every treaty entered into of its own free will and even some more talk of completing the tattered Disarmament Convention. But once Eden had left Berlin there were no signs of any concessions.

The disarmament discussions dragged on a little longer. By the time I left to take up a new post in Egypt in May 1934 there took place what in fact was to be the final meeting of the Conference on which such high hopes had been placed and which was now in total disarray. Soon afterwards a programme for a major increase in the strength of the Royal Air Force was proposed by the government. It was greeted by the Labour Party with a vote of censure.

Much later Eden wrote, 'The head of the delegation, John Simon, was not temperamentally equipped to drive the Conference into action and made skilful attempts to dodge decisions.' This was indeed a fatal flaw in Simon's character. The fact that he often could not easily make decisions even if they were important had been assumed to have been part of his legal background. I am not so sure. It showed up many times in other matters. We always sent him home with two or more – generally three – red boxes each night with the telegrams and the files needing action. Most came back duly in-itialled but there were some which seemed to be almost permanently avoided. One of these was the file dealing with the Four-Power Pact proposed by Mussolini. Under it Britain and France, Italy and Germany were to sign a treaty forbidding any change in the Treaty of Versailles without the agreement of all four parties. It sounded sensible but inevitably detracted from the work of the Disarmament Conference at a critical moment. Simon hesitated and procrastinated and the file came back to us always uninitialled. One day when I pressed him for an urgent decision he said with a faint smile, 'You know if there is one thing that bores me more than Disarmament it is the Four-Power Pact.' It was only eventually signed in the summer of 1934 after I had left for Egypt.

A different and quite unimportant case was worse. A secretary at one of our Balkan legations was having an affair with a lady known as 'Odol the toothy tart'. This was brought to our attention after complaints from the local British community. It was still under consideration when the head of the mission went on leave and the secretary in question was left in charge. A British naval squadron was visiting one of the Black Sea ports headed by a senior naval officer – my old Washington pal Captain Tottenham. At the reception which the chargé d'affaires gave at the legation for the admiral and his officers, Odol helped to receive the guests. This got back to the quarter-deck-minded admiral who reported it to the Admiralty who complained. There was much discussion in our office but ultimately it was decided that the young man had to go. But when this came to the ears of his father, a distinguished former civil servant, all hell broke loose. There were threats of libel appeals to Buckingham Palace and so forth. Week after week, even month after month, the file went back and forth to the secretary of state. He simply could not make up his mind. I forget now how it was ultimately settled.

Another example of Simon's temperament occurred when the Crown Prince of Abyssinia arrived in London on a semi-state visit. A grand dinner of about forty people was arranged for him in the lofty and elegant Locarno room of the Foreign Office and the co-host was to be Mr Baldwin. Uniform was to be worn and this was duly recorded on the foreign secretary's engagement-slip, always placed at the top of his red box. He had evidently not read it carefully for when he arrived he was wearing a tailcoat and white tie with a broad light-blue ribbon of the Star of India across his waistcoat. He took one look at us in our uniforms and exploded. We stood around aghast until Baldwin walked in dressed in the remarkable admiral's uniform of an Elder Brother of the Trinity, a title which so often confused foreigners. Simon at once said he would take no part in the dinner and Baldwin must act as host. Then I had a brain wave. 'Just across the way at No. 10,' I said, 'the prime minister has an identical privy counsellor's uniform. He is a little shorter and stouter but it will fit you and I am sure he will let you borrow it. I will try at once.' Simon demurred but Baldwin nodded to me to go. The prime minister was out to dinner but the butler at No. 10 immediately lent me the clothes and in ten minutes I was back with the gold-braided coat and trousers and the cocked hat.

I had unfortunately forgotten the sword and Simon again grumbled, but surrounded by us all started to undress. All went well and when at last he had got into the trousers and was buttoning his braces, 'Ah,' said Baldwin, 'that's better, a man always feels himself again once he has his braces on.' At the dinner Baldwin sat between the Abyssinian prime minister and one of the princely Rases. He did not exchange a single word with his neighbours during the whole of dinner, merely beaming genially to those on either side.

In the late autumn of 1933 a new Argentine ambassador arrived in London. The court was at Sandringham and they had asked that he should present his letters of credence to the King there. Now the Sandringham clocks in those days were half an hour in advance of the rest of the country. It was a permanent semi-summer-time instituted by King Edward VII to give him an extra half hour of extra daylight for shooting. This had been carefully explained by me beforehand to the secretary at the Argentine embassy. The ambassador was to travel by rail and a suitable train had been selected and agreed.

Shortly after we got back from lunch the telephone in our office rang and the secretary at the Argentine embassy said in great agitation that there had been a mix-up. They had got it wrong and thought that the ambassador was to be at the station half an hour later rather than earlier. He had missed the train and we now had to make new arrangements. We then had to explain the problem to the private secretary at Sandringham. I put in a call but was caught up with something else and when it came through Nigel Ronald answered. We had a dual line and he quickly signalled to me to pick up my receiver. Someone replied and Nigel asked who it was. 'This is the King,' came the reply in King George's gruff voice. Nigel apologised suitably and explained what had happened. It took a little time and soon the young lady operator cut in. 'Another three minutes' she asked, the normal procedure in those days. 'What's that you said?' said the King. 'Another three minutes?' 'What does she say?' said the King. It was clear that he had never made a trunk call before in his life. Nigel broke into the conversation and all was well.

At about this time Walford Selby left on his appointment to the legation in Vienna and was replaced by Horace Seymour. I was sorry to see him go for he had been a good friend to me. Unfortunately his personality clashed with that of the foreign secretary who thereby lost much of the advantage of Selby's knowledge and experience. Seymour was the complete antithesis. Instead of bubbling over with facts and excitement the new private secretary was imperturbable and slow-speaking. He was very good for Simon, simply by refusing to get rattled and pressing his point until he got a decision.

In the course of our private secretarial duties we were required to take all sorts of strange decisions. When I had been briefly in Vienna in 1923 with a friend on a short skiing holiday we spent a night or two in the Bristol Hotel. We were having a drink in the bar when an Englishman came in wearing blue overalls, covered with oil and very pleased with himself. He explained that he was Major Ralph Peto and had won a bet driving the Orient Express from Venice. I did not hear of him again until I was working in the private secretaries' room in about 1933 at the Foreign Office where Peto had once been employed. There had been several warnings about him from Sir Percy Loraine, the high commissioner in Cairo. Peto was staying at Shepheard's Hotel and had drawn some attention to himself by appearing several times at the Gezira Club dressed in full polo kit with a helmet and whip and carrying an enormous American leather bag of polo sticks. He kept asking where his ponies were. It soon transpired that they did not exist.

Now there were fresh signs of eccentricity and the high commissioner asked for authority to instruct the British consular court to send him home. We replied that it would require something far more damaging to justify such drastic action. It came very soon. The old Shepheard's Hotel had a large porte-cochère with a balcony overlooking the terrace on each side. In the mornings the *haut monde* of the tourist world sat sipping their dry martinis before lunch. About midday out came Ralph Peto on to the balcony, stark naked, and started to make a political speech. There was pandemonium. Peto was quickly bundled out of sight but the damage was done. As I remember he sailed in the next P & O boat for home.

It was soon after this incident that I was told that the Appointments Committee wanted me to go to Cairo myself. By this time I felt I had had my fill of private secretarial work and, having rented our house to a friend in the Foreign Office, we sailed from Marseilles to Alexandria in the late spring of 1934.

8

The Nile

'Good,' wrote Archie Clark Kerr from Stockholm when he heard that I was going to Cairo. 'You'll enjoy it, but you must make the effort to get close to the Egyptians – to their hearts I mean – not their little brown bodies.' I was grateful but not surprised at this advice considering while I already knew of his strongly liberal optimistic views while I could make a good guess at some of his more personal tastes.

Our own first aim on arrival in Egypt was to find a pleasant house with a garden, preferably on Gezira Island which lay between the Boulac district of Cairo proper and Imbaba on the Giza bank of the Nile, where Napoleon fought the Battle of the Pyramids. Ronnie Campbell, the counsellor, whom we had known and liked in Washington days and who asked us to stay, had just such a house himself next door to Russell Pasha, the commandant of the Cairo City Police. It was one of a row, white and well cared for, with green shutters, which from the days of Cromer had housed the leading British officials in the Egyptian government as well as senior members of the Residency. As it turned out, we luckily found the house of a young Egyptian named Mamdouh Riad Bey, of Jewish-Turkish descent though a keen nationalist in his politics and married to an attractive Romanian poetess. His grandfather had been foreign minister under the Khedive Ismail. We soon reached agreement on a lease to last for the period of our appointment and became friends.

Ours was just round the corner from the government-owned houses. There was a big drawing room and a dining room, some nice bedrooms and a large room in the basement giving on to the garden which we turned into a games room. The garden was fair-sized with a thick orange-flowered bignonia hedge all round, a large golden mohur tree in the middle, a pale mauve jacaranda and a fine mango tree. Each year we made hundreds of pounds out of the mangoes. There were crimson Clara Butt and russet Sang de Gazelle bougainvilleas climbing up the walls and a little balcony outside our bedroom where I often slept in the summer months.

Although he had left in 1907, there was a remarkable aura of the great Lord Cromer still pervading Egypt. At the Residency we annually received hundreds of letters mostly from *fellaheen*, the village folk, addressed to him sometimes by name but more often 'El Lord', with a large number of petitions also sent to the 'Mandub-is-Samy', the high commissioner. Many complained of landlords cutting off water or diverting small canals; others asked for help in getting a wife back from the arms of a friend, or of the tyrannical behaviour of the local *omdah* of a village. It was rather like an MP's 'consulting room' on a Friday evening. Each year, too, we received a petition from the Honourable Society of Palace Eunuchs for violation of retirement benefits granted by some earlier Khedive. It was said that if you took a taxi or horse-drawn gharry to drive you to the Residency all you need say was, 'Beit el lord' (the house of the Lord) and you would arrive there safely.

The Residency itself also had more the atmosphere of a colonial Government House than a diplomatic mission. It was a handsome white stucco building in a big garden which at that time still ran directly down to the Nile. There was a permanent British military guard on the gates. When the high commissioner drove out in his yellow Rolls he had a car of detectives going ahead and a British motor-cycle outrider on either side. This was all part of security precautions set up after the assassination of the Sirdar, also governor-general of the Sudan, ten years before. There were two service ADCs in uniform and a controller, besides a horde of *suffragis* in scarlet and gold uniforms with high red and white turbans. It was all very grand.

The high commissioner, Sir Miles Lampson, was a mountain of a man with genial features and a cunning razor-sharp mind. He had arrived only a few weeks before me after completing a successful career as minister in Peking. He was exactly the man needed for Egypt at the time. Though not always the soul of tact, his bluff approach and friendly manner were appreciated by Egyptians though puzzling to some accustomed to a more orthodox diplomatic style. I much enjoyed working for him and found him an easy and thoughtful chief. I already had some experience of Egyptian problems: the previous year I had taken part in an important conference in Sir John Simon's room at the House of Commons with Mr Baldwin and various other ministers, meeting Sir Percy Loraine, the retiring high commissioner, to discuss the matter of a treaty.

Putting it crudely, the Egyptians wanted us out whereas it was the key to British policy to ensure at all costs the safety of the Suez Canal and our line of communications to India. This applied as much to the Mediterranean in 1934 as it did to the safeguarding of our oil supplies in 1956. At the same time, our government was anxious to do all it could within these limits to satisfy Egptian desires for greater independence. So far it had eluded all efforts.

Egypt had been technically independent since 1922 but was boxed in by the Four Reserved Points which retained British responsibility for the Suez Canal, the defence of Egypt, the protection of foreigners and the control of the Sudan. In practical terms, this meant the presence of British garrisons in Cairo and Alexandria, the RAF aerodromes, the right of the Mediterranean Fleet to use Alexandria harbour as a base, the control of the Cairo, Alexandria, Port Said and Suez police. There were British advisers in key ministries, and a British inspector general and staff for the Egyptian Army. There were British, American and other foreign judges in the mixed courts which dealt with the affairs of all foreigners and law suits against Egyptians or one another, while there was a consular court purely for British subjects. This latter was all a hangover from the capitulations granted to foreigners under the Ottoman Empire. There was also a British commissioner of the Caisse de la Dette which had been set up to supervise foreign loans in the days of the spendthrift Khedive Ismail II. It was not surprising that Egyptians of all parties wanted to get rid of all this but hitherto every effort to agree on the terms of a treaty had failed. For us the security of imperial communications remained paramount.

One day the high commissioner described Egyptian politics to me as being like a three-legged stool – the Palace, the Residency and the Wafd. The latter was the nationalist party dating back nearly twenty years and the natural vote-getters – though not quite the winners of a hundred and one percent as they claimed at one poll in an election while I was there! If all three were evenly balanced, all went well; but let one leg get a little longer than the others and there was trouble. When I arrived, after two years of Palace government under

Sidky Pasha as prime minister, this was one of those moments. It was the acting high commissioner, Maurice Peterson, who started it soon after Sir Miles left for England on leave. He was the head of the Egyptian Department of the Foreign Office on temporary loan. He made courteous suggestions to the new prime minister, Nessim Pasha, for reform. The Wafd called more blatantly for a return of the constitution. The Palace responded by complaining of Residency interference in Egyptian internal affairs. The results were a general unease and very soon the usual student anti-British riots. As one drove to the office of a morning it was quite common to pass a tramcar lying on its side or even in flames. It was all routine and Russell Pasha's constables could cope quite easily.

But now, looming up ominously, came Italian complaints and demands on Abyssinia with threats of military action. Italian troop-ships poured through the Canal en route for Eritrea. In November I went down to Port Said to meet my father who was coming out by P & O to stay for the winter and I stopped for a moment near Ismailia to watch a crowded Italian transport go past. I suppose they spotted me as an Englishman standing there in my tweeds and a green soft hat in place of the usual red tarbush, for they started singing, laughing and cheering with cries of 'Nice, Tunis, Corsica' their opening claims. Meanwhile Italian garrisons were increasing in Tripolitania and Cyrenaica. None of this was lost either on the British government or on the Egyptian politicians. It seemed to be high time to renew the attempts to achieve a treaty in the interests of both parties. With the warm approval of the King talks began in April the following year.

The King, Fuad I, was a man of nearly seventy, the son of the Khedive Ismail who built the Suez Canal and who had been deposed for his wild extravagances in 1870 when Fuad was still a baby. He was a short, rather tubby man with a Kaiser moustache with waxed upright points. He had been brought up in Italy and was not particularly anglophile but he was determined at all costs not to lose his throne. Queen Nazli was much younger and more frivolously inclined as she was to demonstrate later in life. In my day the only time you saw her was during the King's speech at the opening of Parliament, sitting in the royal box with her ladies all in white gowns with their white veils covering all but their eyes. The King had a curious affliction which took the form of a sharp dog-like bark when he was slightly nervous. It was always said to have been caused by having been shot as a young man in the throat at the Mohamet Ali Club in Cairo by an infuriated brother-in-law as a result of an affair or some other mistreatment of his first wife, Princess Shuwekar.

The Residency was still established in its Alexandria summer quarters when Sir Miles came back from leave. When he went to pay his respects to the King at Montaza Palace he took me with him to present me to His Majesty. I was waiting in the next room talking to the royal ADC with the door slightly ajar when I heard a series of sharp barks like those of a dachshund and realised that the conversation had turned a little sticky. When I was finally invited in, all the King asked me was whether I liked water melon which he said was excellent for the kidneys.

In Cairo the official royal residence was Abdin Palace, a solid stone neo-classical building with iron railings and gates and a forecourt similar to that at Buckingham Palace. However, the King actually lived with his family at Koubbeh, a cosy old-fashioned Turkish palace still with its traditional quarters for the former seraglio. Prince Farouk was then fourteen years old and the King was anxious that he should have part of his education in England. After much discussion it was decided that he should go to Woolwich. When the time came, the entrance examination which was of course in English was beyond him, so he was allowed to take part of the course while living on Kingston Hill with his tutor and guide Hassanein Bey. This arrangement was then brought to an end by the death of King Fuad. Sir Miles described Farouk in his diary at the time as 'a nice simple boy' and 'refreshingly unspoilt'. I can remember watching him learning to ride under a rough-riding sergeant of the 12th Lancers who taught him to jump and knock a polo ball about.

Though Cairo was fairly dirty, with dust everywhere and the strong and unforgettable smell of spices, it was in many respects most civilised. There was for example the Opera House built by the Khedive Ismail in honour of the Empress Eugénie who came to open the Suez Canal in 1869. It was for this occasion that *Aïda* was written and first performed. Court society was still largely Turkish with the Turkish titles of pasha, bey and effendi roughly the equivalent of lord, knight and esquire. The scarlet tarbush was universal except for the Moslem imams' turbans and the peasant *fellaheen*'s loose turban or white skull cap and pale blue gown. There were luxurious men's clubs, notably the Mahomet Ali in Cairo, which could compare for comfort and cuisine with any club in St James's. The Turf, the large but less luxurious British equivalent, was later burnt down by the Nasser mob with horrifying brutality.

Cairo was also a tourist's delight. Apart from the Pyramids and the fabulous Cairo Museum, there was the whole of the Old City of the Mamelukes. Over the years we got well used to playing the part of dragoman to guests at the beautiful Blue Mosque, or the Citadel, home of a regiment of Highlanders, or the famous City of the Dead. We often ended up with a visit to the monastery of the Whirling Dervishes back in the desert where the monks danced themselves into a stupor, finally crashing to the ground. A non-dancer then passed the hat round.

The King was accustomed to give an annual dinner at Abdin in the spring in honour of the high commissioner. They were grand affairs with all the Palace officials dressed in green Stambouli frock-coats and the inevitable tarbush. Among them was the royal chemist, an Englishman named Titterington, whom we always regarded as the King's taster for possible poison. It is interesting, as an indication of how little religious prejudice there was at that time, that the lady who acted as hostess was a leading light in the Cairo Jewish community, Madame Cattaoui, the 'Grand Maîtresse des Robes'. They were big affairs for about fifty guests, including the British commandant, General Weir, and Air Vice-Marshal Newall, later to become wartime chief of the Air Staff. A number of senior officers and their wives were asked as well as the Residency staff. Many younger officers, dressed in their smart white mess jackets, were invited to the reception afterwards which took the form of a cabaret performance in the big ballroom which had a stage.

Whoever chose the programme must have had a poor opinion of British taste for the turns generally came from the lower type of Cairo night club. On one occasion – before my time – the curtain went up and there standing in front with nothing on at all except for a large rose in an appropriate spot was a lady about to do a belly dance. There was a deadly silence when suddenly there was one sharp royal bark from the centre of the front row. After a second or two a gentle ripple of laughter spread through the audience and the girl was able to get on with her dance. During my time I attended several of these functions. Once, after the King and the high commissioner had left, I was horrified to see a number of British officers emptying all the silver cigar boxes and stuffing their pockets with cigars.

In May 1936 King Fuad, who had been ill for a short while, died unexpectedly. His funeral took place in a temperature of nearly 100 degrees. The high commissioner and his staff, all of us in our dark blue and gold broadcloth uniforms and ostrich-feathered hats, joined the Cabinet and hundreds of leading Egyptians in a great procession, shuffling and sweating behind the coffin, past large weeping crowds and up the long winding hill which led to the mosque in Old Cairo. As we approached there was a terrible gurgling sound which I could not place, but a little later we passed six unfortunate oxen lying at intervals on either side with their throats cut. It was an age-old token of sorrow. We were all glad to get away once the grim ceremony in the mosque was over.

As the King was not of age, three regents were appointed, one the brother of Queen Nazli. Sir Miles, paying his respects to the new King, now found him speaking excellent English but already showing unfortunate signs of wanting to get rid of British influences in the Palace in the shape of his sisters' governess and even his old English nanny who had brought him up and of whom he was believed to be very fond. It was a foretaste of things to come, though at the same time the young monarch was keen to excel in British sports, especially shooting and riding

Office hours for Egyptian government officials were from eight to two o'clock. Then, except for emergencies, they closed down for the day. The chancery opened at nine in the morning, but we returned at six in the evening for two hours unless required longer. This gave us a full afternoon for a siesta followed by sporting activities.

I was lucky in my Residency colleagues, many of whom became close friends. On the diplomatic side, apart from the counsellor, Ronnie Campbell, there was Arthur Yencken, the head of chancery, George Labouchere, the high commissioner's private secretary, and myself. Very soon afterwards Campbell was replaced by David Kelly. In the Oriental Secretariat, part of the old Levant Consular Service, there was Sir Walter Smart, with his superb knowledge of Egypt, and two assistants. All spoke perfect classical Arabic. Additionally there was an important Commercial Secretariat under Gerald Selous, the nephew of the famous white hunter of Central

Africa. I was allotted the Sudan desk in addition to other normal office work. Later Labouchere's place was later taken by Frank Roberts with his charming Lebanese wife.

My other work consisted mostly of complaints from Egyptians of ill-treatment by landlords or the *mamurs* or mayors of towns and the *omdahs* of villages. In particular, interference in the flow of water in the small canals raised perpetual problems in which we at the Residency, with the Irrigation Service by now entirely in Egyptian hands, could do little to help. One also had visits from Egyptians with all sorts of requests and complaints, sometimes about the activities of the British forces, in all of which we did our best to help. One offered the visitor the predictable little cup of Turkish coffee – medium, sweet or a dark thick mud, carefully avoiding the classic insult to an Arab of crossing one's legs and so displaying the soles of the feet. Very often there were visits from Sir Frank Watson, the financial adviser, or the judicial adviser whose assistant, John Besly, an English barrister, had married an old friend of my family. On our arrival he and his wife looked after us like children. Sometimes it was Thomas Russell Pasha, in uniform, taking off his tall tarbush and mopping his forehead, wanting to put one in the picture about some incident or other, or Alexander Keown-Boyd from the Ministry of the Interior to report complaints of foreigners or just to chat about the political situation. Or there was the elderly Sir Robert Greg with a nice American wife, seconded from our own Diplomatic Service, who was British commissioner on the Caisse de la Dette.

As far as the Sudan was concerned, I had already made some study of its history. I was absorbed by the work, although much of it consisted in passing on the reports to the Foreign Office with suitable comments. For practical purposes the Sudan was internally self-governing, the main Egyptian interest being confined to the preservation of the free flow of the waters of the Nile. We in Cairo were in effect the Foreign Office of the Sudan government. The senior staff of the Sudan Political Service were all British. It was generally accepted that though small it was probably the most effective service of a colonial nature anywhere in the world in spite of sneers that it only consisted of Oxford and Cambridge firsts and blues. After the murder of Sir Lee Stack all Egyptian troops had been withdrawn, but the Sudan Defence Force under its British officers was impeccable. The governor general addressed dispatches to Sir Miles as high commissioner for Egypt and the Sudan. The only major political incident affecting the Sudan proper in my time was the occupation in 1935 by the Italians of the hilly Oweinat triangle in Western Halfa province, an empty arid area separating South Tripolitania from French Equatorial Africa. With the threats of Italian military action in Abyssinia and the build up of troops in Libya, this had to be taken seriously. There were protests and troop movements and finally a compromise which gave part of the triangle to Italy.

In the spring of 1935 Sir Miles decided to make a wide tour of the Condominium. He and his new and very attractive wife were accompanied by Laurence Grafftey Smith, the assistant oriental secretary, and myself, together with an ADC and the Chinese valet. The tour was unforgettable, first by plane and then by train. After a few days in Khartoum spent in the palace where General Gordon was killed, we visited all the main provinces except the extreme south. Apart from the local sights such as the battlefield of Omdurman, we saw the Gezira cotton scheme at Wadi Medani on the Blue Nile, Kassala on the River Gash near the frontier of Italian-held Eritrea, where we slept in tents, Suakin, the ancient and beautiful half-deserted Arab island port on the Red Sea, and Port Sudan, its busy neighbour. In the dam at Sennar Sir Miles caught a giant Nile perch of over 600 lb. We also made friends with many local tribesmen such as the Hadendoa, the woolly-headed 'fuzzy-wuzzies' of Kipling. It was a prosperous and happy country with the tourist posters proclaiming 'Visit the sunny Sudan' – in distressing contrast to today, with the whole country torn in two and practically bankrupt after appalling droughts and a deadly civil war between the Arab Sudanese and the Nilotic tribesmen of the Upper Nile.

On our flight back in the RAF De Havilland bomber we stopped a night at Luxor. Next day we visited the Valley of the Kings and had the good luck to find Howard Carter waiting to conduct us through the tomb of Tutankhamen which he, with Lord Carnarvon, had discovered in 1922. We spent a riveting hour or two listening to his description of how he found the small triangular area leading to the twenty-six steps – still creamy-white as on the day they were laid 2,400 years before – near the entry to the tomb of Rameses VI and then down to the door with its seals intact and the golden treasure still within.

Alice and I had always been fascinated by Pharaonic art. She as a young girl had made the trip up the Nile with her family to Aswan in the *dahabieh*, while I had studied James Henry Breasted up at Cambridge. We went to the Palace Hotel at Luxor for our first New Year in Egypt and spent hours in the temples of Luxor and Amon at Karnak and at the tombs in the Valley of the Kings. We adored it. Historically there is nothing, it seems to me, to compare with the remains of this 3,500 years' civilisation in the size, quality and quantity of the monuments, and in a condition which could only have been made possible by the Egyptian climate. There are conflicting views about the artistic value of some of the buildings with their traditional style followed with such devotion for so many centuries. But about the beauty and workmanship of the hieroglyphs and carvings and the contents of the tombs, many now to be found in the Cairo museum, there can be no question.

For the next four years we made it a point to spend the New Year in Luxor and invariably found something new there or elsewhere on the Nile to entrance us. At the end we felt we were almost on terms of personal acquaintance with the gods and goddesses. In 1935 my old father and a nurse came with us and stayed on there for a month after we had gone back. It was a great joy for me to see him in such happiness in what was to be the last full year of his life. Later we became familiar with the older but equally interesting remains of ancient Memphis, Saqqara and Abu Suweir, near Cairo. We had an English friend who was operating his own dig near Saqqara and visited him several times. He once invited us to look at a tomb he had opened up only the day before. The coloured frescoes on the walls shone with an oily freshness.

Over the centuries little seemed to have changed. I remember once riding one of my ponies along the banks of the Nile near Cairo where a big *felucca*, the workboat of the *fellaheen*, was badly stuck on a sand bank. It had eight or ten men trying hard to get it off. As they heaved and pushed they chanted in unison, in time with their work, 'Amon-Ra, Amon-Ra' – a straight throwback to the days of the Pharaohs.

Social life in Cairo centred around the Gezira Sporting Club, then basically a British club for Army officers and officials, with a sprinkling of Egyptians and foreign diplomats. In my day there were about 800 members; now I am told there are 20,000. There was a racecourse, three polo grounds, cricket and football fields, tennis courts, squash courts and a new swimming pool, as well as an eighteen-hole golf course. The greens were saucers of hard sand and the sky swarmed with red kites; if one of them swooped down and flew away with your golf ball, in hopes of incubating it, you could drop another without a penalty. After we had finished our chosen exercise we all congregated in the clubhouse for tea and 'gentleman's toast' – Fortnum's patum peperium – as it was called by the immaculate *suffragis*, before we went back to the chancery. There were weekly dances at the club and on our own King's birthday a full-blooded review was held there at eight in the morning. It was commanded by the GOC, with the air vice-marshal in his RAF uniform and black boots, sitting rather uncomfortably on a restless polo pony. The high commissioner, magnificent in grey frock-coat and top hat, stood to take the salute during the march past.

There were three British divisions in Egypt, with two Guards battalions, one in Cairo and one in Alexandria, and a battalion of Highlanders in the Citadel. There were three regiments of cavalry and Royal Artillery; other technical units made up the total. The Royal Air Force had its headquarters in Heliopolis and flying boats on the Nile. I came across old friends and acquired many new ones. One of my oldest and closest was Bill Carr, then a major in the 12th Lancers who had been my exact contemporary at Eton and was married to a beautiful and scintillating Italian. He was a first-rate polo player and watching him playing revived memories of my days at our summer embassy in Massachusetts. With his encouragement I decided, while it was still not too late, to take it up again. He found me two reliable ponies belonging to an officer who was going home. The cost of keeping a polo pony in Cairo was about £100 a year. I never became a high-class player, but by getting up early every morning to practise I reached a stage where I could play without causing anyone undue embarrassment. I would play chukkers and occasional tournaments three days a week. Alice, though she often rode with me before breakfast, preferred playing tennis to watching what was often rather inferior polo.

Though we had to work hard, it was a very pleasant life. The one bane from which we all suffered was the ever-recurrent bacterial dysentery – the 'gyppy tummy' of the tourist guide warnings. It was due to improperly washed vegetables, dirty implements or just unwashed brown hands. We ourselves were ultra-particular; every single bit of fresh fruit or raw vegetables had to be washed in a purple solution of permanganate of potash. Even so, some unfortunates like myself went down with amoebic dysentery, which could damage one's colon for life.

We entertained in our playroom with its table tennis, bar and backgammon tables. We mixed our parties freely, bringing in the soldiers and their wives to meet the pretty Greeks, Italians and Copts who made up Cairo feminine society. Later some of the more audacious Moslem girls, starting with junior members of the royal family, also came into our lives. We saw little of other diplomats either on matters of business or in social life, nor was it encouraged. The Residency stood alone. Ironically my best diplomat friends were the Italian minister, Pelegrini Ghigi, and his second secretary, Roberto Caracciolo, now Duke of San Vito. In a desert trip we made to Siwa at the height of alarms of war, they arranged for our little party on leaving Siwa to cross the border into the oasis of Giarabub, so that we could visit the tomb of the Grand Senussi, the forebear of the gallant King Idris of Libya – so unceremoniously turned out by Gaddafi. We were conducted to the mosque by an Italian major with a sword and spurs on his riding boots which tinkled on the tiles as he walked. For obvious reasons he could hardly take them off to don the regulation padded slippers, as we did. It was, I fear, another black mark for the Italians who were not exactly popular in those parts. The Italians also kindly gave us a meal in their mess, ladies and all, and when it was time to leave on our long drive back to Mersa Matruh, allowed us to use a well-constructed road on their side of the high wire, passing through Fort Maddalena and Bardia instead of going back by our long desert track. When we recrossed the frontier at Sollum it was already getting dark and we were very grateful for the time we had saved.

We had brought our English butler, Peachey, out to Cairo with us as well as our son Nicky's nanny. They were invaluable. Nicky flourished, being wheeled down to Gezira every morning to play with the other children. Very soon he got his own white donkey, the long-legged, graceful animal of Egypt with the small neat head, so different from its hairy, dumpy little cousins at home. Peachey meanwhile adapted himself at once to living alongside five Arabs in the basement with whom he could not exchange one word. Our cook, Ahmed, like all the best Egyptian chefs, came from Abu Simbel in Nubia. His *ful Sudani* soup made from ground nuts could not be beaten. The head *suffragi* was Hassan, in white robes and white and scarlet turban; little Ahmed, his assistant, looked after the nursery and taught my son Arabic. We had a gardener who later also drove the car, and a garden boy who invariably did his heavy watering at eleven in the morning, paying no attention whatever to the blazing Egyptian sun. The flower beds, even the roses, were never any the worse.

Egypt is the Nile and the Nile is Eygpt. With the introduction of the fine long staple cotton by Mohammed Ali the Great in the early nineteenth century, the old system of basin-flooding of the Nile once a year was gradually replaced by perennial irrigation. This meant the building of one dam after another, supplying water to thousands of canals. When I first arrived in Egypt there were still immense areas above Cairo flooded every autumn. Slowly the water drained away leaving behind many little lakes called *birkas*. Three friends and I rented one near the Pyramids for a small sum for the winter season of 1934. We had good but modest sport with the wildfowl that frequented the *birka*, sometimes bringing back twenty or even thirty duck between us on a Sunday morning, having got out there before dawn. We set up small butts of reeds and brought with us two or three small boys – no one used dogs – to pick up the game in the shallow water. Quite apart from the sport, it was each time a fresh thrill to watch the sun rise on the very tip of the Great Pyramid nearby. Often we had come straight from the Continental cabaret having abandoned our dinner jackets to take a quick bath on the way. Two years later our little *birka* disappeared for ever under the new irrigation system.

The Residency itself had a big but neglected duck-shoot at Ekiad, approached through Bilbeis on the fringe of the desert. Once, driving through that town to the shoot, I commented to a friend sitting in the car beside me on the extraordinary number of children with red hair and blue eyes. 'Oh didn't you know?' he said. 'The Scots Guards spent six months here in 1922.' At nearby Tel el Kebir, the site of the battle which brought about the British occupation of Egypt in 1882, there was another big shoot run by British officials and others in the Egyptian service in which the Residency also had two guns, so that one had the chance of a morning's shooting on both Fridays and Sundays.

Sir Miles Lampson was a keen – some would say over-keen – shot. By careful manipulation of the water level at Ekiad and plentiful feeding of the duck population, he improved the bag from a total of 250 birds on the opening day in 1934, which I attended, to a world record of 1,660 five years later. He himself had a record bag of 550 duck, mostly teal. I was by that time stationed at Athens but the ambassador invited us to come over for his second shoot. On that occasion, we shot 1,100 with some eighteen guns. I was no star and was more than satisfied to get about sixty. It was early November and very hot. I only wore an old khaki drill bush-shirt and trousers, but shooting with two guns, and any way quite out of condition, my right shoulder had soon turned into pulp. Towards eleven o'clock there was a lull and I lay down on the floor of the butt exhausted. The small boy who was loading for me jumped into the water, shouting wildly to his friend who was picking up, 'The Pasha is dying, the Pasha is dying.'

These expeditions into the villages along the edge of the cultivation gave me the best opportunities of getting to know the *fellaheen*. Their sun-baked houses were built of mud bricks; if they collapsed or were washed away in a storm they were simply rebuilt from the surrounding soil. With little or no Arab blood and their heavy eyebrows, long eyelashes and turned up noses, the *fellaheen* might well have come straight out of some Pharaoh's tomb. They were cheerful, friendly and always out to help. In spite of my fragmentary Arabic, I found that they were quick to see a joke. Equally one came to realise they had short, sharp tempers, which could lead them to knife their best friend for some obscure insult. According to Thomas Russell there were some 3,000 murders or attempted murders a year in Egypt of which only about a couple of hundred were in the four main cities.

Russell Pasha himself occasionally took some of us out south of Cairo shooting sand grouse. They would sweep down to drink at some little expanse of water, swirling in by the thousand so that the sky was black and you could often do little more than 'brown' them – not very sporting but an extraordinary experience. Alice and I also spent one lovely day with him in the big game sanctuary founded by Prince Kamal-ed-Din in the eastern desert south of Cairo in the Wadi Rish-Rash. There by dint of much walking and long strenuous climbs we were able to get close views of the giant ibex to be found in that area. Alas, my photographs have been lost. Later it led to a clash between Russell and King Farouk who wanted to shoot the biggest head in the world. Russell won.

Above all, Russell was a good friend of Egypt and deeply interested in the affairs of its people. As the drug smuggling increased there in the Thirties, he put all his efforts into the fight against it. He formed the Central Narcotics Bureau to take things in hand. Hashish was the problem at first, penetrating from Greece of all places, and when that was stopped, from Lebanon and Syria. Later on opium was an even greater threat. Russell as usual made himself an expert and was nominated to the Advisory Committee on Drugs at the League of Nations in Geneva. One day he walked into my office with a large zinc tubular object looking like a giant suppository. It was indeed just that. When full of hashish or opium, it was stuffed into a wretched camel and safely driven across the frontiers – safe, that is to say, until Russell got on to it and had them all X-rayed before they crossed the Suez Canal.

I was told the *fellaheen*, though 80 per cent illiterate, when well led make excellent soldiers. If that was not always apparent, I am afraid we should take a fair part of the blame; for in spite of their British senior officers, we were never keen, for obvious reasons, to provide the Egyptians with the latest type of rifle or machine gun. Their own top officers in those days, many of them fat and lazy, did nothing much to inspire respect. The *Egyptian Mail*, one of the two English-language newspapers in Cairo, once printed two photographs whose captions had been, perhaps intentionally, transposed. The first photograph of a group of rather fat staff officers in uniform seated at the dinner table was captioned: 'These peaceful gharry-horses eat their mid-day meal.' The other one, of some old Cairo cab-horses wearing nosebags, purported to be 'The annual dinner of the Egyptian General Staff'.

The 8th Army activities in the Western Desert made the area more generally familiar to the public, but in 1934 it was still very much a closed book – except for Mersa Matruh where there was a nice hotel with a superb beach on the road half way to the Libyan frontier. There was no one apart from the Frontier Administration Camel Corps, whose existence lay out in the Siwa oasis, and the Bedouin with their camels along the Darb-el-Arbain, the track leading south west from the Nile Delta. This was the road taken by Alexander the

Great and his army. It was left to one man, Captain Ralph Bagnold of the Royal Signals, with a few Army friends, to carry out the private expeditions which were to make possible the knowledge of this desert and lead eventually to the establishment in wartime of the Long Range Desert Group which were such a thorn in the side of Rommel and the Afrika Korps. In our time the secret lay in mastering the behaviour of rubber tyres in relation to soft desert sand and the methods of extracting a vehicle once it became stuck. An essential was the fitting of large balloon tyres with low air pressure made especially for desert use, together with sand-mats and shovels for digging out. Bagnold had also written a book called *Libyan Sands* which many of us who were interested had acquired and studied carefully.

Soon after we arrived it became fashionable among young and adventurous officers and some civilians to make these desert trips. There were comfortable rest houses in all the oases put up by the old Cromer régime for the Frontier Administration and it became a popular way of spending a long weekend or a short local leave. Compasses were essential and the invention of the sun-compass, though I myself never used one, greatly helped. We always took at least two cars.

Alice and I took to this new sport with enthusiasm. I bought a good second-hand Ford two-seater with a dicky seat for valises and supplies, put on balloon tyres, and over three years we visited the western oases of Kharga and Dakhla, where there is a beautiful temple built by Darius, King of Persia, the Sinai peninsula and Siwa. It was while returning from one of these oases to stay with our Coptic friends, the Wissa family, in their country house near Assiut that we heard on the car radio on a cold January desert night the voice of Sir Thomas Horder announce: 'The King's life is drawing peacefully to its close.' We all got out and stood for a minute silently in the moonlight.

The lovely oasis of Siwa was reached by the coast road from Alexandria passing through El Alamein and other later famous battlefields and turning south-west by the old caravan route used by Alexander the Great. It was the site of the temple and oracle of Jupiter – Amon. A few remains of this lie close to a small round warm-water pool where we swam. The sand around it was so permeated with the urine of the camels which used to water there (in more senses than one) that it is said that it gave its name to the substance ammonia. It had two other claims to fame – first, the silver plaques on a great silver ring which the virgins of Siwa wore around their necks until their marriage; and secondly, the curious custom of male marriages for those so inclined. During the course of these desert trips we also visited the beautiful Coptic sixth-century monasteries of Natrun in the west and the hermitage of Saint Anthony down the Red Sea coast.

These journeys were encouraged by the military authorities as war loomed closer just as they proved to be of interest to some of our future enemies. The German minister, Baron von Stohrer, a giant of a man, also took to it with Teutonic zest and ranged over large areas of the Western Desert with his chauffeur. One day they disappeared and the Frontier Administration laid on a large-scale search but failed to find them. The amateur desert travellers like ourselves also went out to look but with no success. Finally the RAF were called in but it was not till several days later that they were discovered lost just a few miles from the Fayoum, the enormous cultivated oasis lying to the south-west of Cairo. Another enthusiast was a young Hungarian, Count Almazy, who acquired such proficiency in desert travel that he became a skilled explorer himself. He was to become Rommel's leading expert on the desert. We all liked him but I have never known whether in earlier days he was a professional agent or not.

Another casualty of the desert was the famous French novelist and aviator Antoine de Saint-Exupéry. He was flying his own plane to Cairo when the engine failed and he had to come down in the desert. There he sat for two days eating the remains of his sandwiches and drinking dew water which he collected from the dope-impregnated fabric wings. When he was finally found we went to meet him and he appeared completely unperturbed. He was a delightful companion and years later became a pilot in the Free French Air Force. One day in 1944 he failed to return from flight from Algiers to Corsica, shot down by a German fighter.

During the winter of 1934 the Italian pressures on Abyssinia had come to a head with an armed clash between their two forces at Wal Wal in the Abyssinian province of Ogaden. The whole issue then came before the League of Nations, and the Council and later the Assembly passed strong resolutions condemning of the Italians. One ingenious plan for resolving the matter followed another. Eden paid a visit to Mussolini and warned him of the wider dangers of an open breach of the Covenant of the League. Contrary to what is generally believed, there was no battle royal between them and even the Duce seemed to speak more in resignation than anger. It was all to no avail. It was a test of the League which was to have serious effects for the future.

A tripartite Anglo-French-Italian conference was due to take place in April 1935 at Stresa at which plans to bolster resistance to Germany's threatening moves were to be discussed. It had been generally assumed that the Abyssinian question would be raised there. Unfortunately when the time came, only the prime minister and Simon attended it; Eden, owing to illness, could not be there. In the event, the topic of Abyssinia was never raised. This was to prove disastrous, for Mussolini took it to be the green light and acted accordingly. More Italian troopships followed one another through the Canal till by the summer there were some 150,000 troops in the Italian colony of Eritrea next door to Abyssinia. It was feared that we might become directly involved and in late August the Mediterranean Fleet in Malta was ordered to Alexandria under the command of Admiral Pound, thirty-five vessels in all. All attempts by the League at persuasion had failed.

The Residency had moved down to Alexandria in June as it did every year. The King was as usual installed in Montaza Palace and the skeleton staffs of the Egyptian ministries had moved into their summer quarters. Most of our staff moved down too while my baby son went home to my parents. Alice and I settled down in a rather decrepit hotel in San Stefano. This was on the magnificent beach which stretched alongside the new corniche road from the harbour for twenty miles to Montaza.

As far as we were concerned, life went on much as usual. The polo season had opened at the Alexandria Sporting Club and many of my friends in the 8th Hussars and the newly arrived 11th Hussars also came down. I had brought my ponies too, and though we had become excessively busy in our summer chancery, I rode before breakfast and got a few games from time to time. We soon got to know many of the younger naval officers and a converted barge moored by the Hole in the Wall in Alexandria harbour which Duncan McCallum, the Residency controller, had lent us for the summer now became a centre for swimming parties and picnic lunches on Sundays. The great attraction was our Cris-Craft which we had arranged to have sent from Stockholm and on which I taught our guests to use the freeboard and later to water-ski.

Late in September I had arranged to take the Cris-Craft with our ex-RAF chauffeur up the Nile to Cairo, thinking we might wish to do trips to visit temples and other antiquities further up the river. We left through the Mahmoudia Canal, starting from the centre of Alexandria and running between the cultivation and the marshy lakes for fifty kilometres to join the Rosetta branch of the river. It was full Nile, as we soon found once we had got through the lock which led through to the river itself. That meant that we had to face a swirling current of about ten knots. At times it came with such force that, obliged as we were to keep the bow of the speedboat down by easing back the throttle, we were hardly able to maintain headway. Every sort of object swept past us: torn palm trees, dead camels, goats, a big black gamous, the domestic water buffalo. It was with some relief that we were able to tie up for the night beside the Irrigation Department *dahabeah* where they had kindly agreed to put us up at Kasr-el-Zayat. We had a quieter journey up the next day, passing finally through the Barrage with its beautiful Victorian garden till we tied up at our destination at the little Residency dock. We had covered almost 1,100 kilometres.

Since the days of Cromer there had always been a British governor of Sinai living at El Arish with his small command of Frontier Administration Camel Corps Police. The incumbent in my time was Kaimakam C. S. Jarvis Bey. We stayed with him and his wife several times, including one Christmas when he took a party of us down to Taba, near the Palestinian border on the Gulf of Akaba, where many years later the Israelis were to build a luxury hotel. It became the subject of international controversy when the Israelis pulled out their occupying troops from Sinai but claimed Taba as Israeli territory. In our day it just consisted of a wooden hut with the most perfect snow-white beach one could imagine and not far off a small island with the ruins of a little Crusader castle – but all certainly well inside Egyptian territory.

Shortly before Easter 1936 we had arranged to take a short holiday with two Army friends and their wives in Transjordan and Palestine, travelling in two cars. We drove via Sinai and Akaba, having been invited to spend a few days at Taba on the way. We finally left there through the small Palestine Police post at what is now Eilat just along the beach. One of our party, Francis Jayne, an 8th Hussar, had been on secondment to the Transjordan Frontier Force, a mounted unit of the Emir Abdullah's army long since disbanded, with British officers and Circassian NCOs. It was a regiment which people were inclined to join if they fancied themselves as budding T. E. Lawrences or if they had had a particularly bad Ascot. He volunteered to conduct us up through the stark red rocks and peaks of the Wadi Rumm on the Saudi-Arabian border. We passed on through Maan and spent the night in Kerak, a town of 18,000 people all within the battlements of a vast Crusader castle which had once belonged to the villainous Reynald de Chatillon, Lord of Oultre-Jourdain. It is said that it was his burning of two Moslem pilgrim ships in the Red Sea, full of innocent people returning from the Haj, that so infuriated Saladin that it sealed his determination to expel the Crusaders from the Holy Land at any cost. The only European in the place was a Dominican father who ran a Catholic school and kindly let us put down our bedding rolls in one of his schoolrooms.

After a few days in Amman we went on to Jerusalem, arriving on Good Friday. General Sir Arthur Wauchope, the high commissioner, had arranged for us to attend the ceremony of the Holy Fire the following morning in the Church of the Holy Sepulchre. It was packed to overflowing, with everyone carrying an unlit candle. The tomb itself is a small rectangular building in the centre of the great round parterre, with no windows, except for a small square hole in one wall. On either side of the doors into the tomb there are two small marble benches on which I and a few others were placed. The rest of our party were in the Wauchopes' box. At a few minutes before twelve the Orthodox Patriarch, in full regalia and carrying his unlighted candle, accompanied by the Armenian Patriarch, entered with a guard of eight kilted officers of the Cameron Highlanders wearing their claymores and marching on each side in two columns. I could not help thinking of the Roman legionary guard which had escorted Our Lord. As the clock tolled midday the doors of the tomb closed. There was a total silence for perhaps five minutes while the clerics prayed inside waiting for the fire to strike. Suddenly out of the little trapdoor was passed a burning candle and immediately other candles were thrust into the flame; soon the candle flames spread through the crowd in every direction. Then first from the lower balcony and afterwards from the top tier, down came more and more candles on strings, all to be lit and hoisted up until they opened into two giant circles of light round the church's galleries. Finally the doors of the tomb swung open and out came the Orthodox Patriarch carrying a candle. The Camerons standing beside me pressed around him and marched him through the crowd. But the poor little Armenian Partriarch, left behind, had to be passed out lying flat on his back by hand over the heads of the crowd to his own chapel.

In the evening came another ceremony. The Copts of the Abyssinian Church over the centuries have been squeezed out of their chapels in the Church of the Holy Sepulchre till all they have left is a part of the roof over the chapel of St Helena. After dinner at Government House we were taken by the Wauchopes to the Abyssinian ceremony of the Searching for the Body. Up on the church roof we all sat on gilt chairs with a lighted candle in our hands; then round the corner from the darkness came a procession of black and bearded clerics in their shining robes and round golden crowns, wailing and beating tom-toms, and carrying candles and vast coloured umbrellas for the search of the roof. We rose and obediently followed the high commissioner four times round the cupola of St Helena with our candles searching in the darkness for the Body which had been removed. Finally, when midnight came we had all arrived back where we started. With cries of joy the cortège stopped on the floor in front of us proclaiming loudly that our search was over. Our Lord had indeed risen from the empty tomb.

It was deeply impressive and we returned drained by emotion to the King David Hotel. The next night, after a day of sightseeing, we gave a small dinner for an old Cairo friend, Colonel Dudley-Clark, now director of intelligence at Jerusalem Command. During dinner, just when the champagne got going, he was called to the telephone. He came back badly shaken. 'I'm sorry,' he said, 'I've got to leave at once.' The expected wholesale Arab violence against the Jews had flared up all over Palestine. The first Arab rebellion of 1936-39, forerunner of the Intifada, had begun. Some modern writers have compared the measured British response to the Israeli violent suppression of the 'Intifada'. Nothing can be further from the truth.

The occupation of the Abyssinian Empire by Italy and the continuous threats to the Canal meant a constant state of alert and alarm in Egypt. It was against this background that Egypt and Great Britain decided to start fresh talks on a treaty of friendship and alliance. In January the opening moves were made on the way to negotiations and by February they were in full swing. The difference between this and previous discussions was that now both sides really wanted a treaty. The presence of considerable numbers of Fascist troops across the border in Libya had served to concentrate the minds of all concerned. The talks were to take place in Cairo with a large Egyptian delegation headed by Nahas Pasha and representing every Egyptian political party. There were at least three former prime ministers and also two Wafdist ministers who had both been labelled murderers after the assassination of Sir Lee Stack but who now proved to be most helpful. Sadly both were later to be murdered themselves, as was my dear friend Sir Amin Osman. He was secretary to the Egyptian side, a most remarkable young man who had studied at Oxford and had an English wife. He acted as the main go-between to the two delegations. Ours was headed by the high commissioner and it was he who made the running. In addition there were the GOC, General Sir 'Rosy' Weir, the AOC, Air Marshal Sir Robert Brook-Popham and the commander-in-chief of the Mediterranean Fleet, Admiral Sir Dudley Pound. Walter Smart, our talented oriental counsellor, was to be an adviser while I became secretary of our delegation. Later Eric Becket, a legal adviser of the Foreign Office was brought in. He was brilliant, lucid but a little intolerant and often put the Egyptians' backs up.

Stiff demands, insisted upon by the War Office, were put forward in the first instance and stiff rejection and counter-proposals came back from the other side. The location of the troops, the number deemed to be essential and the ability to reinforce in case of emergency all formed the crucial issues. The Egyptians were adamant that their two great cities should be cleared of foreign troops altogether and eventually offered generous alternative accommodation in the Canal Zone in barracks to be built and paid for by them. The numbers of troops were fixed by them at 10,000 with eventual agreement over satisfactory arrangements for reinforcement. In the event war came in 1939 and no barracks were ever built.

Arguments were protracted, even bitter at times. One point after another had to be reserved for further discussion and sometimes it seemed that agreement would never be possible. So it became the practice for further discussion behind the scenes to be relegated to the little group consisting of Makram Obeid Pasha, the able but loquacious Coptic lawyer and finance minister and Amin Osman on the one hand, and Walter Smart and myself on the other. Our little drafting party would work into the night and with luck come up with something which we could defend the following day. Becket came along for legal intricacies and superb drafting if needed. Amin of course was invaluable. I was hoping and praying for a treaty because I feared that otherwise we might have to hold Egypt down by force. With the unsettled state of Europe and Africa this would have been disastrous. We could never get better terms.

We progressed slowly through the spring with rising bad temper till we reached a point in June when we got stuck. Lampson was summoned home by Eden, by now secretary of state, and a little psychological warfare was applied. But the log-jam broke when Nahas himself came out with a proposal to David Kelly, the acting high commissioner, that our troops could be returned to Cairo and Alexandria in case of dire need at any time and without limit. The treaty was to last for twenty years, subject to renewal after reference to the League of Nations. Lampson came back to Cairo and in a short month or so the remaining clauses on the protection of foreigners and the Sudan were agreed without too much difficulty.

By this time the talks had moved to Alexandria. When agreement was finally reached there was great jubilation with a huge government dinner and reception on a liner in Alexandria harbour. This was accompanied by fireworks with a large raft anchored beside us full of bands, belly dancers and acrobats to add to the gaiety. Nöel Coward was staying at the Residency and we found ourselves sitting side by side at the dinner. After it was all over he and I went to the Fennina cabaret where we sat laughing and reminiscing until the small hours.

The ceremony over, I myself departed thankfully by air to join Olive and Adrian Baillie with Alice and half a dozen other friends at Heraklion in Crete in the good ship *Eros*. She was a French Rothschild yacht of 900 tons, chartered by Olive and already half way through their cruise of the Greek Islands. I felt I had deserved the holiday.

The treaty was finally signed on 28 August 1936 in London by the thirteen Egyptian delegates and Anthony Eden, with Ramsay

MacDonald, Simon, Halifax and Lampson present to give it their blessing. Sir Miles's 'three-legged stool' stood for the first time solidly balanced, and all three parties concerned settled down to try to make the new scheme work.

9
Kenya Adventure

In Egypt under the new treaty arrangements 1937 passed peacefully enough. Early on I was asked by the Foreign Office if I would be available to take on a minor function at the Coronation of King George VI in June when we were to go on leave. I was turning it over in my mind when we received an invitation from Sir Robert and Lady Brook-Popham to stay at Government House, Nairobi and make it our headquarters for a month of big-game hunting. During the treaty negotiations the Air Marshal and I had become friends and he had now been appointed Governor of Kenya. I am afraid we did not hesitate long between my duty to the Sovereign and the appeal of the Great Rift Valley and the Mara River. These were the days when the excitement of big-game hunting was not tainted with guilt.

I had always been interested in big game. Brought up on an American great-uncle's tales of hunting moose, wapiti and grizzly bear in Canada and Alaska, later I turned to the standard works of C.E. Selous and other famous African white hunters. An embassy friend, the controller, Major Duncan McCallum, who himself had a house at Nanyuki near Mount Kenya, lent me his big double-barrelled Holland and Holland rifle and I bought myself a light 13.9 Austrian Mannlicher for use with smaller game. I was able to get some practice with both on one of the British army ranges in the desert behind the cavalry barracks at Abassiyeh. I also spent a day getting familiar with the various East African species of game in the Cairo Zoo.

We decided to fly down to Kenya by one of the new Imperial Airways Short flying-boats and make a leisurely return by Nile steamer from Lake Albert in Uganda. Apart from the interest of the river journey, I knew that those steamers stopped two or three times a day to discharge cargo and take on passengers. As far as I could make out I would be the first member of the Cairo staff to visit the

Upper Nile Province for many years, so I could combine pleasure with a little business calling on the various district officers as we went along.

The aircraft in which we were to travel was of a comfort undreamed of today. It took some fifty passengers and had a special promenade deck for exercise. We dropped down on to the river each evening at sundown to spend the night at comfortable hotels. It took us three days. These planes also carried the Royal Mail at the cost of a penny per letter from England to every part of the Empire. Later, as Sunderlands, they were to render wonderful service to the RAF.

We spent one night in Khartoum and the next in Juba, seeing remarkably little on the way except hundreds of miles of scrub and green papyrus grass, the famous Sudd. Now we found ourselves deep in the country of such Nilotic tribes as the Nuer and Shilluk whom we were to meet again on our way back. They were primitive to a degree, in general going about completely naked except perhaps for a short shoulder skin. Today, headed by the cattle-breeding Dinkas, they form part of the Sudan People's Liberation Army which is holding a large part of the provinces of the Upper Nile and the Bahr-el-Ghazal against the troops of the Moslem Sudanese government. We flew next day over Rippon Falls in Uganda, the very source of the Nile, then quite low over Lake Victoria, spectacular with a faint heat-haze on the blue water and the hundreds of little green islands dotted about. Here it was that I got my first glimpse of East Africa which was to become so familiar and so much loved in later years. I still think that for natural beauty, clarity of air and sheer exhilaration no place can compete. We came down at Kisumu with a ten-foot bow wave and quickly transferred to the little Wilson Air Line plane to take us to Nairobi.

On arrival we plunged straight into a world of pomp and circumstance with an ADC from Government House to meet us in his immaculate white uniform and gold-spiked helmet. For civilians in Kenya the khaki 'Bombay bowler' (still universal in the Sudan) had been virtually abandoned and replaced by the 'double-terai', the two soft wide-brimmed felt hats of India stuck one inside the other. The household was headed by a Kikuyu major-domo and almost all the white-robed house servants were of the same tribe. There was a sprinkling of Moslem Somalis in turbans, devoted if they happened to take a liking to you. Gradually I got to know the Kikuyus better –

small, intelligent, reserved, shrewd and hardworking and, as far as could be perceived, most friendly, though fifteen years later Mau-Mau was to teach us some harsh lessons. The little Kikuyu women dressed in leather aprons and cloaks would be bent over double with loads of brushwood or fresh cut maize piled on their backs and held in place with a narrow leather band on the forehead.

Government House was large and elegant, white stucco with a classical portico. There was always a King's African Rifles sentry on duty outside the door, and up the steps after dark there was also a little wizened watchman squatting with a small bow and arrow and a few short spears. I suppose they represented the belt and braces of security, though which was which I couldn't say. There was a beautiful park with tropical, semi-tropical and European shrubs and flowers all mixed up together. As I remember, Nairobi itself, apart from 'G.H' and a few municipal buildings, had little to commend it. There were a few streets of well-stocked shops, Indian and otherwise, some churches and several very nice hotels, then acres of tin shanties built for the most part out of old two-gallon petrol tins beaten flat.

The governor was a man of about fifty-five with blue eyes and grey hair and a neat moustache. He was quiet and gentle, but as firm in his views as he was acute in his judgement. At his official dinner parties he had a strange habit – one might almost call it an affliction – of dozing off in his chair. It did not happen when we were alone with them and nobody seemed to be the least embarrassed when it occurred. It had nothing to do with alcohol. His wife Opal was tall with auburn hair and as much charm as she had energy. Years later after his death she settled down in a big house in a remote village in my Taunton constituency where she took charge of the local Tory committee with the same efficiency she had shown with the Red Cross and St John Ambulance in Kenya.

Not long before, under the previous governor, there had been demonstrations at Government House by large numbers of white settlers who were apprehensive about their future. It all arose out of a demand for formal recognition and guarantee of the White Highlands area by the British government as the permanent home of the white inhabitants in the area mostly lying in Kikuyuland on both sides of the Great Rift Valley. By the time we arrived it had quietened down and as far as the whites were concerned all was peace and contentment.

In conjunction with the members of the Assembly, the country was run impeccably by the mainly white hierarchy of provincial commissioners, district commissioners and the rest; but we had little to do with officialdom except for the Game Department. The game laws were very strict under the watchful eye of Major Archie Ritchie, a tough but most efficient and courteous chief game warden. All game on licence was tightly controlled by wardens and scouts; all ivory had to be carefully weighed in Ritchie's little tin-roofed office, and any tusk under fifteen pounds was confiscated. Poaching took place, of course, but against constant watch, and once discovered was harshly dealt with. The situation was well in hand.

We soon found ourselves plunged into the company of settlers visiting Nairobi from near and far, to some of whom we had letters of introduction, while one or two we knew well from earlier days. They came in, male and female alike, dressed in trousers of corduroy or drill with flannel or cotton shirts of every hue and pattern – blues, purples and greens or great square checks, all worn with what would today be called a 'cravat'. Others just passing through on return from safari would be in smartly-cut khaki bush shirts and trousers or shorts, elaborating on their exploits and the weight of their ivory (then fetching a price of ten shillings a pound). They congregated every morning from eleven o'clock on at Torr's Hotel in Delamere Avenue. Lord Delamere was already dead, but Lady Delamere was still very much alive and was mayor of Nairobi. They came in their cars with 'box-bodies', with metal compartments built over each wheel for extra room and baggage-racks on the roof – they were often old American models which seemed to do well on the corrugated red laterite roads of Kenya.

One day were were introduced to a white hunter, Baron Blixen, a tall, fair, stout Swede very partial to alcohol, with an admiring young relative named Romulus who never left his side. 'Blix' had a nice sense of humour and later we spent many good times together. He was very different from the pathetic syphilis-ridden character described in Out of Africa, though I dare say he had suffered from that affliction. We very soon began drifting daily to the long bar room at Torr's with its noisy chatter, finding it to be the best way of meeting and making friends in a short time. Dry martinis were the favourite drink of the day, though not really suited to the height or climate. Fortunately we both had good heads.

We got to know Nairobi and its surroundings. We visited Safari-land, which organised hunting parties and was owned by an old Eton friend of mine, Alistair Gibb, but we found their propositions too grand and expensive. Then through the grapevine at Torr's we heard of Major Jack Kingdon of Nyeri up north, who was an honorary game warden and part-time white hunter. He was charming and unassuming, but knew his job. At a meeting at Torr's it was soon settled.

We then set out together to collect the members of our safari team and the necessary equipment and supplies. There was first a good box-body car to be hired and then a driver. We found a solid old red Buick and a Kikuyu chauffeur, Juma, who turned out to be superb, a good driver and calm in emergencies. Then we acquired Musa, my gun bearer, a Moslem with a dirty tarbush, two Wakamba trackers with their teeth filed to a point in cannibal fashion, a cook from Mozambique, and a boy to act as general handyman. We took two small tents and used the fly of our one as a dining room. There were camp-beds with mosquito nets and two canvas baths, crockery and the rest of the paraphernalia. There were also tinned supplies of all sorts as well as a few fresh vegetables and always a couple of demijohns of fresh water for emergencies; there was also plenty of *posho* – pounded maize – for the boys. In those days we were generally able to drink safely from the local streams and even bathe in them if not too cold. The dread bilharzia disease had not yet spread from the Nile to East Africa.

We counted on our own shooting for fresh meat. Our supplementary stores contained a bottle or two of whisky, some gin and dry vermouth and a folding loo seat. Our stores and equipment had to go into a lorry with a tarpaulin cover, which Juma found for us. At night the boys slept under the tarpaulin if dangerous animal intruders were about, or if it was raining.

We had decided to divide our hunting into two separate safaris. The first, in search of general game but more particularly lion, was to be in the Masai country due east of Nairobi towards the Mara river. I had a game department licence for two lions, and one each for the other dangerous game, including one elephant, which we reserved for the second safari.

The rains were very late that year and we set out in mid-June in a heavy storm. We took few clothes – a bush shirt and trousers and shorts, a sweater or two and tweed coats for the cold. We headed north past Kikuyu township and left the main road after about thirty miles, turning sharp east into the Kadong valley on our left just before reaching the Rift escarpment. There was no traffic and little sign of human life. But the game began to appear almost at once, though on account of the streaming rain they were often seeking shelter under the clumps of thorn trees or in the scattered scrub. There were zebra, kongoni and impala, giraffe, wildebeest and the Thomson gazelle, but in the downpour we could not give them much attention. On we went to Narok, the only little town in Masai-land with just a *boma,* the office of the district officer, and a few tin-roofed shanties and Indian shops. We spent the night there, continuing next day, still in streaming rain, towards the Mara river and the Tanganyika frontier. The sky was dark and heavy and as we drove through the deep mud the car and lorry were slipping in every direction. Several times we had to stop to dig them out. After about forty miles the lorry stuck altogether with a loud clanking sound at the rear. It was jacked up and Juma, crawling underneath, announced that the crown wheel in the rear axle was broken in two. There was no alternative but to send him back to Nairobi for a new one – luckily the owner of an Indian *duka* store coming the other way gave him a lift. The rain had eased off and we made camp as best we could, though the fire would only blaze intermittently; however, thanks to our excellent cook and with the help of a few dry martinis and whisky for Jack Kingdon, we soon settled down to a good supper.

We were in a plain with low hills on either side. Soon after we ate we began to hear the grunting of lion and realised that we had bogged down in the middle of a wonderful piece of lion country. They were starting their evening hunt and having come down from the hills were spread out to drive the game down on either side of the valley.

We stoked up the fire before going to bed, though the wood was damp, and surprisingly were soon asleep. About eleven I woke Alice, apparently having called out half asleep 'I smell a lion.' A few seconds later there was a terrific grunt a few feet from out tent. It was a petrifying noise, the most frightening thing I had ever experienced. Then we heard the lion padding its way round the side of the tent and going off through the long grass. We were badly shaken and spent an hour or more with our rifles sitting near the fire with Kingdon in case it returned.

We awoke the next day to find ourselves in full sunshine, the ground around us spick and span as an English park with its scattered thorn trees, tall and twisted acacias, mimosa, and the small coverts of tangled bush. The place was teeming with game all moving northwards to the fresh rains and we spent the morning picking out the different varieties with our field-glasses. Late in the afternoon Juma got back with the new crown-wheel, driven by our Cairo friend Captain Gerald Kilkelly of the 8th Hussars who had come to join us. We were near a virtually non-existent village called Lemek, now I believe the site of a rather unattractive little town.

There we settled down to our lion hunt in earnest. We learned that the best method was to put down a kill – a zebra in our case – in a suitable place the evening before. Most likely it would be partly devoured during the night and the ideal was to find the lion still on the kill the next day. Though she much wanted to do so, Alice was not allowed to come with us after lion: Kingdon thought it was too risky.

It was our first night in the bush. Being on the Equator, there is little real twilight in Kenya but when the dawn comes it has a clarity and freshness all of its own. Along with the solitary melodious notes of the birds of the African bush, the dawn was an experience so unique that I have remembered it all my life.

When we were hunting we rose at four and were out before dawn. To begin with we had no luck and saw only two large striped hyena on the kill which slunk off before we could take them. But on the third day we found the kill had disappeared. It had been dragged to a patch of thick bush about a quarter of a mile away. The drill was to follow the lion's spoor till you found where it had gone in and send the boys round behind to drive it out with a crackle of broken twigs. But just as they left us there was a loud grunt and a beautiful black-maned lion shot out ahead of us. Incredibly fast, Kingdon, who was standing in front with his rifle half up, shot it straight through the heart. Much singing by our party when they had skinned it and returned with us to camp.

One of the great pleasures of safari was that after an early lunch you were able to relax entirely, sleeping, reading or playing the gramophone. This was especially so after a successful hunt when one had had a drink or two to celebrate, after duly inspecting the trophy and watching the alum and salt being rubbed into the skins. These had to be very carefully put away. On one occasion I had shot two zebras intending to take the skins home. They had been rough-cured and corded up in two parcels which were put high in the branches of a thorn tree over one side of our tent. That night we were awoken by an unholy noise above our heads, snarls and tearing and breaking of branches. We shouted and it quickly stopped. But next morning we found that both our trophies had disappeared; hyenas had somehow been able to climb high enough to drag them down.

The striped hyena, the *fesi* in Swahili, is a repulsive beast. A big one stands nearly four foot high at the shoulder, sloping down to about two feet at the tail. It has a vile smell and its voice always seemed to me to be far removed from the proverbial hyena's 'laugh' – more a series of loud, moaning screams. It has immense jaws and though cowardly with lion or other big beasts will boldly come close up to your campfire hoping to snatch some piece of discarded bone or offal. In the fire its eyes reflect a green light (I was told that a lion's eyes will show up red) and there was generally a half circle of them round us as we ate our dinner. Often Kingdon or I would pick up a shotgun to blast them away, but we never succeeded in putting them off.

In the late afternoon you went out with your light rifle hoping to pick out a good specimen of the high-springing impala or Grant's gazelle as a trophy or perhaps taking a shotgun to try for one or two of the crested blue guinea fowl or a Francolin partridge for the pot. Or you could climb a little up the hillside and through your field-glasses lie watching the procession of game of every description as they moved endlessly northwards in their thousands. I believe there were estimated to be over a million wildebeest in the valley alone. I had a Bell and Howell motion camera which I used on a single-leg rotating stand with a telephoto lens and I got some wonderful coloured picture of game – alas, with the years they all faded to nothing.

After an early tea there was the ceremony of the 'first toasti' handed round by one of the boys – a little gentleman's relish or tinned sardines on a piece of toast accompanied by a whisky and soda. At six came the call 'Bathi, bwana!' which we took in round canvas baths in the tents. At six-thirty came the 'second toasti', with a dry martini, and finally dinner in our dressing gowns. We were always in bed by eight for we had to rise early.

After our first success with the lion we spent several days searching and interrogating wandering Masai tribesmen, but to no avail. We were taken to one Masai *manyatta* (village) and shown a twelve-foot *zariba* (hedge), which they said a lioness had been known to clear with a large calf in her mouth. The Masai tribe were the easy-going aristocrats of Kenya with their scarlet blankets, shiny plumes, plaited ochred hair and rows of beads. They did little work other than moving their cattle about from place to place, existing on a diet of mixed milk and blood taken direct from the cattle vein through a straw. We were told that half a dozen tribesmen were still quite prepared to take on a lion with spears if it stole their cattle. A few of them liked to look in on us in the afternoons, squatting down to listen to the gramophone and following all our doings with intense interest.

Finally we tried putting down kills at several different places, but always found them untouched or torn to bits or being devoured by vultures or the gaunt marabou cranes by the time we arrived. One morning we visited our nearest kill and there at last were the tracks of a big lion dragging its victim into a nearby thicket, which was so dense that we had to send two scouts right in at the back. We could hear them breaking twigs or cracking their fingers as they advanced. We did not have to wait long. We were lined up with Kingdon on my right and Gerald on my left when a large male lion burst out and came straight at me. A lion charges at about forty miles an hour so decisions have to made swiftly. As I raised my rifle he saw me move and swung sharp right to pass in between us. Gerald fired but missed and I also swung round and fired just after the lion passed me. It was not an easy angle and the bullet caught him just behind the heart. He stumbled but pulled up and ran on leaving a heavy spoor. We followed him up with myself nervously in the lead through the high grass for a few hundred yards. There we found him anchored under a small thorn tree where I was able to finish him off.

We watched as they skinned him and Musa insisted that I should learn exactly how it should be done, a neat but unattractive process. The stink was terrible and fortunately I have never had an occasion to show off my skill. He was a big specimen with a golden mane and he measured twelve foot two inches 'between pegs' i.e., from nose to tip of tail.

[127]

For four more days we tried to find a third lion for Gerald, but without success. Our last hope involved an overnight foot safari through a dense forest area impossible to reach by car. This meant taking on eighteen villagers as porters who followed us in Indian file down the narrow game-paths carrying all our belongings, including tents and bedding, on their heads and often singing. 'We might meet a rhino through here,' said Kingdon, 'so have the big rifle ready.' I had the licence for one rhino, but I must admit as a raw beginner I was not particularly keen to meet one. We saw plenty of signs in the form of heaps of dung which Kingdon told us a rhino, like some fox terriers, will turn and scatter vigorously with his hind legs. In one dark, narrow place Kingdon shouted, 'Rhino, look out!' I was aghast at the danger to Alice and our big party strung out behind us. It came crashing by just a few yards to our side, quite invisible but snorting like an express train. We saw no more of it – perhaps our scent was not strong enough – but we also saw no lion. We came back to camp and loaded up for our return to Nairobi and Government House the next day.

When we first arrived we had been put up as temporary members of the Muthaiga Country Club in the suburbs of Nairobi with its golf course, tennis courts and swimming pool. It was the social centre of the capital, an agreeable place with comfortable bedrooms for those living up-country. The food was excellent and after five o'clock it was practically impossible to move in the bar. All day long the box-bodies rolled in with their coats of white, brown or red dust from distant places like Eldoret, Nanyuki or the Happy Valley, each with their servants, all to be accommodated at Muthaiga. We had made many friends there and when we got back found invitations waiting for us to stay up-country during the ten short days before our next safari.

We kept the Buick on and after several nights at Government House set off in a party of friends to stay at different places in the Happy Valley. Strictly speaking, this name only applied to the valley of the Wanjohi river, rising in the foothills of the Aberdare Mountains and running down to where it changed its name and flowed into Lake Naivasha. Notionally, however, it included several small places not in the valley itself but all centred round Gilgil, a charming cattle-market town.

Our route took us north for Naivasha. To do so we had to enter the Great Rift Valley, that vast gash on the earth's surface which starts with the River Jordan in the Wadi Araba and includes the Red Sea and Lake Rudolf in Kenya. It reminded me faintly of the Grand Canyon, though in place of the buttes and pinnacles there were green rocky escarpments. It has been described as the 'cradle of mankind' for it was here and further down in Tanganyika that Dr Leakey and his wife Mary discovered fossilised bones of our earliest ancestors.

Our first hostess, who lived near Gilgil, was Alice de Janzé, a most attractive American whom we had known in Paris. She had been married first to Raymond de Trafford, an Englishman, and later to a French count. The marriage to de Trafford, a ne'er-do-well of some charm, had ended dramatically at the Gare du Nord in Paris when she pumped six shots into him from a revolver. Miraculously it did him no serious harm. It was probably well deserved even if some-what over-demonstrative, and by the time we saw her again at Gilgil she treated it as a huge joke, merely claiming that she was the worst shot in Kenya. She was a kind hostess and took us out to various friends' houses as well as a dance and when we left presented us with a beautiful quilt made up of nine Thomson gazelle skins which I still have. Years later she took her own life, having been much in love with Lord Erroll, the victim in the notorious wartime murder case.

I met several old Eton friends living round about, not perhaps all of them serious farmers but much enjoying the climate and easy life of Kenya. The Happy Valley, with the help of the film *White Mischief,* has tended to give the white settler in Kenya a bad name. The vast majority of the white inhabitants were efficient and hard-working farmers, most of whom had come there with their families as im-migrants on grants to ex-servicemen from the First World War and had bought and built up their farms with official backing.

The Happy Valley was in no way typical. By the time I knew it, it had become a curious mixture of well-to-do British and foreign aris-tocrats, sportsmen, pleasure seekers, sun-lovers and eccentrics, as well as some wanderers and exiles with just enough money to afford to keep a few servants. They were almost all farmers of a sort, some keen and very competent. It was nervously regarded by the world in general as a hotbed of sin and illicit love which as far as I could judge differed little from what went on in London, New York or Paris. I should not have said that there were any more adulterous affairs there than elsewhere, though people were more blatant about them –

helped, or course, by the fact that the servants all regarded it as one of the tribal customs of the white man.

We spent the rest of our time at the house of Lady Idina Haldeman, the sister of my old friend Buck De La Warr. She was still married to her fourth husband, an American. He apparently suffered from the general effects of alcohol which at a height of 6,000 feet can be punitive. He had been finally ejected from the house after emptying an entire magazine from his pistol through the dining-room ceiling. Idina was a curious creature, not beautiful but with great fascination and a kindness of heart and humour which swept all before her. Her previous husbands included a future Cabinet minister, the secretary of the Travellers' Club in Paris, and the 22nd Earl of Erroll. Later on when she came to Cairo during the war she married again – a nice young officer in the RAF. I was never in any way physically attracted but I adored her and last saw her when she was dying of cancer. At her brother's request I fetched her from her bed in the Middlesex Hospital to a small family theatre party. We all had supper at the Savoy Grill and I took her back, never to see her again.

Her house, Clouds, lay at the head of the valley up against the dark backdrop of the Aberdare mountain range with its silvery streams and dense forests of cedars and bamboos. It was full of wild life, including the only specimens in Kenya of the elusive bongo, the rarest and largest of all antelopes, with its red and white striped flanks. The house was a grey clapboard one-storey affair, built in a square like a miniature Cambridge college. The main door facing the entrance arch had above it the bleached skull and horns of a fine buffalo. There was a garden around the house with few flowers but with tall blue gums and cedars where the black and white colobus monkeys with their long tails gambolled and chattered high above our heads. We were a house-party of eight with a few others coming in for lunch or dinner. As was then the custom in the White Highlands, after one's evening bath one got straight into a dressing-gown and pyjamas for dinner. This had, as far as we could judge, no erotic significance, but was simply the continuation at home of the general custom on safari – namely changing straight from your bath into sleeping attire. We dined well and it was all very respectable, even if we stayed up late and drank a fair amount of whisky.

I must admit that I can remember once being awoken about ten in the morning by the rattle of a cocktail shaker somewhere nearby, but at lunch no one seemed to be any the worse. We left before dawn two nights later, so as to get back to Government House for a luncheon in honour of the governors of Uganda and Tanganyika who were assembled for their annual meeting. I was driving and soon after leaving Clouds we entered a deep cutting about twenty foot high. We could hardly believe our eyes when out sprang a big cock ostrich with its black and white tail feathers waving and set off at speed down the middle of the narrow road ahead of us. We were late and obliged to press on, but the bird kept ahead of us until there was a small game-path on one bank up which it could scramble to safety. We arrived at Government House with half an hour to spare.

A few days later our little party and vehicles left for our second safari. I had already had a brief experience of elephant earlier on, having been asked by Jack Kingdon to stay with him on his farm near Nyeri for a couple of days. He was an honorary game warden and owing to the late rains raiding elephants from Mount Kenya had been doing terrible damage to the *shambas* and crops of the Kikuyu villagers near Nanyuki. A hunt had been organised and several elephants were killed and the herds driven away. In considerable trepidation, I had managed to get one of them myself.

This time the hunt took us to the Athi plains south east of Nairobi beyond the river of that name. It was mostly yellow savannah country with woodland patches – mimosa, acacia and even swamps of papyrus with high elephant grass. There were wonderful views of Mount Kilimanjaro. Here we slept not in tents but in a primitive red mud and wattle rest-hut with a thatched roof and no door. There were, so we were assured, no malaria mosquitoes in the area so we did not bother to unpack our bed-nets or mosquito boots. We sent our scouts, recruited from the nearby village, to reconnoitre on all sides. After one disappointing hunt a scout came back with tales of a large tusker described as having to walk backwards up hills as his tusks would otherwise stick into the ground! His oval footprints they said were over eighteen inches which should certainly ensure good ivory. He was obviously a fine specimen of the African elephant, so much more handsome than his button-eared Indian cousins.

We left before dawn, at first easily finding the large prints in the dew as the sun rose. An elephant swings along at about six miles an hour and we had to walk fast to catch up with the herd, for such it was. The head Kamba tracker was testing the wind all the time with a little dust from the palm of his hand and his colleague running, head bent low, to examine every stony patch. Kingdon himself always carried a little salt cellar in his pocket against such emergencies. After two hours we began to find more direct signs, tidy heaps of dung shaped like old-fashioned country loaves of bread. Then we noticed these heaps beginning to steam in the cool air and knew we were very close. Soon we heard a cracking of broken boughs and small trees or the tearing of branches. From the herd came every conceivable sort of noise – light trumpeting, loud squeals from the little *totos* and above all the unmistakable rumbling of the great stomachs. I cannot describe the combination of fear and exultation of that slow foot by foot advance. Pushing aside the thick clumps of bush, we suddenly saw them all together under a patch of thorn trees just in front of us.

We put Alice up a twisted acacia tree where she could see to some extent what was going on but which would have given little protection had an elephant come crashing her way. We went cautiously on. Then in a wooded dip we seemed surrounded by the huge beasts, many bright red from the mud where they had been wallowing. There were some twenty or thirty cows and calves but no sign of the big bull. We moved forward again a little; then a little more . . . stop! A dry leaf ahead crackled and you hardly dared breathe. Suddenly Kingdon, just behind me, pulled sharply at my coat and pointed through a thorn bush just ahead. There was a grey flat patch which I realised was our quarry. He could not have been more than five yards away. There could be no question of shooting from there, so backwards I went slowly, foot by foot, silently, back – one – two – three – with the heavy double-barrelled rifle held forward. Then they must have got wind of us for suddenly there was dead silence and the whole lot unbelievably melted away, without a sound, like a picture fading out in a silent film.

We tried a new approach. Soon we were following some fresh tracks and came across the herd again in another clump of trees. This time I had a clear view. It was a good-sized bull but no real tusker in spite of the size of his footprints and I took him easily with the first shot. It was getting dark and we were far from our camp so decided to leave a guard for the night and return the next day.

When we came back next morning at dawn we found half the population of a nearby village assembled, some already at work with axes cutting out the tusks while others were helping themselves with their pangas to vast square steaks to take home. The tusks weighed about fifty pounds each – nothing wonderful. That night, after our thirty-five mile walk the previous day, we were stiff and exhausted but strong enough to attend an *ngoma* dance to celebrate the occasion with full plumes and drums in our honour. With the long line of slim bare-breasted girls dancing interminably, their hips thrusting backwards and forwards, eyes locked into those of the plumed young warriors opposite and the drums beating their endless rhythm, any idea of sleep soon melted away.

I never hunted elephant again but over thirty years later I was charged by one in the Parc National Albert in the Congo. He was a big bull who was helping himself to the contents of the dustbins at our camp at four in the afternoon. When I tried to take a photograph he gave a loud squeal, spread his ears, raised his trunk and came straight at me. I am told that an elephant charges at over thirty miles an hour but I was still well ahead when I fell head over heels into a ditch. I split my drill trousers from top to bottom but he kindly then gave up the chase and went back to our dustbins. It was just a warning!

Next day, back at Government House, we said our grateful farewells to our host and hostess and left by car for Uganda and Lake Albert, crossing the Rift again on our way to Nakuru and then to Njoro. There we stayed with the Kilkelly family and watched a polo game of which one could see nothing but the dust of a dirt ground leaving players and ponies all the same chocolate brown.

We went to lunch with Gerald Kilkelly's sister, married to the agent of Lord Francis Scott, a great public figure in Kenya, at their farm in Menengai, an extinct volcano crater. We were sitting over a pink gin beforehand which I found remarkably strong for I suddenly began to feel dizzy. I went shakily into lunch and no sooner had I sat down than I was violently sick. After that I remember nothing until I came round in a small bed with Alice bending anxiously over me. I was ice-cold and shivering. It turned out that I had a severe attack of malignant malaria. I must have picked it up ten days before on the so-called 'malaria-free' Athi plains. I was delirious for four days with a temperature of 105 and woke up to find myself being well cared for in the Nakuru Cottage Hospital. My main recollection is of the dozens of bats that flew round my netted bed at night and, despite the always open windows, the appalling stench.

I was in hospital for nearly three weeks and our journey through Uganda had to be cancelled. At last one fine day at dawn we took off for Juba on the Nile in a chartered light plane. The sun rose as we crossed Lake Nakuru and simultaneously thousands of flamingos all took to the air below us rising like a vast pink quilt in the morning sun. We spent the night at Juba in the house of an old friend, Martin Parr, the governor of the Upper Nile province, who was away on leave. Shortly after we had got to bed, we were awakened by a harsh rasping sound like a heavy saw out on the balcony. 'It's only a leopard,' I could say nonchalantly to Alice's nervous gasp. He soon went off, no doubt to seek a pi-dog in the village, his favourite dinner. It was my last encounter with big game.

The next day we had time to see something more of our Shilluk friends. The men, stark-naked and very tall and slender with just a plume in their hair, were often completely covered with white ash or mud which made their nudity slightly less obvious. The women, equally tall with the same straight noses and narrow build, wore a loose band of cloth or rows of beads round their flat stomachs. We saw Shilluks nearly seven foot tall standing for hours on one leg in water like cranes, with the other foot resting on the opposite knee and supporting themselves with a long slender staff. They were, we were told, very vain and fascinated by elaborate headdresses of plumes or leaves. Some of the men we saw had let their straight hair grow down to their shoulders in a bob but dyed it a bright golden colour.

Many missionaries and their wives worked in the area, of every denomination and with great influence over their converts. There were apparently two schools of missionary thought on the questions of nudity. Some, the more prudish, insisted on putting people into khaki shorts or bright-coloured gingham frocks as the case might be. Traditionalists favoured the unspoilt native in his own primitive state. We were told by a district officer about one missionary family where if you were invited to a tea party you were apt to find the immensely long implement of the butler dangling dangerously close to the cucumber sandwiches.

Our steamer was driven by a stern paddle-wheel with a barge lashed firmly to the starboard side for the third-class passengers. Looking down at it I found myself facing an elderly and skinny little Shilluk, completely nude but with an old green Homburg hat not unlike my own on his head and a short white clay pipe in his mouth. I waved and he ceremoniously took off his hat and bowed. I did likewise.

The cabins were comfortable but like the few other passengers on board we soon realised that the sensible thing if one wanted to breathe was to sleep on the upper deck in a giant square wire 'meat-safe'. We also found a surprising but very welcome present in the shape of a case of Pimms No. 1 Cup sent up somehow by our American photographer friend Lee Miller. We were very popular on board. I was still weak from malaria and we spent most of our time sitting in the stern with our books, with a rifle across my knee to pot some of the numerous crocodiles along our route. It was a difficult shot as only the bulging eyes and two nostrils show above the surface. I felt no compunction knowing the terrible suffering they inflict on the dwellers on the river banks, but I doubt that I ever killed one.

The Nile soon opened up to nearly a mile in width with heavy trees and bush on its banks and occasionally a Shilluk or a Nuer village in the pale yellow or magenta sunset. There were clumps of trees and open savannah with much matted scrub and an occasional distant mountain top. After two days the river narrowed as we entered the Sudd – the 300 miles of floating islands of papyrus and bright blue lotus flowers lying ahead. Sometimes the islands were small and slim; more often they were immense so that you could not believe that it was not a solid part of the mainland. There the dense stalks towered twenty or thirty feet into the sky and day after day the nose of our small craft had to knife its way through the tangle of rotting plants and ill-smelling weeds. Sometimes the current swept the Sudd aside and you could see forests or a small grassy village, and if you were near inshore, a bank with horrible grey twenty-foot crocodiles lying basking in the sun with their mouths open.

One day after another we slid through the Sudd until at last we were joined by the mighty Bahr-el Ghazal river at Lake No near Malakal, where it comes down from the Congo. Now it became the White Nile and widened again, with villages and little Arab towns on either side of the plain until we came to our goal of Kosti and to Khartoum itself.

There we spent the night at the house of a friend, a famous character named Major Pongo Barker, the jovial director of the Khartoum Zoo. We all three slept on the roof and were woken early next morning by the lions below us, hungry for their breakfast. It was the only zoo I have ever been where all the animals that were not actually dangerous were left to wander about to graze and drink together as they wished. You would find the damp nose of a large waterbuck pushing into your pocket in search of some delicacy. Pongo also handed us a telegram from the embassy to say that our little son was seriously ill with typhoid in Alexandria. Though he was said to be out of danger, we left by flying boat the following day for Aboukir Bay and the blue Mediterranean.

10

On the Brink

Towards the end of 1937 I had learned that I was to be transferred to the British agency in Burgos, the headquarters of General Franco. Loving Spain as I did and anxious to be of some help in her agony, I was delighted, especially as it came under the orders of none other than my old Washington friend Sir Henry Chilton as ambassador – he actually resided at Hendaye on the French border. However, shortly after the New Year the first secretary of the legation in Greece drove his car into a tree at night and was killed instantly. I was switched to Athens at short notice.

We crossed the Mediterranean in some state. Accompanying us were our son, his nanny, Peachey, three dogs, including a beautiful cream Rhodesian ridgeback bitch we had been given in Kenya, two polo ponies with my old wall-eyed groom Hassan Said Hassan, and a Ford station waggon. The Foreign Office in those days allowed you to take on transfer three lift-vans of furniture – ten and half tons in all. Not till the day after our arrival did the American Export Line agent appear, very crestfallen, to inform us that in Alexandria harbour a crane cable had broken high up in the air and our lift van had dropped straight into the hold where it collapsed like a crushed matchbox. It was a sad blow because though insured it had contained much of our most loved family English and French furniture.

We arrived in Athens at an awkward moment with the annual national carnival festivities clashing with the state funeral of Prince Nicholas of Greece, the father of Princess Marina the Duchess of Kent. We watched the procession from the balcony of the Hotel Grande Bretagne with our friends Nardo Mercati and the Michael Arlens who with their family were also staying at the hotel.

We all paid nightly visits to the restaurant-night-clubs in the Plaka district below the Parthenon. The evenings began sedately enough with a little jazz music, a xylophone and an emotional singer. Then suddenly things began to happen. Hundreds of wax eggs, filled with confetti and sold by the dozen, would be thrown about – at friends and strangers alike – followed by glasses and plates tossed over the shoulder against the walls. By midnight, as far as one could judge, all the crockery in the place lay in shattered piles. We were never able to learn the origin of this orgy of destruction. Peter Wilson, a major in the Transjordan Frontier Force who stayed with us the following year after chasing Arab terrorists in Palestine, thought Athens at carnival time was far more dangerous.

The legation was a dignified but dull building which had belonged to the liberal leader Eleutherios Venizelos in the First World War. It has a small garden overlooking Kifissia Avenue, in which the Greek Foreign Office was also located. The minister, Sir Sydney Waterlow, was a large and formidable figure with a luxuriant walrus moustache which he fondled continuously into an elegant upward curl at each end and which had earned him the nickname of 'The Water-Buffalo'. A great classicist, he was, I fear it must be said, in other respects a figure of fun. He wore a *ceinture réglante* which kept his ample stomach flat but blew out his thorax to give him the appearance of a pouter pigeon. He had had a curious diplomatic career, having had to resign in the early 1900s on account of an adulterous divorce – something, to their own misfortune, not then tolerated by the Foreign Office. I understood that he had the unlikely distinction of having been cited as a co-respondent by some man at the same time as his wife was suing him for divorce on grounds of impotence. He had re-entered the Diplomatic Service through the backdoor of the Commercial Diplomatic Service and had been a successful and I believe popular minister in Sofia. For some reason he took an instant dislike to me. Six weeks after my arrival I wrote to my mother that I had experienced nothing but criticism, bad temper and downright rudeness since I had arrived. I told her that if things didn't improve by the autumn I would ask for a transfer. It was the course adopted by two previous heads of chancery.

I had only one secretary to help in the chancery – Edward Warner, the son of my late chief in the Treaty Department. There was an honorary attaché, Aubrey Moody, a commercial secretary, a naval attaché and a translator and that was all. The naval attaché, Captain Herbert Packer, RN, and his wife, the novelist Joyce Packer, became our closest friends in Athens. In due course he was to command HMS *Norfolk* which played a big part in the sinking of the *Bismarck*.

After many years of exile the Greek monarchy had been restored in 1935, and King George II had resumed his reign. He had lived for a long time at Brown's Hotel in Dover Street and was completely anglicised. He was separated from his Romanian wife Queen Elizabeth and had no children. I had known him slightly when he was in exile in London. He was of medium height with a clear complexion and blue eyes, a little shy in manner but with an easy smile. He was immensely pro-British and embarrassed by the autocratic régime in Athens, but after the political confusion of recent years was determined to restore stability. From my own conversations with him I have no shadow of doubt that King George sincerely believed that the régime's policy would in due course lead to the return of democratic rule.

The heir to the throne was his brother Paul, very nice if not highly intelligent, who had quite recently married a Hanoverian princess, later to become Queen Frederika. She was a beautiful but strong-minded young lady who made many enemies but played a very gallant part during the Communist rising of 1948. Paul also had two charming sisters, Princes Irene and Princess Catherine. The latter married a British army officer and came to live in England with her family.

The restoration of the monarchy had been the work of General Metaxas, one of several military dictators of both the right and the left. He had done his military training in Germany before the 1914 war and was by instinct favourably disposed to Germany. When it came to the crunch, however, he stood up stalwartly first to Mussolini and later to Hitler. It was he who, under King Constantine I, when it came to the question of an Allied attack on Turkey in 1915, had put forward a carefully elaborated plan for an overland march on Constantinople in place of the Gallipoli landings.

The Metaxas régime was not in itself a Fascist system, though it had some of the frills and the parliamentary constitution had been suspended. There was a rather half-baked blue-shirt organisation which played no real part. The only visible sign of Fascism in the streets was the Youth Movement, which was little more than a revamped edition of the Boy Scouts. Still, the régime was undoubtedly unpopular and there was continual plotting and scheming among the Venizalist opposition leaders. As in several other countries the leadership tended to pro-German – with the King and the people pro-British.

[139]

In those days Athens was still a beautiful city, unblighted by smog, with its ancient monuments and its sedate Germanic boulevards, coupled with the little byways of the Plaka. However, we decided to look further afield for a house in the suburb of Psychiko with its attractive villas and a striking view of Mount Hymettus. With the help of Nardo we found a remarkable building owned, designed and just completed by a modern architect, Kondoleon. He had recently married a young millionaire poetess, with advanced political views, who six years later emerged as the champion of the Communist ELAS party which tried to pocket Greece under the nose of the British liberating forces. The house was on a circular plot on the top of a tree-covered ridge which ran from the city out towards Kifissia and the marble quarries of Pendelikon. It was surrounded by a five-foot wall with clumps of Mediterranean pines within. Down on the other side lay a shoddy little village of Greek refugees from Asia Minor, part of the million-a-side population exchange with Turks from Greece in 1924. I am told the whole valley now teems with houses and people.

The design of the house was just as unconventional as its owners – a large garage, a small round front hall with a lift, and a large drawing room was all there was on the ground flour. The high draw-ing-room windows slid into the walls and turned it into a garden room. Everything else was on the floor above, with a large terrace running the length of the house. It was surprisingly attractive. Our broken furniture was in part repaired by a skilled restorer and, with the rest, created a sensational room with white Greek satin curtains almost twenty foot high. Six years later the house was for a time occupied by Archbishop Damaskinos, the Regent, and was shelled by the Communists as they retreated down the far side of the ridge. Later still it relapsed into a rather poorly tended old people's home.

I kept my horses across the valley at a riding club at the foot of Mount Hymettus. Hassan brought them up every morning and Nicky and I would ride for an hour along the ridge with the dogs. It was delightfully countrified considering it was only a quarter of an hour's drive to my office. Sometimes I rode with Princess Frederika whom I came to like and admire. Though German she certainly deplored and feared Hitler as much as we did. Poor Hassan, a month later he asked to be sent back to Egypt. He who had robbed me steadily for years explained that he could not survive alongside the Greeks who, he said, cheated him right and left!

Count Nardo Mercati, who was my son's godfather, made our social life for us. His father was the Grand Chamberlain and with the help of King George's personal ADC, Major Levidis, who also became a close friend, we were soon invited everywhere. We had mixed feelings about Athens society. After the free and easy life of Cairo with British army officers dropping in for meals at all times, the formal dinner parties, the hours of bridge, the haute couture and, above all, the spiteful gossip dismayed us. It took time to adjust ourselves. Alice described it as 'black satin and pearls'. But by the winter we had settled down and were really enjoying ourselves. Above all we discovered the kindness and unfailing loyalty to the British connection of the Greeks high and low.

We had made particular friends with one family, the Melas, well off and leaders in the Athens social world. One was a senior member of the Foreign Office who became the ambassador in London; the second, George, was a Venizelist with a rich wife; and the third, a bachelor, Basil, was a great admirer of Alice. We were out with George and his wife one night at a night-club when at three in the morning she started complaining that she had a fine thoroughbred jumper for which she could not find a rider for the show-jumping tournament at the riding club that afternoon. I had plenty of experience of jumping but never in the show ring. However, after a few glasses of Lanson 1929 I agreed to take it on provided I could have a trial ride that morning. At 7 a.m. I presented myself, rather bleary-eyed, at the club, where I found the horse, a beautiful deep chestnut but equipped with a side saddle. I asked for a replacement saddle, and while waiting for it had a short and dizzy ride round the ring side saddle. With the steep drop on one side, it reminded me of a tall camel. When the actual performance took place in the afternoon, I was surprised to find I had had two faultless rounds and was apparently the winner; but no, I had gone the wrong side of one of the guide flags.

In the summer we had a short holiday in England where we visited my family and friends. Alice went on with Nicky to America while I returned to Athens as chargé d'affaires. German pressures were becoming intense and unfortunately their inroads into Greek commerce swamped anything that British efforts, pitifully weak and in many respects unsuccessful, could accomplish. Greeks would ask me how I could expect them to buy British cars when spare parts would take over two months to come out by rail, while a German Mercedes agent would receive them back by air in twenty-four hours. I had no answer.

In Athens we already had the advantage of several well-established British institutions, commercial and otherwise. Apart from the famous British School of Archaeology run by George Young, which attracted many visitors, there was the more recent British Institute under the aegis of its chairman, Lord Lloyd, which had already had such success in Egypt. It was modelled on the Institut de France, already going strong throughout the world for many years. The teaching of the English language was its prime function and by the end of a few weeks we already had 3,000 inscribed students with another 2,000 on the waiting list. This was not just evidence of a desire to learn English for its commercial advantages, but a symbol of support for democracy not wholly welcome to the régime.

Rumours of war appeared almost daily in the press, concentrating mainly on the free city of Danzig. Later in the summer attention had swung to the Sudeten-deutsch of Czechoslovakia and reached its crisis at Munich. Lee Miller had come to stay for a few days on her way to Romania and I must admit that both of us – I an old-fashioned but bitterly anti-Nazi Conservative and she a near-Communist surrealist – breathed with equal relief when news of the Munich agreement came over on the evening wireless news and we drank Neville Chamberlain's health in champagne.

With only three of us to do the cyphering and with instructions for war pouring in we often worked well into the night. We still, however, found time for relaxation. The little golf course at Glifada was one of our standbys. Not only had it a nice nine-hole course, though with mud 'greens', but it also had a little beach where we could swim and water ski with Nardo and his friends. There was a small harbour where we were able to tie up the Cris-Craft on its arrival from Alexandria. I also went underwater spear-fishing for the first time with Chris Baker of the Naval Mission. To begin with we used the long primitive three-pronged spears of ancient Greece and flying goggles – but he soon designed some sharp single-pointed steel spears and had them made at the Greek naval workshops on the island of Salamis where he was posted.

During the summer I had been introduced by a friend to fishing for tunny all night and I went out with him several times. The aim was to locate the sardine fleet which used one huge net attached to the stern of twenty or thirty small boats in a ring, each with a lantern in the stern. The sparkling lights in the black water were a lovely sight. When the net was hauled in full of thousands of squirming sardines, a tunny was often brought in as well. It had followed the sardines in and our role was to hang about outside the circle of lights in a rowing boat and fish with the aid of sardines we had brought with us and sprinkled on the water. In the heat of the July night we worked stripped to the waist, sweating heavily. My friend once caught a 200 lb tunny and we ourselves got a number of smaller ones. One night, with an army friend on a visit from Cairo, I got a big fish on the line. I tried to wind in but it was too strong for me and we found our little boat being towed backwards out to sea in the darkness. The boatman said it was far too big for any tunny and must be a dolphin; so I was glad when the line finally broke.

I also had occasional days shooting snipe at Lake Copaïs and elsewhere and Alice had some good tennis, especially with her old friend Didi Vlastos, the Wimbledon player who lived out at Tatoï near the royal country palace and family mausoleum. I had come to know the King quite well and we now formed a friendship which lasted throughout the war. It has been said by some historians that he was a homosexual. This I can categorically deny, for in his London years he had formed a close attachment to a beautiful and charming English lady, Mrs Joyce Britten Jones. At Churchill's request I had the job of arranging for her to fly out to Athens in the early part of 1941, 'to stiffen the King of Greece' as the Prime Minister put it in his directive.

The King and his sisters came to dine with us several times at Psychiko and on one occasion he brought Joyce. He was sitting at the head of the table on our dining-room terrace with Alice on his left and myself opposite. I was a little taken aback to hear Peachey saying, 'No, Your Majesty, not that fork, the next one!' Crown Prince Paul and Princess Frederika lived in a more traditional villa in Psychiko half way up the hill leading to our house and with them too we had an easy friendship. I remember in 1939 showing him my new S.S. Special Jaguar tourer with its elegant half-hood which had just come out – 'the poor man's Bentley' it was called in those days. He was determined to buy one himself but I expect that the war intervened to stop it. The Nazi-like 'S.S. Special' designation was soon dropped once war began.

When winter came and with it snow on Hymettus glowing deep pink in the evening light, Alice and I went skiing on Mount Parnassos. On New Year's Day we skiied in the morning and swam in the sea in the afternoon. Occasionally she came out riding with me along the pine-covered ridge on which our house stood. Nicky meanwhile flourished at his English school. We had settled down happily enough, many friends came out from England to stay, only the German menace hung over us like a pall. In this city of rumours there were continual reports of impending German action – Danzig, Memel and now above all Poland. In the spring it came in a sudden take-over of the whole of truncated Czechoslovakia. Despite all the Allied Franco-British pledges given to President Benes no one moved.

Easter was early that year and the following week I was due to go up to Salonika with Alice to open a new branch of the British Council. Then on Good Friday came the news of the invasion of Albania by Ciano and his minions. On Holy Saturday there was to be a great Te Deum in the Mitropol Cathedral to celebrate at midnight the Resurrection of Our Lord, to be attended by the King, the Government and the Diplomatic Corps. Sir Sydney was recovering from a bout of influenza and I was deputed to take his place. In full diplomatic uniform I stood with my candle amid the rest of the diplomats in the gold mosaic sanctuary, in front of the high altar amid the chanting of priests in their rounded golden crowns and glittering vestments. The great bell tolled overhead. As we stood waiting for the King and his brother to arrive, a Foreign Office official slipped in beside me to whisper that, after the service, General Metaxas wanted to see me immediately at the Foreign Office.

It was a little time before I could find my car and present myself at the Foreign Office. When I was finally ushered in to the general's room, I was astonished to find him bent over his desk sobbing with his hands to his forehead. He pulled himself together at once and explained that they had received information from a sure source that the Italians were going into Corfu that morning. He begged me to notify His Majesty's Government at once and ask them what they proposed to do. I commiserated suitably but pointed out that time was a little short though I would do my best. Bidding me goodbye, he put both hands on my shoulders and with emotion said that he knew that he could always trust the British.

Back in my office – still dressed in gold and blue coatee – I composed a telegram to the Foreign Office with a 'Most Immediate and Top Secret' heading. With some hesitation I also decided to repeat the telegram to the commander-in-chief Mediterranean Fleet in Malta. I summoned Warner from his bed to help with the cyphering and took the draft to the minister's bedroom. Half asleep and still no doubt full of sedatives, he sat up to proclaim that the black forces of evil were at that moment swirling in the skies above us and the clash could not be long delayed. Otherwise he made no comment. Returning early next morning to my office for a reply from the Foreign Office, I found on my desk a decyphered signal from the commander-in-chief. It stated simply that units of the Mediterranean Fleet had sailed at first light north east of Malta. We waited anxiously but the invasion of Corfu did not take place.

The same day, at his farm outside Athens, Nardo had arranged an *al fresco* lunch for King George and a few friends, where a lamb was barbecued whole on an iron spit. The King arrived late in khaki uniform, British style. He was accompanied by Levidis and a fair-haired, good-looking boy in a grey check suit. He turned out to be Prince Philip, now Duke of Edinburgh, who was about to join the British Navy. The King looked me hard in the eye but said nothing except that they had been delayed at the ceremony of his break-ing hard-boiled eggs with each of his Evzone guards. These famous troops in their frilled white ballet skirts and floppy red-tasselled caps also supplied the guard to the Unknown Soldier's tomb in front of the yellow Royal Palace in Syntagma Square (now the Parliament building).

Early on Easter Monday Alice and I left for the North by car, spending a night en route at the small town of Larissa in Thes-saly. We had just come down to the hall for dinner when there was a clatter outside and by lamplight a cavalcade of cars drew up. Out from a Rolls-Royce stepped King Zog and Queen Geraldine of Albania with her brand-new baby and the King's four sisters, fleeing from the Italian invasion. As we watched in the dim light, out of the third vehicle, carried in by attendants, were several aged iron-studded chests which we assumed to contain the national gold of Albania.

Our British Council opening passed off successfully and within two days we were again overwhelmed by a multitude of applications. We had decided to spend the weekend in Thrace along the coast towards

Turkey. At Cavalla with its ancient walls, the original home of the Egyptian royal family, we visited the huge tobacco depositories, the home of much of the Oriental tobacco generally known as Turkish. I had brought a gun with me so we passed one pleasant day walking up the innumerable snipe in the marshy areas to the east. I had been advised to put two ball cartridges in my pocket in case I disturbed a water buffalo at his toilette and was charged. This was a very different type of animal from his lethargic cousins in the villages of Egypt.

Towards the end of 1938 the minister's attitude towards me had changed suddenly and totally. He became friendly, jocular and considerate, full of praise for the operations of the chancery and anxious for advice and help. It was several weeks before I discovered the cause of this welcome transformation – Sir Sydney Waterlow had fallen in love! The leading Greek actress of the day, soon to gain worldwide fame, was Katina Paxinou. She starred above all in modern versions of the ancient Greek tragedies of Aeschylus and others. She was striking-looking with fine classical features and deep eyes and a particularly charming personality. Waterlow had met her at a small reception of the Venizelist group of political dissidents which frequently met to gossip and plan. It was a strange place for him to find himself, for he had been a admirer of General Metaxas and an upholder of the monarchy. It had been love at first sight; from then on the minister could think of nothing else. When there were no formal meetings he would often go off after dinner to Madame Paxinou's villa until late at night, with the legation Rolls parked stark on the highway and the Union flag fluttering on its mudguard. Inevitably the news spread like wildfire to the drawing rooms of society and no doubt to the coffee tables of Syntagma Square. Inevitably also the stories came back to me and naturally I sought to damp them down. As far as I was concerned the crux came when the minister took me into his confidence and pathetically revealed to me his joys and dreams, his eyes full of tears.

The position was further complicated when we learnt that Sir Sydney, who was due to retire in May, was to be given a year's extension by the Foreign Office. He went off on leave and I found myself left in charge. Bewildered and quite uncertain as to what I should do, I was suddenly sent for by the King. In the chintzy setting of the morning room at the palace, with its copies of the *Illustrated London*

News on the table, he told me that though he liked the old 'Walrus' as he called him, he simply could not overlook the public support which the minister was now giving to his political foes. He had just heard a rumour of the renewal of the appointment. This was the last straw and it had to stop. I said I would do the best I could to put over his views. I went home with deep misgivings to concoct a straightforward account of the facts to the private secretary at the Foreign Office, Derick Hoyer-Millar. I had finished my letter but the diplomatic bag had not yet left. At this point Lord Lloyd turned up on a visit to the British Council establishment and was summoned to an audience with the King, who duly repeated his complaints. Lloyd came straight to me and I showed him what I had written. He offered to take my letter with him the next day and deliver it in person. Within a few weeks the appointment of Sir Michael Palairet as British minister in Athens was announced. It was not an event I could look back on with any satisfaction.

Sir Sydney took his farewell in May and soon afterwards Sir Michael and Lady Palairet took his place. Sir Michael was destined to play a vital part in the events of 1940 and 1941 before he and his wife finally escaped from Greece with the King. For the moment we somehow gave a party for 240 people to meet them, then soon afterwards left on leave for England. We expected to spend the years of the coming war in Athens. It was not to be. During a short visit to Dublin for the Horse Show festivities and a lovely tour in our new car thorough the glories of Killarney and Connemara in full summer, I had an urgent letter from the Foreign Office. The Cabinet had decided to set up a new Anglo-French Section of the Committee of Imperial Defence – soon to be merged with the War Cabinet – to rebuild the machinery of cooperation as it had been left in 1918 from the Supreme War Council downward. A naval captain and an Army colonel had been appointed to this and I was to become the Foreign Office representative. I was asked to return to London forthwith.

II

Liaison

Next door to the Banqueting House in Whitehall is one of the lesser-known treasures of eighteenth-century London, Gwydyr House. This was to be the home of the new Anglo-French Liaison section of the Committee of Imperial Defence, soon to become part of the War Cabinet Secretariat. It was built by William Adam and the interior, including its fine marble fireplaces, was practically untouched. On my arrival there towards the end of August 1939 I found my two service colleagues already installed – Captain A.W. Clarke, RN (inevitably 'Nobby' to everyone) and Colonel Harold Redman of the King's Own Yorkshire Light Infantry. From the beginning we got on well and I cannot recall a single sour word or serious disagreement in the eleven months we worked together. We occupied the big ground-floor room with its blue and white Wedgwood plaques on the wall. The members of the brand new Allied Military Committee, British and French, were accommodated upstairs while another big room held the long blue-baize-covered conference table.

It had been decided during the summer between Chamberlain and Daladier to revive the various inter-allied bodies of Anglo-French liaison as they had existed at the time of the Armistice in 1918. Starting with the Supreme War Council they were to cover Anglo-French cooperation in every sphere but above all military matters and vital affairs of economic cooperation. These War Councils were supposed to be held alternately in France and Britain. Twelve took place in all, the first being at Abbeville on 12 September 1939. The next was held at the Town Hall in Hove – representing, I suppose, a defiance to invaders. The prime ministers of course attended these and were joined by the Cabinet ministers appropriate to the decisions in hand. General Hastings Ismay, who now became deputy secretary at the War Cabinet, was invariably present as secretary, as was generally a member of our own secretariat.

The Supreme War Council handled every conceivable topic. There were matters of major strategy such as the possibility of a French breakout on the Maginot Line – which never came. There were issues of Allied policy in Scandinavia; there was some question of Allied occupation of Petsamo in Finland for its iron ore; of an Italian invasion of Greece or Yugoslavia with a possible British pre-emption of Crete; or an Allied landing in Salonika and Thrace where I had so recently been happily shooting snipe. There were plans against an Italian invasion of Egypt and even some talk of an Allied occupation of the Soviet oil fields in the Caucasus. Needless to say there were reams of accompanying documents.

All sorts of other military, economic and technical committees were also set up, including the Allied Military Committee of the Supreme War Council for which we acted as secretaries. Its members mirrored the respective chiefs of staff. The permanent members on our side were Rear-Admiral Chalmers, Major-General Sir James Marshall Cornwall, whom I had known as the first head of the military mission to the Egyptian Army in 1936, and Air Vice-Marshal Evill. Their French opposite numbers were Vice-Admiral Odend'hal, DSC, General Lelong, who was also military attaché in London, and Colonel Rozoy of the French Air Force. It soon became fairly obvious, not only here but in many other ways, that the French Air Force came off a bad third to their other services as compared with the RAF. The committee members had their own staff officers, some of whom always attended the meetings. In the early days I found myself doing most of the translation but we soon secured a superb translator in the form of Captain Humphrey Berkeley who was much later to become a controversial member of Parliament for Lancaster and a distinguished writer and broadcaster.

I attended almost all their meetings, helping to keep records of no less then 97 of them before the end of 1939 and 148 more before the French collapse in 1940. I must have cut a rather peculiar figure as the sole civilian among all the khaki and blue but we soon all made friends and got along very happily together. Our proceedings began with the reading by Nobby Clarke of the intelligence summary for the day prepared by the British Joint Intelligence Committee, later to have as chairman that brilliant diplomat Bill Cavendish-Bentinck. Much of it came from intercepts.

I always felt that as a civilian my presence caused slightly raised eyebrows among the staff. With the three chiefs of staff I was quite at ease, as General Ironside took a liking to me and I had known Admiral Pound and Air Marshal Newall quite well in Alexandria and Cairo.

On Sunday 3 September 1939 the Allied Military Committees assembled earlier than usual. The British ultimatum to Germany was due to expire at eleven o'clock. We got through our business in a desultory way and ten minutes later the prime minister came on the wireless to announce that war had been declared. Not many minutes later we heard the wailing siren of an air-raid warning. It was a dramatic and lugubrious moment. We all picked up our gas masks and headed for the lift and the air-raid shelter below. I can see us now: little General Lelong in his scarlet and gold *képi*, Admiral Odend'hal, grey-haired and distinguished, Evill in his light blue uniform and wings and a little typist squeezed in between us. It was a horrible procedure and it was the last time I ever went down there. As if in mockery it turned out to have been set off by some private aircraft that had gone astray on the south coast.

At our own meetings we discussed every conceivable plan, situation or eventuality, members voicing requests for information from either side. It was also agreed that we should establish a branch in France to carry out similar functions. Their main role was to act as a continuing means of communication between the French High Command of General Gamelin through General Jamet (an unfortunate name I thought) at Vincennes and ourselves, the Cabinet Office and chiefs of staff in London. We also had the duty of maintaining close contact with the Conseil Supérieur de la Défense Nationale and were given an office in the Invalides headquarters. Colonel Redman was deputed to head this office though he frequently came back for consultation with us or General Ismay. He also had duties at the Supreme War Council when it met in France.

We shared other Cabinet Office duties with our fellow assistant secretaries, headed by Colonel Joe Hollis of the Royal Marines, who good-humouredly kept us in order. We each did one night a week as duty officer at Richmond Terrace, shared generally with a service colleague, manning the telephones to No. 10 and to the Foreign Office, and handling air-raid arrangements.

A friend of mine from Alexandria days, Richard Coleridge, then flag lieutenant to Admiral Pound, had unfortunately been forced to resign from the Navy after an attack of tuberculosis in Malta. He had recovered well and was looking for a war job. He was offered the post of chief constable for Huntingdon, which I thought a ridiculous waste of a brilliant mind and great experience. As we were very short-staffed I managed to get him posted to our liaison section. He became assistant to Redman in Paris and filled the bill perfectly.

No chapter on the Cabinet Office would be complete without a reference to two remarkable men who led our small team of assistant secretaries during the first year of war. There was first the secretary of the Cabinet, Sir Edward Bridges. He had started life in the Civil Service and risen to the very top. Behind his kindly smile and gold-rimmed glasses there was a genius for administration and a will of iron; but he was always anxious to help and always fair. In a Cabinet full of stars and under a leader who however brilliant and inspiring was not always easy, Bridges smoothed the way and all seemed to fall into place.

Totally unlike him except in brain-power and decision was Hastings Ismay, the deputy secretary of the War Cabinet and former secretary of the Committee of Imperial Defence. He had originally been in the Indian Cavalry – Skinner's Horse – and was later attached to the Somalia Camel Corps. There he chased and finally ran to ground the Mad Mullah, who was what would now be called a Moslem fundamentalist, and whose supporters spent their time cutting the throats of all who did not agree with them. As his nickname 'Pug' implies he had a small turned-up nose and rather bulging eyes. I had met him in Egypt preparing the treaty negotiations in 1936 and with our common interest in horses had soon become friends. His military knowledge and toughness were considerable, and in addition he had a most remarkable facility for ironing out some apparently hopeless conflict of opinions.

Long before war was declared, conversations had been going on between the two governments on arrangements for complete economic and financial cooperation in case of war. This had existed to a certain degree in 1918, notably on purchasing in America. The great exponent and head of the Allied Purchasing Commission in Washington at that time was Jean Monnet. Small and slightly balding, he was a remarkable character – brilliant, dynamic, tough, ruthless perhaps, and totally up-to-date in that he was to be the first 'European'. From the beginning he insisted that the prospect of future suicidal wars, with poor Europe as ever the cockpit, could only be avoided by union of a sort including Germany – even if full union was beyond reach. When I first met him in 1939 he expounded these ideas to me. He was the father of united Europe. By some miracle the French government in September had had the sense to send him over to London to lead the arrangements for Anglo-French integration and coordination of their economic war efforts. Within days the wheels began to turn, fast.

Negotiations between Monnet and Sir Edward Bridges and the permanent heads of a number of British departments led to an exchange of letters between the two prime ministers towards the end of October. They set up permanent Anglo-French executive committees dealing with food, shipping, armaments and raw materials, oil, air, production and finally economic warfare. The members were drawn from already existing French committees in London and the relevant British departments. The chairmen consisted of the mandarins of Whitehall and equally eminent Frenchmen sent over from France. Soon afterwards the two prime ministers set up an Anglo-French coordinating committee with Jean Monnet as chairman. I became its secretary.

By the spring of the next year all these bodies were working well, though one or two lagged a little. The executive committee met regularly, the coordinating committee I think only four times. There was also an Anglo-French Purchasing Board in Washington under Arthur Purvis, which functioned superbly. Under a secret agreement worked out under the authority of President Roosevelt, Purvis also became a channel of cooperation in preventing essential materials from reaching 'dangerous destinations'.

Soon afterwards I found that my other work was making it impossible for me to keep a proper watch on all these economic affairs and I was given an assistant, Bill Gorell Barnes of the Foreign Office, who took my place as secretary. I also became personal assistant to Monnet together with René Pleven, much later to become prime minister of France, and one other. We met early every morning at Monnet's office in Richmond Terrace.

When we first got to London in August Alice and I had nowhere to live so we moved into a small and uncomfortable furnished flat in Old Burlington Street, conveniently close to Buck's Club. Then came a stroke of luck. In the previous spring a joyous party had descended on us in Athens, as far as I can remember pushing the sale of some variety of English fashion materials. It consisted of Lady Maureen Stanley, the wife of Oliver who was then president of the Board of Trade, Lady O'Neill, later to marry Esmond Rothermere and Ian Fleming, and John Fox-Strangways whose only claim to fame is that he tried to kick Aneurin Bevan down the steps of White's when after the war Air Chief Marshal Slessor brought Bevan into the club one evening for a drink. We had shown them all the sights, given a couple of cheerful dinner parties and generally introduced them around. They much enjoyed themselves. The Stanleys had a large house in Tufton Street where they entertained actively and when Maureen heard we were in London she and Oliver asked us to come and stay 'for the duration' as paying guests. We were only too pleased to accept, for London in the first weeks of the blackout was a dim and dismal place. People were scattered far and wide and we, having been abroad for six years, had lost contact with many of our friends. We had a nice big bedroom and there were still sufficient staff to make us very comfortable. Lunch parties and dinners were quite frequent and bridge was played almost every night. I played at first but with people of the class of Oliver and Ian Fleming felt rather out of my depth. Also I had to be in my office, though conveniently close, soon after eight o'clock each morning.

There were leading diplomats like Joe Kennedy, the American ambassador, and others in and out of the house and it was not long before we found ourselves being subjected by Kennedy to his extreme pessimism about the war (coupled with warnings to the President not to get tangled up with Britain or her fate). To be honest we were glad when during the Blitz the following year he and Mrs Kennedy retired to a country retreat for greater safety. Signor Bastianini, the Italian ambassador, was another frequent visitor though I found him a dull dog. On one occasion I overheard Euan Wallace, the Minister of Transport, whose French was limited, saying to him, 'Excellence, connaissez-vous le "Sac des Clous"?' – the Bag o' Nails was a disreputable night-haunt of the times. Very soon after this we were joined by another friend of the Stanleys, Hugh Fenwick, an American, the representative in London of the Boeing Company then in its very early days. He was a huge ruffian with a good sense of humour and an admirer of Maureen. We were a cheerful party.

The blackout in Britain was almost complete. The slightest chink of light would call for a visit by an air-raid warden or the police followed by a stiff reprimand or even a fine. The rules for cars were remarkably strict. Sidelights were allowed but the glass of the head-lamps had to be blacked out except for a small round hole the size of a modern penny. When in due time the Blitz came in earnest, it became practical to follow Mr Jorrocks's motto of 'Where I dines I sleeps', sometimes with embarrassing results.

I had settled down comfortably in my job and still believe that the systems of liaison which we helped to build up in London on both the military and economic sides were really close to perfection. In France, where things were a little more haphazard, the system also worked reasonably well. Meanwhile Alice had enlisted in the FANY and was driving a large electric canteen for troops on leave around the main railway stations. It had been presented by some ladies' business association. The FANYs, the earliest of all British women's paramilitary bodies, had been formed in the Boer War as the First Aid Nursing Yeomanry. They had initially carried out their duties riding side-saddle!

Before the war whenever we had been in England on leave we used to look spasmodically at country houses, notably in the Cotswolds. Everything turned out to be too dear in that part of Gloucestershire. Staying with friends near Exeter in the summer of 1938 we had been attracted by an advertisement and photograph in *The Times* of a reasonably priced Jacobean house in East Devon near the Dorset border. We visited it and were much taken by it. Netherton Hall, between Honiton and Colyton, had been built by the Prideaux family on to an older Tudor manor house in 1604 and had most of the things which we sought. There was little original woodwork left but the stone fireplaces were large and authentic with mullion windows in every room, including a big saloon with a screen. The position, the view, the garden, the stables, the farm acreage and, above all, the price were just right. There was even a tame ghost! But we could not quite make up our minds and decided to wait till the next year in case anything turned up near Cirencester. When the autumn of 1939 came, with war imminent and all our furniture bottled up in Greece and nowhere to store it in London, we decided to go banco and bought Netherton.

We never regretted it for a moment. It was my heart's desire and filled the gap left when my father had sold Duntisbourne twenty-five years before. We were both deep in our new jobs and so sent our faithful Peachey to Athens to pack up and bring everything home. Being in wartime it might have frightened a lesser character; not so him. He had it all packed and loaded in three lift-vans, put them abroad a Greek freighter and brought them through a hostile Mediterranean safely to their new home.

We realised that we might well have a hoard of evacuees descending on us, but as it turned out they found that we were too close to the sea at Branscombe to be considered suitable. We were in our own home at last and I was to remain there for thirty-five years. We spent Christmas at Netherton with Nicky, back home after his first term at Summerfields. After dinner on Christmas Eve the carol singers came round and serenaded us and then we all came in to drink a hot Christmas punch together. Then came New Year's Eve and the Stanleys gave a big party at Tufton Street and we all saw the New Year in. Winston Churchill, the First Lord of the Admiralty, was there and before 'Auld Lang Syne' we sang 'Run rabbit, run rabbit, run, run run,' with Churchill singing and conducting with his podgy forefinger. This was followed by 'We'll hang out the washing on the Siegfried Line, if the Siegfried Line's still there.' Little did we know.

I found myself obliged to make frequent visits to Paris. Often it was to confer with our opposite numbers or to deal with specific problems. We travelled by military transport planes of which there was no apparent shortage. Sometimes it was to accompany some grandee Cabinet minister, such as my old boss Sir John Simon, now chancellor of the Exchequer. I stayed with him in state at the Hotel Crillon and had two meetings with the future prime minister Paul Reynaud, then still finance minister. I also met for the first time Gaston Palewski, his *Chef de Cabinet*, who was destined to become de Gaulle's right-hand man. We became close friends and remained so till the end of his life.

Paris itself was reasonably defended but there was not the complete blackout we had in London. The mood of the city, if not of all France, was superficially tough; under the surface, however, the French were deeply divided. I bought Alice a handbag in Paris which aroused much envy in London. It was inscribed in gold with the motto 'Il faut en finir'. The sentiment, in English, might be 'Let's finish with these bastards!' Unfortunately in France it was not to be found in every heart. There was – and they were still in the big majority – the *'durs'* who sought a German defeat at all costs; but there were also the *'mous'*, the 'wets', who looked down their noses and murmured not just about the discomforts of war but their deep doubts of success. They were headed by men like Laval and Flandin. There were also a number of right-wing potentates who shared their views. The outstanding man of strength was Georges Mandel, the Jewish minister of the Colonies, unbendingly firm and courageous throughout, who was to suffer death at the hands of his Vichy adversaries.

During one of my trips I found myself deputed by Ismay to visit Mandel personally. It was in connection with an ultra-secret project known as 'Royal Marine' to which Churchill attached particular importance. It was a well-conceived British plan to mine the upper section of the Rhine, where it left French territory below Strasbourg, so that it would not only disrupt the heavy German shipping lanes, but with luck damage a few important bridges as well. The French saw the merits of the plan but immediately voiced fears that the Germans would retaliate by bombing French cities. I was instructed to do my utmost to persuade Mandel to take the lead in pressing the vital importance of carrying out this plan while the Germans were still reinforcing and strengthening the Siegfried Line from the Ruhr and Rhineland factories. It could hamper the water-borne transport of troops and tanks before the sweeping attack through the Low Countries and Northern France.

But it was the deeply-felt French fears of the bombardment of their cities that again came to the surface. Mandel understood the importance of Royal Marine as clearly as we ourselves; but said it had been discussed by the French Cabinet and turned down flat. He would press it again but could hold out little hope. In the end, and after further pressure from our side, it was agreed to allow us to go ahead with preparations for mining the Rhine and the Meuse – but only once the Germans carried out a full-scale invasion. When that moment came, it was indeed carried out with considerable disadvantage to the Germans – but it was far too late.

I have often pondered as to why with such careful preparation, with genuine trust and carefully integrated plans between our two governments and military leaders, everything nevertheless came tumbling down. There were many explanations. Belgian and Dutch neutrality meant that before the war no solid fortified line lay between the Allies and the Germans. There had been elaborate staff talks between us but plans and liaison, however perfect, do not defend frontiers against armoured divisions. It was the Maginot mentality which I fear to some extent had affected others as strongly as it had the French. General de Gaulle saw clearly the need for a 'force de frappe'. He mentions in his book *The Call to Honour* that General von Seeckt (whom I remembered from my days in Hanover) 'depicted the possibilities which an army of quality', meaning the Reichswehr, with 100,000 men on long-term service, had as opposed to 'masses without cohesion'. He was referring to the French. His own book on the subject *Vers l'Armée de Métier,* in which he launched his ideas, was generally disregarded or pooh-poohed by his colleagues.

Remarkably, the only official warning – which I saw – of the dangers of the gap on the left of the Maginot Line came from, of all people, the Duke of Windsor. He had asked for an active job at the outbreak of war and had been offered a liaison post (carrying a temporary demotion from field-marshal to major-general) between Lord Gort's command and the French armies on the Belgian frontier, as well as the more general job of reporting on the Maginot Line itself. Between his first visit to General Gamelin's headquarters in October 1939 till February 1940, he went to all the French armies of Northern France in turn. In one section on the Maginot Line, the Duke's report (presumably compiled by his small but competent staff) mentioned that there was one dominant obsession among the French officers he had met which was the impregnability of the Maginot Line which he said 'does not seem to be an insuperable barrier'. He concluded with the remark that 'if the crust were broken there would be nothing but a few demolitions in the open to stop an advance to Paris', adding that it was perhaps fortunate that the Germans did not attack through Belgium and Luxemburg in November. This report, with all its unnerving implications got little credence or support in Whitehall and its warning of trouble to come went unheeded.

Alice and I stayed with the Stanleys for six happy months before finally deciding we wanted a place in London of our own. We were lucky to find a nice furnished house in Gayfere Street, Westminster, just around the corner. It was the end of the Phoney War, after the disastrous Norway landings the Chamberlain government succumbed to Parliamentary pressure and the advent to power of Winston Churchill coincided precisely on 10 May with the vast German armoured sweep through the Ardennes and the Low Countries.

Each morning during those anxious days, after I had read the intelligence reports, Monnet questioned me as to how the Battle of the Bulge was going. Surely, he said, it was not beyond the power of the combined forces of France and Britain to nip off the serpent's head? Sadly it was not to be, and the final failure to effect a juncture at Abbeville seemed to have doomed vast numbers of British and French troops to be prisoners. The heroic story of Dunkirk and how they were saved needs no retelling.

By the time the great German thrust came our Paris branch was firmly established. Work at the Invalides had proved to be light, so a small office had been set up at Vincennes, the real centre of activity. Redman had built up a solid position for himself and was on excellent terms with General Jamet. He got on well with Brigadier Howard-Vyse, the prime minister's personal envoy, and Spears, the god of liaison, if not always of discretion, worked equally closely with Reynaud. The embassy itself stood solid as a rock with Sir Ronald Campbell at its head and Oliver Harvey at his side. Campbell, calm in adversity as in success, was precise and indomitable with his little touch of Scottish humour to lighten any situation.

The swift march of events swept most of this smooth-running machinery away as in a cyclone. Under the rapid German advance, starting with the French defeat at Sedan, all became uncertainty. On 20 May Gamelin was replaced as commander-in-chief by General Weygand who enjoyed wide public esteem, but de Gaulle expressed the view that Weygand at no time had the will to succeed. I fear this was all too true. He was unfortunately soon joined by the eighty-year-old Marshal Pétain who had been brought back from the embassy at Madrid to join the government as a symbol of 'determination' when his views were in fact exactly contrary. It seems clear that almost from the start both of them contemplated an armistice as the inevitable outcome. Thus there was launched the final battle between the *durs* and the *mous* – Reynaud, Mandel, Campinchi, Dautry on the one hand, Pétain, with Weygand, Flandin, Baudouin and finally even Admiral Darlan on the other. We all knew where Laval stood.

In a reshuffle of the Cabinet on 5 June, de Gaulle, straight from the battlefield, was brought into the government as under-secretary for National Defence. He was at once deputed by Reynaud to go to London to make clear personally to Churchill that France would hold out at any cost. He was also told to make a further plea for more fighter planes. Before doing so he called on Weygand. He records that as a minister he made it quite clear to the new commander-in-chief that the government had formally undertaken that it would in no circumstances give up the struggle. From then on they both knew exactly where they stood. For instance, de Gaulle had advocated the defence of Paris; on 10 June Weygand off his own bat declared it an open city. That same day the French government, with all that that implied, left Paris to establish themselves near Tours. The British embassy, General Spears and Redman's little band went with it.

So in those terrible days in early June, while the battle in the field still raged, the battle within the French Cabinet too went back and forth in Paris, Tours or Bordeaux. Churchill and his colleagues came over three times to emergency Supreme War Councils, doing their best to urge a retirement to North Africa and no surrender. It was all of no avail. Those who prevailed were those two former generals who were now too old or too tired to realise the dreadful consequences to France of their decision to ask for terms for an armistice.

Looking back it seems to me that it was perhaps the fear of the bombing of the cities which at the time lay behind much French and indeed some British thinking. So many decisions seem to have been taken with it in mind. Though later in England the effects of air raids were horrifying and devastating, they were not disastrous. We may have been a little more stoical than the French, but we must not forget that in London 10,000 coffins had been prepared for the possible effects of the first night! It is not surprising that the fear of this coloured so much French thought and action. Such, for example, was their decision after Italy declared war to thwart an RAF raid via Marseilles on Genoa and other Italian cities (previously fully agreed) by blocking the runways. Such, too, was their opposition to Royal Marine, when it might have proved to be invaluable.

On 14 June the government withdrew to Bordeaux and de Gaulle again left for London to get help in the form of shipping for the still hoped for grand-scale move to North Africa. Arriving on the 16th before dawn, he was at once presented by Monsieur Corbin and Jean Monnet with the text of a plan worked out with Vansittart – though I think originating with Monnet – for a solemn and total union between Britain and France. It would mean little at the moment but at least as a gesture of confidence it might delay surrender. De Gaulle was attracted by the scheme and at a lunch at the Carlton Club raised the issue. Churchill at once summoned the Cabinet to meet at Downing Street.

The night before I had been duty officer at the Cabinet Office with one of my service colleagues. It had been a night of very heavy work with continual 'Most Immediate' telegrams from the ambassador in Bordeaux. Telephones had been cut but during the night I managed to discover a private telephone line open to the consulate there. I spoke a number of times to Sir Ronald Campbell and made a record of my conversations for the Foreign Office. I went to bed at eight o'clock for a few hours. Later in the morning I went to the Foreign Office to answer any questions they might have. On leaving, to my great surprise I ran into a little party crossing Downing Street. It consisted of the French ambassador, Monnet, Vansittart and a tall khaki figure in French uniform whom I did not recognise. It was in fact my first sight of General de Gaulle.

They were there to put forward this formidable proposal of a total union between Great Britain and France. After explaining the plan to the War Cabinet, the French members remained in a small office at No. 10 next to the Cabinet Room. At last, after two hours' discussion, the prime minister came in to say the declaration was agreed. It was at once telephoned through to Bordeaux for discussion at Raynaud's Cabinet, meeting, but it was all too late to change the outcome. General de Gaulle, still ignorant of the upshot, returned in an RAF plane to Bordeaux. The only hope would have been for Reynaud to sack Weygand and re-form the government without Pétain. Unfortunately he was not strong enough to do so.

During these hectic weeks Alice and I had to face a serious personal problem. We wanted to be as near Nicky as possible, yet here we were at a most uncertain moment in the war and when apart from anything else we never knew when I might be sent abroad. My American brother-in-law, with a nice house in Princeton and an excellent day-school nearby, had offered to take our son for the rest of the war. Reluctantly we decided that this was the best course, and he left in the *Duchess of Richmond* with our nanny and three small friends from Cairo days, also going to join relations in America. They were sailing in convoy and lay immediately behind the *Arandora Star* which was taking a shipload of interned Italian waiters including Luigi, maître d'hôtel of the Savoy, on their way to Canada. Some days out to sea the *Arandora Star* was struck by a torpedo and most of them lost their lives. Fortunately we did not hear of this at the time.

When the French collapse became imminent, a small Cabinet sub-committee had been set up under Vansittart to consider all possible means of saving as much of the French Empire as possible. With Vansittart in the chair, it consisted of Lord Lloyd, now colonial secretary, William Strang of the Foreign Office, Desmond Morton, the prime minister's personal adviser on Intelligence Affairs (indiscreet and unpopular), someone from each of the three services, and myself. The secretary was Richard Speaight of the Foreign Office but I have never been able to find any record of our proceedings. We were in touch with some of the principal French commanders and at first had hopeful responses from General Mittelhauser in Syria and some others. On 17 June, to suit Lord Lloyd's convenience, as he was about to leave for North Africa, we met in his room at the Colonial Office in the early afternoon. As we went out we passed two office-keepers sitting by the Downing Street entrance. One of them had an early edition of the *Evening Standard* in his hands with the story of the French Armistice splashed all over it. Turning to the other he said, 'Heard the news, Bill? We're in the final!' From then on I had no doubt about the outcome.

Later in the day I was sent for by General Ismay to learn that General de Gaulle had arrived and I was instructed to do everything necessary to look after him. We were to meet in Ismay's office at six o'clock. De Gaulle arrived accompanied by an ADC. Very tall and slim, he was wearing his uniform and *képi* with the two little stars of a brigadier general on the khaki cover. He had a neat moustache under his rather heavy nose and a curious, almost feminine, bulge of the hips. I glanced at his ADC in a pale blue *képi* and the heavy cloak of the Spahi cavalry and gasped. It was an old friend, Geoffroy de Courcel, whom I had left in Athens where he was second secretary at the French embassy just a few months before.

The prime minister's instructions to me included the provision for de Gaulle by the next morning of a suitable office, fully furnished with desks, carpets and telephones. In wartime London this was something of a task but Spears, who was also with him, came up with a suggestion of an empty flat in St Stephen's House on the Embankment. Sir Eric de Norman, head of the office of the Commissioner for Works, working with me through the night, miraculously provided the rest. At nine o'clock next morning I was able to call for General de Gaulle and show him round.

I spent much of my time with the General during the next two months, and the more I saw the more I liked and admired him. The Vansittart Committee did all they could to help, but except for General Catroux, General Legentilhomme and Admiral Muselier, few big names and only a handful of troops came to join him. No doubt the tragic necessity of our bombardment of the French fleet at Mersa-el-Kibir put many Frenchmen off their intention to rally. Almost the whole of the other large contingent of French officers and businessmen in London on the various French missions left as a body. I said my sad farewells to them in the Golden Arrow at Victoria Station. Jean Monnet in due course joined the Purchasing Committee in Washington where he played a vital part in furnishing our supplies from America. The despondency among my French colleagues who stayed behind was appalling – only Jean Monnet seemed to have no doubts as to the outcome. René Pleven wanted to join the 22nd (French Canadian) Infantry as a private soldier. I can remember spending several hours arguing with him in an effort (fortunately successful) to put his brilliant abilities at the disposal of General de Gaulle.

I also had to handle some personal matters for de Gaulle, such as helping with his arrangements for meeting Madame de Gaulle and the children who had, if you please, been put in a British camp for persons 'of doubtful reliability'! There were constant new arrivals to be catered for, accommodation to be found, interviews with British leaders to be arranged, and so forth. Much of this was carried out by General Spears, but he did not know the intricacies of Whitehall as I did. Lady Spears, with her ambulances, had managed to get back safely from France. One day de Gaulle arranged a little luncheon in a private room at the Ritz to enable the Spearses and ourselves to meet Madame de Gaulle. We had a totally delightful and relaxed lunch with the general ruminating over his experiences and the affairs of the world. He could be a man of enchantment. He was, however, no lover of England. In his books he talks of the withdrawal of French troops from Fashoda in the Upper Nile fifty years before as a shameful episode. He also had a contempt for the musical chairs of French politics, especially as his books, urging 'an army of manoeuvre and mechanised attack', had been largely ignored. The King of the Belgians too, later held in such contempt or his surrender, had long before justified his withdrawal from the Locarno arrangements on the grounds that in practice, given what mechanised forces are capable of doing, we would in any case be alone'.

But once the die was cast with Reynaud's defeat, the general did not hesitate; he was determined to obey 'the call to honour' and, once he was in England, to continue the fight. He broadcast his famous initial call to his countrymen on the night of 18 June and asked permission to make a more formal appeal on 23 June. It was referred to the Vansittart Committee who asked me to try my hand on a draft. I did so, and it was very properly at once torn up by the general. He produced an eloquent and far better alternative which was also turned into posters, with the tricolour at the top, calling for volunteers.

Naturally every effort to keep French forces in the war had all possible help from our side. De Gaulle was given the vast hall at Olympia as quarters for French troops returning from Norway or Dunkirk. He was given the means of paying them and looking after their dependents and for setting up a civil establishment for any administration services required. All this was embodied in a formal agreement between the prime minister and the general in July. Unfortunately the threat of punishment for treason, the danger to their own relations at home and many other psychological factors led to a very, very poor response to recruiting. When General Béthouart's whole brigade got back from Narvik, they were also accommodated at Olympia. De Gaulle was asked to address them and I accompanied him and his staff. He stalked coldly up and down the ranks saluting from time to time. He did not stop once to say a word or even ask about a war medal. Only at the end came a very short speech, the band played the Marseillaise, he saluted again and that was all. Only a handful of the whole brigade fell out to join up. A select few preferred to join the RAF. I never quite understood the general's approach to the matter – nor did I dare ask.

Time went by. The Spears mission to the Free French took over the work of liaison and our premises at Gwydyr House. Nobby Clarke took a command at sea and Redman went back to the Army, later to become a general and finally governor of Gibraltar. With the formation of SOE under Dr Dalton and its instructions from the prime minister to 'set Europe on fire', Gladwyn Jebb was appointed chief executive of the new department with my cousin Sir Frank Nelson as director of operations. Sir Alec Cadogan asked me to become his private secretary in his stead. I was very sad to sever my links with the French and especially with de Gaulle. But it was wartime and there was nothing more to be said.

12

Blitz

On New Year's Day 1938 Sir Robert Vansittart had been kicked upstairs. His bitterly anti-German views together with the Cassandra-like forebodings of his Cabinet memoranda had convinced the prime minister and to a lesser degree Eden that there had to be a change. At the same time Van's refusal to accept an embassy coupled with his age – still well below retirement – led to the creation of a new post. He became chief diplomatic adviser on the analogy of Sir Horace Wilson, the chief industrial adviser, with the great difference that he was not installed in a room in No. 10 next to the prime minister, but remained ensconced and lonely in his big corner room at the Foreign Office.

Sir Alexander Cadogan had been promoted to be permanent under-secretary of state for Foreign Affairs in his place. I had met him in 1932 in Geneva where he led our disarmament team, but had never known him well. Now I was joining him at almost the worst moment of the war, but a couple of days sufficed to convince me that I should be able to work with him. He lacked Van's sparkling charm, but I found a calm, shrewd mind and a gentle, welcoming smile. He did not suffer fools gladly and had a caustic wit which bordered on sarcasm, yet by the straightforward simplicity of his approach he could put the most nervous or irascible visitor at his ease. He was small in stature with a little moustache and steel-grey eyes. He always wore a bowler hat. His judgement became more and more to be relied upon at the highest level.

The Foreign Office was the only government department where the permanent under-secretary outranked his Parliamentary colleague, which much irked Rab Butler. In addition to being the principal political adviser to the secretary of state, Cadogan was also very much the head of the Office. If the secretary of state was the divisional commander, the P.U.S. was the colonel of the regiment. I as his private secretary found myself in the role of adjutant of a diverse and somewhat temperamental unit – with the chief clerk as quartermaster.

While matters of pay, pension and hours of work were the functions of the chief clerk, grievances, disagreements or questions of discipline all came to me. In practice, the constant pressures of war and soon, above all, the Blitz preoccupied us. My first job was to familiarise myself with every file that was sent up to Cadogan, to ensure that it was given the proper level of priority and to set up meetings where necessary. From my previous position in the Cabinet Office I already had experience of matters of state and my days with Simon had given me some practice in the workings of the Foreign Office.

One thing I had cetainly not expected was that apart from Cadogan himself I had now by some quirk of fortune become the only direct link between the Foreign Office and MI6 – the Secret Service. Every morning on my table there would appear reams of telegraph intercepts between foreign diplomats in London and their headquarters as well as recordings of their telephone conversations with members of the Foreign Office, their foreign colleagues and sometimes even their mistresses. (I am afraid some of our own colleagues, too, were not the acme of discretion!) There were also copies of deciphered diplomatic wireless messages or telegrams from all over the world. These all had to be read and sent on if necessary by special Victorian snuff-coloured boxes to heads of departments in the Office or direct to the prime minister at No. 10. On most mornings I also had a visit from 'C', Colonel Stewart Menzies, the head of the Secret Service, or occasionally from his opposite number at MI5. Menzies would come to see Cadogan or to leave letters over some startling development, written in his bright green ink with 'C' for a signature. We had many common interests and soon became close friends.

The SIS, or MI6 as it was also called, had been set up during the First World War under Captain Mansfield Cumming, RN, who had bequeathed the initial 'C' to his successor, Admiral Hugh Sinclair, who had in turn passed it on soon after the beginning of the war to his deputy Menzies. He was both a highly professional intelligence officer and a well-to-do Household Cavalry officer with a passion for fox-hunting, which some might have supposed was skilful deception in itself. He was of medium height with thinning light brown hair, very blue eyes and a neat military moustache. He had heavy lids which made his eyes look half-closed. When he talked he tended to muddle his speech a little as if his tongue were too large. Cadogan sometimes described him as a 'babbler', which I thought unfair. Certainly it did not apply in any way to his use of secret material. He was unassuming with a youthful zest which made him attractive. He suffered much sorrow in his private life.

As poor Sinclair lay dying of cancer, Menzies found himself in hot water. He was not alone in his conviction that many of the German general staff were so bitterly hostile to Hitler that this might, if skilfully exploited, lead to an army take-over and peace. Two senior British SIS officials in the Netherlands appeared to have found an opening leading to Admiral Canaris, the head of the Abwehr – the German Foreign Intelligence Sevice – and to General Beck, formerly the chief of staff. Unfortunately it turned out to be a plot cleverly concocted by Schellenberg, the head of the Sicherheitsdienst, and culminated in the kidnapping of two British agents at Venlo. There was hell to pay and Menzies's fitness for the top post was called in question. It was some months before his appointment to the succession as 'C' was confirmed. However he clung to his views about Canaris and the German general staff and on 20 July 1944, with the generals' attempted revolt, he was proved right – all too late. I believe, though I have no proof, that he and Canaris were later actually in touch with one another. Canaris ended his life hanged on a meathook some months after the coup failed.

My first few weeks there came at a period when Hitler, in public speeches or through various individuals operating in neutral countries, was trying to persuade Great Britain to agree to make peace. At the same time German plans were going forward for invasion which Cadogan expected at any time.

When the Local Defence Volunteers came into being, with a branch set up in the Foreign Office, I joined at once. To begin with we just wore an arm-band with LDV on it. Later, when we became the Home Guard, we were issued with khaki drill, very cold when you were on the Foreign Office roof in an air raid looking out for incendiaries. Rifles and bayonets were kept at the Foreign Office. With our khaki fore-and-aft forage caps, we looked a pretty ragged lot as we were taught to charge down a strip of grass on the St James's

Park side and bayonet sacks of straw, giving a good grunt as the blade went home.

I had been given a week's leave on 15 September – the first for many months – and we motored down to Netherton to enjoy ourselves. The next morning there was a telephone call from the resident clerk at the Foreign Office saying our house in Gayfere Street had been hit in the first heavy raid and all the windows had been blown out. There were apparently no casualties but we were much disturbed because our beloved Peachey – by now an RASC corporal working at Gwydyr House for the Spears Mission but lodging in our house – had completely disappeared. I decided to drive straight back to London to look for him and spent the night at the Carlton Hotel nearby. There was a raid and I went down to the underground Grill-cum-air-raid shelter, but I could not stand the atmosphere and resolved never to do it again. After a worrying night I called at the office in Gwydyr House to see if they had any news of him. There was nothing. Two minutes later Peachey came in whistling, safe and sound. I drove back to Devon.

That was the first of many noisy nights for the next ten months. The air-raid sirens went off most evenings about eight o'clock. The all clear sounded about eight o'clock the next morning. With our house wrecked we moved into Claridge's and slept on the third floor on mattresses pulled out into the corridor. This would reduce the risk of injury from flying glass, though it made little allowance for a direct hit. On our first night we were reluctantly persuaded to try the air-raid shelter which was somewhere below ground down a long corridor of brightly painted pipes. In the middle of the cellar itself there was a large silk screen obscuring the old Queen of the Netherlands, Princess Juliana, and her husband at her side. The old lady was snoring heavily. On the way out next morning I happened to touch one of the pipes. It was scalding. As we didn't fancy being both mangled and then boiled alive if there were a direct hit, we decided not to sleep there again. In fact the safest place to sleep at Claridge's was always said to be the big first floor landing at the head of the stairs, where the beds seemed to be permanently bespoken by very rich couples.

One evening there was an unexploded bomb nearby and we were shifted for the night to the old Berkeley Hotel in Piccadilly. It was surprising how we all took it in our stride. Then, three weeks later, I managed to find a furnished flat belonging to a friend in Cadogan Lane next door to Smith's riding school. At the beginning of the Blitz Alice had been chosen by the FANY commandant to drive for Sir Warren Fisher, the former head of the Civil Service and now in charge of all civilian anti-aircraft protection for Central London. She used our Jaguar and was constantly called day and night to drive her chief to one incident after another. Early one morning she had to turn out and drive him to the Café de Paris which had received a direct hit during the night. The large room below ground with its twin staircase was still littered with broken tables and chairs, crockery, clothing, girls' shoes, and the instruments of the band. They had ben playing 'Oh Johnny, How You Can Love!' when the bomb struck; they were all killed. Alice was badly upset by the work, but stuck to it until the raids began to tail off in the summer of 1942.

Meanwhile I often found myself obliged to walk to work. Sometimes I went by underground, until Sloane Square station itself was destroyed. One night I was walking back from the station up Cadogan Lane to the back door of our flat. I had my tin hat on as the red specks from our own Ack-Ack shrapnel were falling all around me. Suddenly there was an explosion and a loud blast some way down the little street. Smith's stables, almost next door to us, had been hit.

Our new home, Netherton, was a big house and there was furniture to be bought, not to mention curtains to relieve the otherwise gloomy uniformity of the blackout material. We were able to make an occasional flying visit to Exeter and sometimes I would manage to do a little shopping in London in the early morning before going to work. After a heavy bombing it was a sad and disjointed place. If the area had been under direct attack there would be whole sections roped off with crews digging ominously in the rubble or awaiting the visit of the bomb disposal squad for an unexploded bomb. Water would be lying everywhere from the efforts of the fire brigade and there was always a nauseous smell of sodden half-burned furnishings. The shopkeepers who had 'caught it' would be outside their broken plate glass windows totally disoriented or even in tears. It certainly affected prices, for quite often they were almost inviting prospective customers to take things away. There was a great stillness overall and it almost broke one's heart.

Sometimes there were some little attempts at humour. There was a story going the rounds of the lady of easy virtue who had become the owner of a fish and chip shop near Paddington and who, after a near miss, put up a sign in the window, 'Owing to Hitler the fish will be littler'. Soon after, when a bomb blew out her front door, she added, 'Owing to Hess, chips will be less'. Finally, when the whole shop window was blown in she wrote a third notice, 'Owing to Goring, I'm going back to my old profession!'

The Foreign Office building also came in for its share of damage. Our windows overlooking the park went first. People usually replaced broken windows with thin cellophane strips which soon tore, or even brown paper. I had seen at a friend's house some firm cellophane sheeting criss-crossed with string, and managed to order a big consignment of this for our own office and the rest of the building. It did us very well. We had decided that in spite of the inconvenience it was important to get people home in daylight, which meant the main office closing down at four o'clock, with the staff expected to arrive in the morning soon after eight. The rest of us tried to get home by eight if possible, when the sirens normally sounded the alarm.

Cadogan and his wife moved into the Carlton Hotel. When it was gutted they went to the Dorchester. It was there that the élite, including the Halifaxes and the Duff Coopers, congregated at night to face the Blitz. Being new and built of reinforced concrete, the hotel was believed to be one of the safest places in London. In fact I learnt at the time that there was nothing between the roof and the ceiling of the cellar-shelter. It was not long, however, before the Prime Minister asked Halifax to move into his rooms at the Foreign Office to be nearer at hand. This caused much inconvenience to all concerned. I hardly knew Halifax, meeting him only from time to time at conferences. I found him easy and attractive; perhaps, too, his frequent use of fox-hunting expressions in normal conversation rather appealed to me. I had also always thought that he had been unfairly criticised over his attitude to appeasement. Certainly he became much more uncompromising after Hitler's design and methods had become all too clear at Munich. Sitting as he did in the Lords, he was politically seriously handicapped, but in the final stage of his career as ambassador in Washington, after the sudden death of Lord Lothian, his personal and very English appeal was exactly what was wanted. He had accepted the appointment reluctantly, after Lloyd

George and Eden turned it down. Probably the prime minister was glad to be rid of him in day-to-day affairs in the Cabinet, not so much because of what he did or said, as because of what his views, so often distorted in the press, were believed to represent. The prime minister was also anxious to bring Eden back to the Foreign Office.

My office was the centre for receiving all diplomatic intercepts. The carefully selected traffic was picked up *en clair* or in cypher and them broken down by skilled cryptographers. Some were quite simple code messages; others highly secret diplomatic documents of state written with the use of a double code, the so-called 'one time' pad such as we used so many years before at the Washington embassy.

Its control all stemmed from one of 'C''s auxiliary departments, the Government Code and Cypher School. This was where British cyphers were actually put together and also where cryptologists were employed in dealing with the daily traffic or seeking to break some apparently cast-iron foreign cypher. The head of it was Commander Denniston, a distinguished scholar. At the beginning of the war it had been moved to Bletchley Park, a red brick mansion in Buckinghamshire. There it had grown rapidly in strength, reinforced by numerous Cambridge mathematicians who much improved its scope. At the end of the war the staff was about 9,000.

The story of Ultra, the top German cyphering machine, is now well known and it is safe to say that the discovery of its secret was a major factor in the winning of the war. The German leaders remained convinced that their machine was still impenetrable. For the prime minister, Ultra had become a vital weapon of war; he waited eagerly every morning for 'C' to bring round the day's bag to No. 10. Churchill's code name for it was 'Boniface', after the seventh-century Devonshire saint who evangelised North Germany. It was on his feast day that the breakthrough came. It was all shrouded in the deepest secrecy – I was told that only thirty people knew of it, though that I very much doubt.

On 14 July Colonel 'Wild Bill' Donovan arrived from America on a mission from President Roosevelt. He was a successful lawyer and a former attorney general under Coolidge. His orders were to examine all aspects of British intelligence and to make recommendations for similar arrangements in the United States, where all such secret activities had been shut down after the First World War. 'C' brought him round to meet Cadogan, with whom he established a good relationship. He and I also had a long talk, including a chat about our old days in Washington. Menzies had given him access to all the different fields of operation – apart only from Ultra. This led in due course to the setting up of the American OSS, which after the war became the CIA.

During the early weeks after my appointment, 'C' had made it his business to familiarise me with other aspects of his work, including contact with a number of double agents who were doing a most valuable job in counter-espionage. They came under fancy names like 'Tricycle' and 'Garbo' and 'Tate' and were simply taken over with their radio equipment and played back to their masters in Germany. 'Tricycle', a Yugoslav of good family, had come over deliberately; others had been captured and 'turned' or had lost their nerve and surrendered. Others, after being listened to carefully for a few weeks, had been arrested and locked up while their equipment coninued to be played back with their own characteristic touch and language carefully imitated. Meanwhile 'C' continued to rebuild his network in France – occupied or otherwise. Some old links with French colleagues now in Vichy had been cautiously restored and our new allies in Poland, Norway, Belgium and the Netherlands were also brought into play.

'C' took me round to visit his headquarters at 54 Broadway, a tall block next to St James's underground station and overlooking the park. He was on the fourth floor and I can still remember the slight shiver of excitement when I entered his private office with its green baize door and the red and green lights outside indicating whether one might go in. He had a cosy Victorian room with an open fire. Inside was his trusty secretary Miss Pettigrew, later fictionalised as the formidable Miss Moneypenny of the James Bond series. I was duly introduced to Colonel Claude Dansey and Colonel Valentine Vivian, the two principal assistants. Dansey was a small man, highly skilled in espionage with experience in the field; not a very nice man perhaps, but able and ambitious and hoping to succeed – or supplant Menzies. He had a sardonic sense of humour and few scruples but was brilliant at building up a network of spies. Three years later he sent me out an agent to Rome called Mangot. 'I am sure you will like him,' he wrote, 'he's quite a neat little box of tricks.' His colleague Vivian was more commonplace, a veteran of the Indian Army with a gift for administration. He also aspired to 'C''s throne and was unfortunate in that it was he who later brought Philby into the Secret Service. Philby's father had been Vivian's close friend.

I was also taken round the office itself by 'C' and introduced to some of his junior specialist assistants, men like Commander Kenneth Cohen, RN, who operated with the Free French, or Commander Dunderdale who dealt with Vichy affairs and had just had to leave the SIS premises in Paris in a hurry. Then there were the technical experts with their modified gramophone machines listening in to the diplomatic telephone traffic. At the end of my visit 'C' took me on through a secret passage from his office to the house adjoining it in Queen Anne's Gate which was his official residence.

Once we became more or less inured to the bombs, we began to wonder what would come next. There had been much talk of a German drive in the Balkans, while there were continual indications from our sources of plans for a grand-scale invasion of the Soviet Union in the spring. Meanwhile de Gaulle had had a serious setback in the ill-fated Free French expedition to Dakar. It suffered, it seems to me, rather like the famous Bay of Pigs in Cuba many years later, from lack of preparation, over-confidence and the incomplete and only half-hearted support given by its backers.

General Catroux, the former governor-general of Indo-China, arrived at Liverpool from the Far East. As a sort of Free French receptionist, I was called back into action again and found myself forced to cope by telephone not only with the formidable Madame Catroux, but with several tons of luggage and wines, two Annamite servants and two Pekingese dogs which got loose on the dock. When they were finally captured, Madame Catroux absolutely refused to put them into quarantine. As it was wartime, with more crucial issues at stake, I am afraid I decided that this requirement might perhaps be disregarded as the lesser evil.

Then on 28 October 1940 the Italians launched their attack on Greece. I was not surprised to learn that General Metaxas had rejected their ultimatum with contempt and while asking Britain for naval and air help had refused participation by British land forces – no doubt so as not to provoke a German response. Though the Italians at first advanced some miles, the Greek line held in the Pindos mountains, and pretty soon it was the Greeks, short of many essentials though they were, who were advancing into Albania. With only British air support, one Greek victory followed another. Dictatorship or not, the Greek people were for the moment united and the church bells rang. I can remember the reports coming over on the news on our little radio in the flat in the early morning. The whole of Britain followed the campaign with bated breath and deep admiration – it was the first gleam of light in the dark shadows of the past six months. Florence Desmond sang: 'Oh what a surprise for the Duce, the Duce, He can't put it over the Greeks!'

We ourselves did not go out much in the evenings; the blackout was not conducive to it, and once the air-raid alarm had sounded, transport became difficult. On the other hand I believe that most of the theatres that were open were generally full. An old Cairo friend, Sir Maurice Peterson, who was ambassador in Madrid, had been shunted out to make way for Sir Samuel Hoare. He was disappointed and lonely, so as we had a spare room we suggested that he should live with us while we were still in London. He and Alice used to play two-handed bridge when I was late coming home and, though I did not encourage it, I was sometimes called in to make a third. We also put away a fair amount of whisky.

At Christmas we went down to Netherton for a day or two. We travelled by rail to Axminster, a gloomy process with the window blinds difficult to control for the blackout and the stations in complete darkness. We were met by our gardener who was medically unfit for military service. He and his wife had put up some simple Christmas decorations and built a huge fire in the big saloon. I remember as we came in and bent down to warm our hands we both, impelled by some emotion, joint and spontaneous, went down on our knees and thanked God for this haven – and for our safety through a troubled time. We had a happy break, with the carol-singers visiting us on Christmas Eve and a day's hunting for me with the local hounds on Boxing Day.

The night I returned to London I had dinner with Maurice at the St James's Club with the glasses and bar-stools literally shaking from the anti-aircraft barrage. As I drove him back to Chesham Street, the sky at Belgrave Square gave out so much light that I stopped the car and found I was able to read the evening paper quite clearly by the crimson glow to the east. It was the City of London in flames. It was not long before we heard that even our own remote village of Farway had not been overlooked: some German raiders returning from an attack on the Midlands had unloaded their bombs there before making the return crossing. One of them killed two cows on our land.

One Sunday evening when I was at the office after a day of golf, I had a surprise visit from John Maude, an old Eton friend. He was in major's uniform and told me that he was employed by MI5 and had a delicate situation to report. It seemed that the Security Service had come across a series of notes said to have been prepared and stamped by the French consulate (when it was still open under Vichy) showing that Admiral Muselier, who commanded de Gaulle's small fleet, had tried to send information to General Rozoy of the Vichy Air Force (my old pal on the Allied Military Committee), giving the plan for the Dakar expedition. It seemed to me most unlikely and I said as much. 'Nevertheless,' said John, 'we've had to take him into custody.' I suggested that all further action should be held up until I had informed Cadogan and the secretary of state. This was agreed; clearly nothing more could be done until the following day. When the news reached No. 10, however, the prime minister went through the roof and demanded that the admiral be tried forthwith and hanged for treason. It was not difficult to imagine the effect on General de Gaulle, who was convinced that it was due either to a serious mistake or to the machinations of Vichy. This proved to be correct, except that the documents in question seem to have been forged not by Vichy but by someone in the Foreign Office – I never learnt who. Admiral Muselier was released from prison with due apologies from Churchill and Eden to General de Gaulle, but it did not exactly improve relations with the Free French.

With the spring the raids became less frequent though I can recall a terrible battering in mid-April when St James's and Pall Mall with some of the clubs were hit. On the weekend of 10 May Alice and I had arranged to go down to Devon for a short break. On my return I went straight to the office and found Cadogan looking distraught and surrounded by red boxes. 'Well,' he said, 'you certainly chose a fine weekend to go away!' He explained that the Führer's deputy, Rudolf Hess, had arrived in Scotland by air during Saturday night. He was asking to meet, of all people, the Duke of Hamilton. Cadogan explained that the Duke, who had never met Hess, was on active service with the RAF, commanding a fighter station not too far away, and had interviewed him and reported that he appeared to be genuine. It seemed that Hess had parachuted from a Messer-schmitt 110 two-seater fighter near Strathcairn on a peace mission unbeknown to Hitler. Described as being 'in the name of humanity', its aim was to bring about an understanding between England and Germany. Hamilton had flown straight to London and reported his conversation to Cadogan. Meanwhile the resident clerk had also told Jock Colville, one of Winston's private secretaries, who had informed the prime minister who was staying in the country at Ditchley. After consulting Eden, Cadogan arranged for the Duke to fly back to Scotland the next day with Ivone Kirkpatrick of the Foreign Office who had been first secretary at the embassy in Berlin and spoke excellent German. He was to interview him and try to extract something more coherent. Meanwhile, nothing at all was to be made public.

Kirkpatrick duly reported from Scotland that Hess was certainly genuine – he had known him personally in Berlin. Hess's proposals boiled down to similar conditions to those which had already been put forward by neutrals – namely that peace could be attained if Germany could be given a free hand in Europe. There would then be no interference with the British Empire (though Germany would want her old colonies back). If there were no understanding, according to Hess, Germany would destroy Britain utterly. Asked by Kirkpatrick if Hitler intended to attack Russia, about which rumours were plentiful, Hess said that the Germans had some demands against the Soviet which had to be satisfied. There was a hint of war if these were not met but Hess hastened to say that there would be no early attack on Russia.

The following day 'C' came round to report on the matter and brought with him a bag containing all Hess's drugs – there were fifteen or twenty small phials, boxes, powders and so forth. I could not distinguish any of them but, after being examined, they were all duly locked up in my safe. Later they were sent for and I suppose carefully listed. One thing, however, was clear: Hess was a confirmed hypochondriac. Apart from the drugs, he was always talking about his health. He was lodged for one night in the Tower of London and then sent down to a country house in the Aldershot area where he was kept under military guard. It seemed that Menzies had been given special instructions about his conditions of detention – I presume by the prime minister, for thanks to the successes of Ultra and their almost daily meetings Stewart's stock with Churchill was very high. There was a special SIS contingent attached to what the prime minister called 'a state prisoner', in the form of the German-speaking heads of the former Berlin and Vienna MI6 stations. The apartment in which he was kept was bugged and every conversation recorded and sent to us. The transcripts appeared on my table every morning.

Several weeks later the prime minister arranged that Hess should be interviewed by Lord Simon, now the lord chancellor. Though it lasted some time the interview produced little that was new. It was long and rambling and I had the full text on my desk the folowing morning. Simon in conversation with Cadogan thought that Hess was telling the truth about the object of his visit. He considered him mentally most unstable and probably deranged. This was also shown in a report from 'C' a few days later and Hess finally confirmed it by throwing himself over the first-floor banisters into the hall and breaking his thigh in two places.

So the 'state prisoner' remained in custody until the end of the war four years later, when he went for trial as a war criminal by the Nuremberg court. He was condemned to life imprisonment and that indeed was what it turned out to be; others served their terms or were in due course paroled, but not he. On Soviet insistence he remained a prisoner in Spandau until he took his own life in 1987. My own belief is that the Russians never forgave him for what they were convinced was his attempt to take the British out of the war before the German attack on the USSR took place.

I am sure there was nothing more to this curious incident than what we learnt from Hess's conversations in those early days; but a mystery of sorts it remained and mysteries give birth to myths. So far there have been two. The first originated with Dr Hugh Thomas, a British Army surgeon in Berlin, who did the post-mortem on the body after the suicide. He noticed that there were no scars on the stomach where Hess was believed to have suffered severe wounds during the First War. From this he concluded that the prisoner was not the real Hess but a 'double' who had been substituted when the original's plane had been shot down by the Germans. I find this impossible to believe for two reasons. Twenty-five years later I and my wife Barbara had lunch with Professor Messerschmitt at his house near Marbella in Spain. He had been a close friend of Hess and wholly in his confidence throughout the affair. He described to us in graphic detail the long preparations they had to make for the flight. The passenger's seat had been filled with spare tanks and other equipment. Messerschmitt had seen Hess off the night of the actual flight. He himself had later been arrested on Hitler's orders and would have been executed had it not been for the desperate need for his services in the aircraft industry.

The other reason why I am bound to reject this theory is that for weeks during the Nuremberg trial the prisoners had been daily together, chatting in the dock. Many of them had known Hess intimately for years and it would have been impossible for a bogus Hess to have fooled them, still less those who later served long sentences with him in Spandau prison. His family visited him in gaol regularly if rarely, and they too had not the slightest doubt about his being genuine. One can only conclude that the wounds which Hess suffered during the First War were less serious than he claimed.

The second myth is of more recent origin. In his book *Ten Days That Saved the West*, published in May 1991, Mr John Costello claimed that an approach to Hamilton by an old personal friend in Germany had been held up for five months while MI6 had concocted letters sent to Hess over his name. These letters, said to have been extracted from KGB files, had supposedly lured Hess into undertaking his peace mission and it was suggested that this had been eagerly welcomed by many eminent people in Britain. These papers were said to corroborate 'claims made by Hess at the time' that he had corresponded with the Duke of Hamilton before he landed. I can only say that I had seen everything of importance that Hess said at the time and that so far as I know no such statement was made by him. I was by this time on very close terms of friendship with Stewart Menzies and he would certainly have kept me informed. Even were it true, it was a trivial matter compared with the top-level secret material which 'C' sent us every day and there was not the slightest reason for him to conceal this minor matter from Cadogan and myself. No doubt the KGB files were full of documents about the Hess adventure. Those quoted sound a little like some attempt by junior officials in the light of Hess's journey to gain kudos for themselves with the men in the Kremlin by cooking up such stories.

To suggest that Philby was in some way involved is even more ludicrous. At the time in question he had not long been transferred from SOE to become a junior member of the Iberian division of Section V of MI6 at St Albans, which could have had nothing whatever to do with the matter. Even if by that time Philby had met 'C', he would have not have been consulted on an issue of this sort. A year later it might have been different.

The desert campaign had ended with the complete rout of the Italians in the field. The hideous decision that lay ahead was in effect whether to honour our promises to Greece by withdrawing troops fron North Africa to support her if the Germans invaded or whether to press on to take Tripoli. Here the position had been altered by the arrival of General Rommel with a small but highly trained Afrika Korps force on 19 February. Cadogan was strongly in favour of our pressing on but General Wavell, the hero of the hour, had doubts. It was decided that Eden, accompanied by General Dill, the CIGS, should visit the Middle East and Greece and make recommendations. Meanwhile limited help should be be sent to Greece, mostly in the form of newly arrived Australian and New Zealand troops with British artillery and air support. I myself felt that we were right to fulfil our pledge.

In the end we got the worst of both worlds. When Prince Paul, the regent of Yugoslavia, was forced by Hitler to take the side of the Axis (contrary to general belief he did not sign the pact), he and his government were overthrown. The Germans at once invaded Yugoslavia, which crumbled after a heavy air bombardment of Belgrade. They also declared war on Greece. The Greeks fought on gallantly with such help as we could give them but soon urged us to evacuate. When the final collapse came the King and some members of the government and the forces managed to leave the country. In Crete in its turn the fates were against us; an airborne invasion could almost certainly have been defeated had not our commanders felt unable to make use of the secret information we had received from Ultra showing we should hold the airfield in force. As it was, we were faced with another costly evacuation with the heroic help of the Royal Navy – though it was even more costly to the enemy. The presence of Rommel in North Africa and the parlous state of the British forces in Cyrenaica also led to a withdrawal to the frontier at Sollum. We were back to square one.

Anthony Eden had now been in the Middle East for two months and while his activities could hardly be described as a success, the fact was that his presence at this particular time had had a useful steadying effect in this battle-zone. It had shown very clearly the need for a top personality with wide powers to decide issues of policy on the spot. The embassy, with the powerful figure of Miles Lampson still in charge, was of course available for consultation, but only on Egyptian issues. Now, with a serious pro-Nazi revolt in Iraq, there was a widening of Middle East involvement.

There were more problems to come. The Germans were making more and more use of Iranian airports and the question of the expulsion of the Vichy forces from Syria was also under serious discussion. I had heard talk in Whitehall of the urgent need for someone to be brought in to coordinate all the multifarious activities of the area, military and otherwise. One morning I was summoned to the secretary of state's room where I found a large smiling figure whom Eden introduced to me as Oliver Lyttelton. He explained that he had been appointed a member of the small War Cabinet and permanent minister of state in the Middle East. I had been chosen to go with him as a Foreign Office adviser. We were to leave immediately.

Nothing ever surprised me in wartime and the propositon seemed to have great attractions. At the same time I was very sad to leave Cadogan. I am glad that he apparently felt the same for he confided to his diary on 27 June: 'This was really the limit but I must agree to the best man going to prevent the thing being a flop.' I broke the news to Alice who I hoped would be able to join me later on.

13
Middle East Satrap

The minister of state was a man of great humanity, with sparkling wit and a gift of mimicry. He excelled in all he did, a wonderful raconteur, a good golfer and a skilled bridge player. He was one of a quartet which included Bob Vansittart and Francis Queensberry who, before the war, played bridge regularly in the late afternoon at the St James's Club for very high stakes. He had a gallant record in the First War as a regular officer in the Grenadiers whom he revered but always with a twinkle in his eye. He was large, balding, well covered, with a small military moustache and a preference for short double-breasted waistcoats with a gold watch chain lying across and generally a discreet pearl tiepin. After he left the Army he had gone into the City where he made a highly successful career in the world of metals and was an intimate friend of all the mining leaders of the day. We became close friends and so remained until his all too early death. Later, when secretary of state for the Colonies, he asked for me to be appointed his minister of state during those dramatic years of the Communist revolt in Malaya, Mau-Mau in Kenya and the Makarios rebellion in Cyprus. He coped with them all with the same placid skill and tact. Lady Moira, his wife, was tall and slender, calm and elegant.

Our party left from Mountbatten Airport near Plymouth at ten o'clock in the evening in a bomber with an Australian crew. The town itself had been hammered during the Luftwaffe's Baedeker raids but Drake's Plymouth Hoe remained intact. Apart from the minister and myself, our small party consisted of Lady Moira, Sir Arthur Rucker, until recently private secretary to Neville Chamberlain, and Harry Lintott, his own private secretary while at the Board of Trade. We flew in a Sunderland flying boat, headed for Gibraltar. In the cabin there were two hard settees on which the Lytteltons stretched out while the rest of us slept, peacefully enough, on a large mattress laid on the floor over the bomb-bay. There were gunners fore and aft. On arrival we were met by General Lord Gort, the new governor, and taken to Government House, 'The Convent', with its medieval cloisters. After breakfast the minister was taken by Gort on a round of the innumerable new tunnels and galleries which now honeycombed the Rock and which included a full-scale hospital as well as military hardware.

I at once found myself involved in a strange affair. An RAF officer, the chairman of the local intelligence committee, came bustling round in some excitement to seek an important decision. It appeared that an Englishman who bore the appropriate name of Black-Hawkins and lived somewhere in the Middle Atlas mountains had turned up with a proposition to put to us. When we met he turned out to be a youngish tow-haired man with a deep brown face who had travelled through hostile French territory to convey an offer from the famous El Glaoui, the Pasha of Marakesh. If the British government were willing to pay the Pasha 40,000 gold sovereigns he would undertake to harry the troops of the Vichy government in Morocco as and when need be. After some discussion with Black-Hawkins I thought we should agree and so advised Oliver Lyttelton. Within twenty minutes it was all settled and in due course received the blessing of the prime minister.

At lunch at the Convent we enjoyed the company of two beautiful Spanish duchesses, the wife and sister, I think, of the Duke of Lerma, the big local landowner, and fully vouched for by the governor. In the afternoon we visited the Upper Rock to meet the three apes which the prime minister had instructed should be imported from Africa to replace those that died. It was widely believed that as long as apes were on the Rock, Gibraltar would remain safe in British hands. In the evening, as the sun set, we returned to our Sunderland and took off for Malta. Since all that went on in Gibraltar was surveyed through long-range field-glasses by German observation posts in adjoining La Linea, I wondered what they made of our little party of civilians travelling in such grand style.

We were arriving in Malta at the beginning of the Luftwaffe campaign to annihilate the island. Wave after wave of bombers each day poured across the island on which the future of North Africa much depended. The air defence was negligible in comparison but single-minded and utterly devoted. It was to become even worse the next year, but it was this dogged defence and above all the people of Malta's own courage which won the island the George Cross.

On arrival we dispersed, the Lytteltons to the governor's palace of San Anton and the rest of us to a hotel nearby. The minister was taken on a tour of the defences of the main airport by the tough old governor, General Dobbie, a real Puritan, fully convinced that he could blast to bits any parachutists who attempted a landing. We were taken to the RAF underground operation rom. A heavy air-raid was in progress. Seated at a large table a number of WRAF girls were moving square chips representing squadrons of enemy bombers while others manipulated the tiny numbers of our fighters. From time to time we could hear over the wireless telephone the 'tally-ho' of our pilots as they went into the attack and on the table a few German chips would disappear. Then a new German squadron would move in. So it went on all day until we left in our Sunderland with the sun setting, a great orange ball behind us.

I was woken by searchlights flashing straight in my face through a porthole. The alarm bells went off and in a second our gunners were ready for action and our plane went into a sickening dive down to a few hundred feet above sea and safety. It was an enemy fighter from Bardia which had picked us up out of the night. Within a short time we were stopping to refuel at Aboukir Bay. Later, on our arrival on the glassy strip of the Nile above the embassy in Cairo, we found in the RAF launch a distinguished party to meet us, headed by Sir Miles Lampson, the ambassador. There was Averill Harriman, President Roosevelt's roving ambassador, General Wavell and, never to be outdone, Randolph Churchill. He buttonholed Oliver Lyttelton at once and by the time we reached the embassy in the car had poured out a horror story of the misdeeds of the local SOE leaders, with a brisk swipe at the alleged incompetence of army intelligence and the military spokesman Colonel Shearer.

Our whole party was invited to stay by the Lampsons at the embassy until our own premises were ready. Next morning I borrowed a polo pony from the controller and went on an early ride on the Gezira Club racecourse. Among the few riders I met was General Wavell himself, who was leaving the next day to take over his new command in India. He was a man of much silence but immense charm, as I discovered later that day when I was able to talk to him at a goodbye cocktail party at his house.

Oliver had been lent a villa by its owner, the American metals king, Chester Beatty. Known as the Beit el Azrak, it had a blue tiled courtyard, a fountain and plenty of spare rooms to accommodate our group. It lay in the desert near the Pyramids and we had a hilarious time there each evening on returning from our work in town. The office itself was a medium-size house in Garden City, at 10 Sharia Tolumbat, the headquarters of the Middle East Command. We started from scratch; all had to be built up bit by bit, but we had every help and soon the office was functioning.

The minister of state's empire was vast and included Egypt and the Sudan, Palestine and Syria, Lebanon, Iraq and Cyprus. Soon afterwards Persia, Abyssinia and Eritrea, British and Italian Somaliland and Aden were added. The British authorities in all these territories were ambassadors, governors or Occupied Enemy Territories officers. From now on they all reported to our minister as well as to their home departments in London on both political and economic matters. Middle East Headquarters and the three commanders-in-chief and other commanders in the area equally had to keep him in touch with all that was going on. Oliver Lyttelton sometimes used to call it his 'satrapy', but it was far larger than any area ever occupied by Darius or Alexander the Great. Some, like the ambassador in Cairo and some of the military, were at first a little suspicious of this invasion of their bailiwick, but I can testify that all came to be more than grateful for the help we could give them in innumerable ways, especially when dealing with their own ministers in London. It was a demanding task which faced the four of us as we gazed at the immense maps covering the walls of the minister's office at 'No 10', as it became known.

Abyssinia came under our wing as a result of a curious episode. OETA, the people dealing with occupied territories, ran the country like an independent principality under Sir Philip Mitchell, who operated directly under Sir P.J. Grigg, the secretary for war. In the autumn, passing through Cairo on his way to England, Mitchell paid a courtesy call on the minister of state. He explained casually that under a scheme hatched in the War Office he was about to sign an agreement with the Emperor which in effect would turn the country into a British Protectorate. Oliver was horrified, for this was just the reason why we had been fighting the Italians. It would have scandalised the free world and would have played straight into the hands of Lord Haw Haw and Dr Goebbels. He explained his doubts to Mitchell and followed it up with a quick visit to London himself,

ABOVE LEFT My father with me aged six months at Duntisbourne.
RIGHT My mother. BELOW The new Renault at Duntisbourne, with my
father, my mother's aunt, Sarah d'Aubigné, my brothers and my mother,
1908.

ABOVE My self-built sidecar, 1918. BELOW Riding with my tutor, Dr Münch, Hanover, 1922.

ABOVE With Commander Knothe, RN, and Corporal Tizzard, Armistice Day 1926, Arlington Cemetery. BELOW The old embassy, Connecticut Avenue, 1926.

ABOVE LEFT Sir Esme Howard. RIGHT Alice. BELOW Presentation of letters by Sir Miles Lampson, by then ambassador, Cairo 1937.

ABOVE, LEFT Sir John Simon. RIGHT 'C', Stewart Menzies, with daughter Fiona at meet of Beaufort Hunt 1938. BELOW, LEFT Vansittart and Cadogan leaving Downing Street. RIGHT Anthony Eden back at the Foreign Office 1940.

ABOVE (behind) General Spears, the author, (foreground) Mrs Casey, Lady Spears, Richard Casey. BELOW August 1942: Churchill and Smuts with Victor Lampson.

ABOVE   Cairo 1942: Roland Penrose, Lee Miller, Alice and the author.
BELOW King George VI and General de Gaulle inspecting Free French
Troops.

ABOVE Spanish News at the Gezira Club. BELOW The murdered victims hanging upside down in Milan. Mussolini and Claretta Petacci centre.

where I joined him after I had arrived with General de Gaulle to see Churchill. The War Cabinet were equally shocked and after a few meetings in London the whole thing was dropped and Abyssinia was brought into our orbit. But it was a near thing.

Oliver Lyttelton was very clear as to what he had to do and tackled each task stolidly, yet with remarkable imagination. He set up an overall Middle East War Council, which I attended, consisting of the three commanders-in-chief, the ambassadors in Cairo and other diplomatic posts and colonial governors whenever they could visit us. General Wavell was succeeded by Sir Claude Auchinleck of the Indian Army. He was tall, smiling and sunburnt in his long baggy shorts and bush-shirt and I took an instant liking to him. He was to have his ups and downs in the desert campaigns against Rommel and above all suffered from the inadequacy of some of his material, notably armour, as compared with that of the Germans. But it is certain that he saved Egypt in the summer of 1942 by his prepared position at El Alamein and the plans which he made for the eventual break-out were built upon by General Montgomery.

The naval C-in-C was Admiral Cunningham. I hardly knew him but his name was a household word from one end of the Mediterranean to the other. Soon afterwards his brother, General Sir Alan Cunningham, the hero of Abyssinia, arrived to command what became the 8th Army. Air Marshal Tedder I got to know well and greatly admired. He was new and showed his mettle from the first day till his eventual achievement of domination of the air by the RAF.

With Sir Miles Lampson, these three also formed the Middle East Defence Committee of the War Council which met once a week under the minister of state's chairmanship. For a while there was also General Sir Robert Haining, who had the title of Intendant General, and who had been given an independent command for all army supply matters in the rear areas. It was an arrangement which worked badly and was soon abandoned. He was a pompous individual who Lyttelton always said had a lieutenant-general's badges sewn on the shoulders of his pyjamas.

Apart from the increasing needs of the forces, it was clear to us from the first that major economies could be made by a determined organisation of civil production in the area as a whole. For this purpose Lyttelton set up a new Middle East Supply Centre. He brought in from Malta a young and dynamic Australian naval officer, Lieutenant-Commander Robert Jackson, who under his direction in quite a short time produced an efficient network in every field of production. (Later he became famous as head of the United Nations Development Organisation.) This naturally grew into a large setup for which we had to acquire extra space.

One of the things which perturbed the minister of state was the vulnerability of our only two deep water harbours, Alexandria and Port Said, with Suez not much better. He therefore proposed the construction of a railway from the ancient port of Safaga some way down in the Red Sea across the desert to the Nile, sixty miles to the west. This was successfully accomplished, as was the extension later of the coastal railway leading across the Western Desert towards the Italian frontier, which proved invaluable to the army in many crises.

Another problem was the number of refugees who appeared in different parts of the area from Greece and elsewhere, causing great dislocation and distress. For this the minister created the Middle East Refugee and Relief Administration, known as MERRA, under direct control of Arthur Rucker, which today still functions as UN-RRA, its international successor.

The needs of the area had been much neglected in terms of publicity and propaganda. The military spokesman – who was also head of Army Intelligence – was Brigadier Shearer, a competent and likeable man who held a daily conference with the press correspondents. This was purely a factual affair and the minister of state saw that something much more vivid and comprehensive was needed. For this he gathered a number of skilled press people while he put out feelers for some high-powered personality from England to head the organisation. In September he and I had to go back to London to clear up various other difficult issues in which I was involved, and my first task was to find someone suitable for the information post. The first name put forward, by the Secretary of the Cabinet was that of William Wedgwood-Benn, Lord Stansgate, a former Liberal MP and Cabinet minister – Tony Benn's father. When I interviewed him he produced such extraordinary ideas about the aims and requirements of the new job that we had to look elsewhere. Lyttelton himself suggested Sir Walter Monckton, the well-known lawyer who had played a key role in the abdication of King Edward VIII. He had plenty of experience and a keen imagination and he readily accepted, so by Christmas we had a Director of Propaganda and Information for the Middle East. He also became a valuable member of the Middle East Defence Committee.

In 'underground' activities, we found ourselves immediately plunged into the storm over the affairs of SOE, the local branch of the subversion and sabotage organisation headed by Dr Dalton, the minister of Economic Warfare. They were in deep trouble, not merely because at that time they had accomplished little or nothing, but on account of a series of scandals which were only too glaring. As a small example, the King David Hotel bar in Jerusalem was one of the favourite haunts of young SOE men with their girl friends. Here, we were told, nylon stockings imported by diplomatic bag from America were sold by them quite openly. Far worse was the chaos in the Cairo headquarters itself; these and many more spicy details were retailed to the minister of state by Randolph Churchill. General Arthur Smith, the chief of staff at Middle East Head-quarters, also raised the matter with me. As a result Lyttelton sent Dalton a stiff telegram bringing all this to his attention and urging that drastic action should be taken. Dalton, after a little havering and a tart reply, sent out the SOE chief executive, Sir Frank Nelson, a former MP, who dealt with the situation – but only temporarily. The heads of the SOE branches were removed in Cairo and Jerusalem. In the former post the SOE head was replaced by Colonel Terence Maxwell, a highly intelligent businessman who did his best to clear things up. For one thing it was arranged that copies of all important signals in and out should be sent to me for the minister of state. This practice was followed up to a point, but I later found that key telegrams were not being sent to me. Some of the junior officials dealing with the important matters in Greek and Yugoslav affairs had Communist affiliations and were in fact doing all they could to further those interests. I remember on one occasion a consignment of 10,000 gold sovereigns being sent by British submarine to Greeece to be divided among the three or four military groups who were fighting the Germans. Later I heard that the whole sum went to the Communist ELAS. I was never satisfied that the evil influence had been removed.

Lyttelton also arranged to set up a Middle East Intelligence Com-mittee of which I was made chairman. It consisted of the representa-tives of MI6, the local MI5, SOE, Military Intelligence and 'A' Force

(Deception). We met once a week in my room and though operational details were not discussed in any depth, at least people knew what was going on. As Lyttelton said, 'At least the canaries will now all be singing the same tune.'

The question of Alice's future had also arisen soon after my arrival. I had assumed that as the wife of a diplomat she would be able to accompany me as she would to any other post. On the other hand, I found that Army wives in Egypt had recently all been repatriated except for those engaged in military or nursing duties. After discussion with Oliver, it was agreed that if she could find a genuine job for which she was properly equipped, it would be quite in order for her to take it up. Our old friend Colonel Dudley Clarke from Jerusalem and Cairo days supplied the answer. He was the head of the remarkable secret organisation known as 'A' Force, formed solely to promote deception plans of every variety which were to play such a vital role in the eventual defeat of Rommel. He needed a personal assistant to run his private office who knew the country and its people and had already put in a formal request. The job involved anything by word or deed which could mislead the enemy as to our plans and intentions, including everything from dummy tanks to leaked 'plans' and false dates. With her membership of the FANYs and her quick mind and common sense, it seemed that Alice would fit the bill. Her appointment was duly approved at Middle East Headquarters and in October, when Oliver and I had finished our visit to London, she returned to Cairo with us. She served with 'A' Force for two hard years and when she emerged with a 'mention in dispatches' and an Africa Star, my pride knew no bounds.

Until the end of the year we lived at the Beit-el-Azrak. It was a joyful company. Though there were setbacks in the desert and major disasters elsewhere, Oliver's stolid courage and above all his invariable wit and good humour kept us all happy and confident. I also managed to hire a nice chestnut Arab stallion and rode every morning in the desert or in the Cultivation, often with Russell Pasha who was building a house out there to which to retire. During that time we had constant visitors, especially at dinner-time – generals, admirals and air marshals as well as even more distinguished guests such as General de Gaulle and General Smuts with 'Ouma', his wonderful old wife. I should mention that Oliver never admitted to his excellent French and thus through his silence overheard many useful little titbits among the Free French commanders whom we met so often.

Meanwhile we were looking for a small furnished flat in Gezira. We eventually found what we wanted in the Sharia Ibn Zanki adjoining our old house, now occupied by Michael Wright, an old Washington friend. He was head of chancery at the embassy and also had close personal ties with the Free French in Egypt. The flat was big enough for us to be able to entertain a bit and it was handy for the Gezira Club and our occasional tennis and polo. The latter was being played regularly, even if not very skilfully, by a few Egyptian residents and it was a joy to our old cavalry friends and others on leave from the front. Also in Cairo at about this time were the last three mounted regiments in the British Army, the Northumberland Hussars, the Yorkshire Dragoons and the West Somerset Yeomanry, all down from Palestine, still with their horses and now in the process of being mechanised. I myself acquired an old English gelding from Duncan McCallum, the controller at the embassy, and a nice lightweight thoroughbred called Spanish News who I found would follow the ball with her nose.

Cairo in wartime, so well described in Artemis Cooper's book, was little changed from when I had been there before, except of course for the khaki mass of service men from all over the Empire. They were everywhere. Much drink was consumed and unfortunately there were occasional instances of hijacking the 'gharries', the horse-drawn carriages of Cairo, and other similar genialities. But on the whole the troops remained popular with the crowd, if only as generous spenders. The officers haunted the night-clubs and everyone had a good time. Alice and I went occasionally to dine in the garden at Shepheard's where many of our younger Egyptian and French friends consorted with officers stationed in Cairo or back from the front. The hotel cuisine remained superb and many items could be had which had not been seen in England for a long time. Drinks of good quality on the other hand were often in short supply. Nicholson's gin was the staple but not very popular. Whisky was obtainable but with difficulty and light local wines from Lake Mariut near Alexandria were only just drinkable. There was also a dangerous local brandy and kümmel suddenly appeared in the shops as if by magic. It was manufactured and put into green beer bottles in Palestine where Herr Wolfschmidt was said to have swum ashore with his recipe in his mouth! In general anything that was produced locally could always be found, though often at high prices, and we were able to give small lunch and dinner parties from time to time.

The embassy itself was still run on a grand scale with scarlet and gold *kavasses* in their baggy Turkish trousers and the red tarbush with a black silk tassle. The Lampsons were very kind in inviting us and there was almost always some personality staying there or passing through. I often met General Smuts and once, sitting next to him at dinner, he fascinated me with his enthusiasm for the then popular scientific book on the universe by J.W.Dunne, *An Experiment with Time*. Once a year on King George VI's birthday in June there was a garden party for several hundred people where Egyptian grandees met the British Army and Air Force as well as the local community. I must say it gave little impression of wartime. Now and then I was asked to shoot at Ekiad, the embassy duck shoot, and once at the King's shoot at Inshasah. I managed to get a game of polo about once a week and Alice, when she could, played tennis at Gezira with her usual success.

Cairo itself was only subject to a mild form of blackout as the then prime minister, Ali Maher, on the entry into the war by Italy in June 1940 had declared it an 'open city', on the model of Paris. Although this was probably a breach of the 1936 treaty and had caused much criticism among the British Army chiefs at the time, it was probably just as well; the effect of a few heavy bombs on the Mousky, the bazaars full of people, would certainly have caused a disastrous panic with the population flooding out into the Cultivation and immense confusion for troop movements. Indeed I often wondered why the Germans did not resort to it at the crucial moment when they arrived at El Alamein in July 1942 when things were touch or go.

Throughout the summer of 1941 there was a lull in the desert fighting as Auchinleck built up his forces. Rommel did so too, with his troops dug in from Fort Capuzzo on the frontier down to Jarabub in the south. Knowing the Western Desert fairly well from pre-war days, I could picture some of the difficulties they had to suffer: the hard surfaces balanced by the occasional drifts of deep sand; the rolling sandbanks to be avoided at all costs; the terrible *khamseen* wind with its sandstorms in the early summer; the digging out of spinning rear wheels; the swarms of pricking flies during the day; the intense heat and then the icy cold nights. The 'Auk', as he soon became known, was very conscious of his military weakness and was not to be hurried. Churchill, on the other hand, became more restless and eager for action every day and the delays angered him. In the event, it was not until November that the commander-in-chief was able to launch his offensive. With increased strength of tanks and guns, his intention was to turn Rommel's flank and relieve Tobruk.

The Battle of Sidi Rezegh, as it came to be known, opened on 18 November. It took Rommel by surprise, though he was planning his own offensive for a few days later. It turned out to be one of the fiercest battles of the whole desert war. The build-up had been continuous on both sides, with New Zealanders, South Africans and Indian divisions now taking their place in the line. The two armies were fairly evenly balanced in numbers, but the Germans were still superior in quality in both tanks and guns. The attack was launched with great confidence – perhaps too much.

After a promising start by the British, Rommel's armour, which he had somehow collected into one German and Italian force, began to get the upper hand in spite of the gallant efforts of the 7th Armoured Division, the famous Desert Rats (my old polo-playing friends of pre-war days). It led to a harrowing retreat and all seemed lost. Unfortunately it then appeared that the new General Cunningham was in no state of mind to ensure victory and wanted to pull out of Libya altogether. In reply to an inquiry from the minister of state, General Auchinleck agreed that such was the case and admitted that he wanted to replace him immediately. As a member of the War Cabinet, Lyttelton at once approved this action and General Ritchie, the deputy chief of staff, took over in his stead. Churchill endorsed it the following day.

After a few days, with Rommel's tanks getting utterly exhausted, his advance was held. Slowly and painfully he was driven back by Brigadier Jock Campbell's desert patrols and the New Zealanders and finally Rommel evacuated all Cyrenaica. Tobruk had been relieved and Benghazi was again in our hands. It was judged to be a victory but no one was happy about these events – least of all the prime minister.

There was, as might be expected, continued criticism of Middle East Headquarters. Auchinleck soon decided to move a large part of the staff out of Cairo altogether into quarters in the desert beyond

Mena House. Cairo, with its mixture of luxury and dirt, and at high Nile in the autumn its steamy heat, was not the ideal place from which to conduct a war. In the desert, in spite of the clouds of flies by day, the nights were icy cold so that one awoke refreshed. The move would also lay to rest unkind jokes about 'the gaberdine swine' in their natty pale uniforms.

I remember an old Army friend, himself a Desert Rat, describing desert warfare to me soon after I arrived in Cairo. He said the tanks and the mechanised units had much more in common with an action at sea than conventional fighting in the field. The 7th Armoured Division had acquired their practical knowledge very quickly and became at the time perhaps the most modern desert fighting force in the world. Rommel soon learnt the same lessons. The result was that battles in the Western Desert tended to move rapidly up and down over great distances, with success often quickly followed by defeat. It was in the quality and power of the weapons, whether tanks or artillery, in which the Germans to begin with so often excelled – the Mark III and Mark IV and the German all-purpose 88 anti-aircraft gun caused devastation. Until the American Grant and, still more, the Sherman tanks came along in 1942, we were constantly at a disadvantage.

Apart from the events in the desert and Greece, poor Wavell before he left had been troubled with other anxieties. In Baghdad a coup d'état was carried out early in April by the pro-German politician Rashid Ali and four Iraqi generals known as ' the Golden Square' against the regent, Prince Abdullilah. This had led to the isolation of the RAF base at Habbaniyah some fifty miles away. There were only a small number of British aircraft available and a minute garrison, beleaguered as it was by Iraqi forces. Yet no frontal attack on the base was ever carried out and when British and Indian troops were landed at Basra the whole thing petered out. The five 'heroes' escaped to Iran where German intrigues were also at work.

In Syria, too, enemy activities had become more sinister. Their commercial aircraft flying through to Baghdad and Teheran were carrying out lengthy stops in Damascus, supposedly for refits, and permanent staff were being left there. While up to now the Germans had ben careful to leave the Levant States alone for fear of pushing the Vichy French garrison of 50,000 men into our arms, they were now getting bolder. A stream of German planes landed at the three main airfields of Syria – allegedly for short periods. Meanwhile the Vichy French orders were that any British plane which appeared over the border was immediately to be shot down. For many months General de Gaulle, strongly backed by Churchill, had been urging Wavell to take action. He, already short of men, munitions and tanks, now still further reduced by Greece and Crete, wanted to maintain the *status quo* at all costs. However, the Germans were soon making full use of the Syrian airports and it became obvious that something had to be done. Slowly the commander-in-chief's views veered round. The fears of the new air commander, Air Marshal Tedder, that with Syria's three main airports occupied by the Germans our position in the Middle East would change perilously, certainly played its part.

Finally our Intelligence intercepted a telephone message from Admiral Darlan to General Dentz which authorised 'collaboration' with the Germans. In the end, though with Wavell still unhappy, it was decided to send in a mixed force of British, Australian and Indian troops under the command of General Wilson with some Free French units under General Legentilhomme. The Vichy French unexpectedly fought back and fought hard, especially on the Litani river, but fairly soon Damascus fell. Stiff fighting still went on for a while with both German bombers and Vichy squadrons from Morocco harassing our small Levant fleet. On one occasion the Free French Foreign Légion found itself fighting its own Vichy comrades, which they did with vigour. Before the campaign opened, a warning to Vichy had been a proclamation signed by General Catroux, now appointed Free French 'Délègué Général' in the Levant, and endorsed by Sir Miles Lampson. Under this the French Mandate over the two states was abolished and their sovereign and independent status was proclaimed and guaranteed by treaty. How this was to be carried out was unfortunately to become the subject of bitter dispute betwen ourselves and the French in the years to come.

The armistice talks took place in the old Crusader town of St Jean d'Acre where Napoleon's Middle East ambitions had met their doom. General Wilson represented the British and General de Verdilhac spoke for Vichy; General Catroux represented the Free French. Although the terms had been vetted by ourselves and the Foreign Office and agreed by Catroux, the wily and charming Vichy commander General de Verdilhac and his political officer had managed to pull the wool over General Wilson's eyes and they emerged in quite a different form. We were aghast when we read them – in particular a secret protocol not at first revealed to us which contradicted the armistice terms by laying down that the Free French should have no access to the Vichy troops who were supposed to be given a free choice to join up with de Gaulle. Just at this moment de Gaulle himself arrived in Cairo. He read the terms and exploded and on a brusque and ill-tempered visit to the minister of state he handed him a letter withdrawing his forces altogether from British command. Lyttelton, incensed but calm, declared the letter in formal diplomat's style to be regarded *'non avenu'* and tore it up. He suggested that they should meet again in the afternoon. At that meeting, which General Spears and I also attended, it was agreed that we two should meet next day with General de Larminat, the local Free French commander, to produce a document putting things right as best we could. After a three-hour session and with great help from Michael Wright, the first secretary at the embassy, we succeeded in producing what was to become known as the Lyttelton-de Gaulle agreement. Not that it settled things by any means

I drove up to Beirut a short time later with Louis Spears, spending two nights with the high commissioner of Palestine where I had my first meeting with his enchanting secretary Lady Ranfurly. We went on by car with Louis dressed in a baggy pair of shorts and a scarlet-tabbed bush shirt and with an enormous quilted pith helmet as used for pig sticking. It was very hot. At the Lebanese frontier at Nakura we pulled up to have a cold drink. We sat in the shade in a little restaurant covered with grape vines in full fruit. Presently a white ambulance came clattering by from the other direction and stopped likewise. Out poured half a dozen walking casualties returning from the 6th Australian Division. They were already rather drunk, and now had a few more beers. Then they started picking the grapes on the trellis. Louis and I looked at one another askance. When they came to leave, a rough red-faced NCO said 'Well let's go', and out they walked – without paying. The owner of the little restaurant rushed after them with the bill but was told to 'beat it'. General Spears with revolver on the hip strode out in the full glory of his pith helmet and placed himself directly in front of the ambulance. He fingered his revolver. 'Get back and pay up,' he said. Sheepishly the NCO obeyed.

Arrived in Beirut, we had no accommodation booked. Rather than trying to find the town major, we went to the splendid new Hotel St Georges which was firmly locked and empty. The guardian took one look at Louis and not only opened up but prepared two rooms and some supper. By noon the next day the hotel was fully open and at lunch I found myself sitting next to a table where there were three young British naval officers and a ravishing Indo-Chinese girl. Her name was Honky Tonk and she turned out to be a Vichy spy. We found everything in Beirut topsy-turvy. The Normandie Hotel was the sole preserve of General de Verdilhac and the Vichy staff. It was out of bounds to the Free French, and Colonel König, later the hero of Bir Hakim, was among those turned away. The Armistice Central Commission was headed by a rather dull-witted Brigadier Chrystall who was on the best of terms with *les gens de Vichy*. There was nothing good enough for them. Under the treaty the Vichy French had been promised the 'honours of war'. These were generously accorded and reached their height when they finally went on board the Vichy SS *Providence* with an Australian detachment presenting arms and the band playing the 'Marseillaise'. General Catroux and his Free French were not amused.

For the next few months the Levant remained eruptive and chaotic. The Free French, headed by the general himself, were determined that we were out to supplant them in the Levant by hook or by crook – as Oliver said, 'They see a T.E. Lawrence behind every bush.' This included our efforts to ensure that some reality should be given to Catroux's pledge on independence, which they only saw as a British ploy to take over the country. We ourselves, powerfully led by General Spears, were determined to adhere to the promises implicit in our guarantee. Personalities became involved and it was not long before de Gaulle and Spears were barely on speaking terms. Louis' relations with General Wilson were little better. For me it was a source of real sadness for I liked and admired them both and indeed in later years Louis Spears was to become a close friend. He had a brilliant mind and a sharp but unkind wit.

I was to return to the Lebanon and Syria many times and got to know those countries quite well. One day in Beirut I saw a strange sight. A large car came down the street with a beautiful woman sitting in it and a cavalry guard in turbans and lances and high scarlet boots came clattering on either side of it. I asked my companion from the Spears Mission who it was. 'Oh, don't you know? That is the Emira.' She was the wife of the Emir Suleiman Attrache, the Syrian minister for war, a Druze prince. I knew her well by repute, for under Vichy, when for the moment she was divorced from the Emir, she had become an agent of ours under the Jerusalem Intelligence Bureau. There had been an incident on the Turkish frontier when she had been caught with some 10,000 gold sovereigns and had been banished to Beirut.

A week or two later I was sitting after dinner in the garden of my old Cairo house, now the home of Michael Wright, beside Colonel Corniglion-Molinier of the Free French Air Force, a man known for his wit. 'I wish you would tell me about the Emira,' I said. 'Oh,' said he, 'J'ai visité une fois l'Emira dans son appartement. J'avais une impression tout-à-fait curieuse. Sous le lit se trouvait l'Air Commodore Buss et dans le lit le Brigadier Evett. Suspendu sur le chandelier était le Général Spears; enfin on ne sentait pas seul.' Except for Spears, I suspect that these assertions were not far off the mark. Poor Emira! After a chequered career in the Cairo night clubs, she ended by being driven in a car under most mysterious circumstances into the Nile, where she was drowned.

On another occasion I flew up with Oliver Lyttelton and a few others to Deir-ez-Zor, a dusty town on the Euphrates, to visit General Slim and the 10th Indian Division. The British political officer there, who had not been long installed, had discovered the scrapbook of the Vichy 'officier des services spéciaux' whose room he had inherited. It contained the names and photographs of half a dozen beautiful French ladies and pinned to the back page was a pair of black lace drawers! Later he came back laughing with a paper which he had found on the floor – evidently written by his Free French colleague. It read. 'Les officiers anglais se partagent en trois catégories: d'abord il y a les 'gentlemen' – parmi eux le Général Slim; ensuite on trouve les 'good fellows' – ceux-là ne se concernent pas de la politique; enfin il y a les gens de l'Intelligence Service – ceux-là je traite avec une certaine réserve.'

Things went from bad to worse. One day returning to Beirut I heard that Colonel Olive, in charge of the Jebel Druze district, had hauled down the Union Jack of our political officer. Someone promptly pulled down the tricolour in return, and so it went on. It reached the point where Spears and I had to go to Damascus to meet de Gaulle in a final attempt to clear things up. It was a stifling hot afternoon and we sat on either side of a small table, the general clad in immaculate white drill with the tips of his long fingers placed together. Little by little we arrived at some sort of *modus vivendi* and flew back to Cairo that same evening. I drafted a telegram to the Foreign Office describing these events; the minister of state read it carefully and only added: 'Needs must when the Jebel Druze.'

Eventually things got so bad that some officers at MEHQ – though I hasten to say not the commander-in-chief – actually put forward a proposal for detaining de Gaulle temporarily in a mental hospital outside Cairo. Needless to say, that was at once stamped upon. Finally de Gaulle himself announced in high dudgeon, 'Je retourne à mes fiefs.' This meant his retirement to Brazzaville in the French Congo. These repeated incidents infuriated the prime minister, who shortly afterwards gave orders that de Gaulle himself should be required to return to London to discuss the whole question. After some demur he agreed to do so. I was deputed to meet him in Nigeria at Lagos and accompany him to London. I flew by military plane via Khartoum and Chad to Takoradi on the Gold Coast – on the way to some hot desert airfield we came across a squadron of Hurricanes making their way across Africa to Cairo. On arrival at Lagos I found awaiting me the governor's Rolls with an ADC complete in spiked white helmet. Surprised, I took my seat with him by my side. I thought he looked a little mystified and then he politely inquired how soon I would be going back to Washington. My arrival had been mistaken for that of Harry Hopkins, President Roosevelt's right hand man, who was travelling in those parts!

General de Gaulle arrived that evening and we left twenty-four hours later for Bathurst where we were to spend the night on the way to Gibraltar. We flew in a small American Catalina flying-boat with only the general and his ADC and myself for passengers. Smoking was not allowed and de Gaulle, who normally smoked incessantly, had supplied himself with a large box of chewing gum. We took off just before a glorious yellow African sunset and very quickly found ourselves over Dakar, which the Free French had failed to capture in 1940. 'Ah,' said the general, 'I wonder what Governor Boisson would say if he knew I was up here above his head.'

Soon he started to talk about what he hoped for France after we had won the war. As we flew on that long journey round the bulge of

Africa he proceeded to describe at some length the constitution which France required to meet the needs and temperament of her people. He defined it as a constitution with many basic French qualities but embodying certain aspects of the American and Swiss constitutions. He wanted, for instance, a strong president with broad executive powers in his relations with the Cabinet and legislative branches and also a wide use of the referendum. I was to recall this journey very often as his proposals unfolded themselves in 1958. It was the blueprint of the Fifth Republic.

After eighteen hours we arrived safely at Gibraltar, to be taken to Government House until the evening. I only hoped that the tall, unmistakable figure in French uniform coming ashore in our little motor-boat had not been recognised by the night-and-day German spotters with their field-glasses on the roof of the Spanish Immigration House beyond no man's land.

The onward journey to Poole and London passed off without incident and I had orders to present myself at No. 10 as soon as I arrived. I waited there kicking my heels for an hour or so, then found myself in the small downstairs dining room at lunch with the prime minister and Mrs Churchill with only their daughter Mary present. In reply to the prime minister's question as to how I had travelled, I briefly described my route. 'Ah,' he said with his eyes lighting up, 'it's a long way to Takoradi.' It was a long story I had to tell and I like to think I may have induced a more favourable reception for General de Gaulle that afternoon. At any rate by the time Oliver Lyttelton arrived in London on other issues a week later, things were comparatively calm.

By September, in spite of the elimination of Vichy in Syria, the Germans had also succeeded in building up their influence in Persia under the pro-German old Shah to such an extent that a long-standing British plan for invasion was put into effect. A joint attack was carried out with the Soviet Union and though there was some resistance it was soon all over. Allied casualties were few and the flow of oil was never interrupted. The Soviet forces confined themselves in the main to the northern province of Persian Azerbaijan, with headquarters at Kasvin adjoining the Caspian Sea. British troops occupied the rest of the country. One great benefit of the situation was that British and American armaments and supplies were able to flow to Russia while General Anders's Polish army moved from the USSR to the Iraqi-Persian border. The Shah was deposed and sent to South Africa. His place was taken by his son who proved to be helpful from the very beginning. Another country was added to the minister of state's satrapy.

We spent a quiet and happy Christmas at the Beit-el-Azrak – but the peaceful atmosphere was not to last long. On 1 February 1942 the prime minister, Hussein Sirry, a good friend of Britain, resigned over our insistence that it was high time for the minister of Vichy France, still recognised by Egypt, to be given his marching orders. A political crisis ensued with the King insisting on bringing back the pro-Axis Ali Maher Pasha and Sir Miles Lampson calling for the appointment of Nahas Pasha, the head of the Wafd, the popular party. After much conferring with the Foreign Office and the minister of state, it was decided to make this a sticking point: if King Farouk did not give way he would have to go. By six o'clock in the evening of 4 February there had been no response from the palace, though at the last minute the Grand Chamberlain, Hassanein Pasha, had sought through me to secure Oliver Lyttelton's intervention – naturally to no purpose. Before nine that night Abdin Palace was surrounded by British troops, including eight guns under the command of Colonel Turnbull of the Royal Horse Artillery. Oliver asked us to dine with him and Moira at Shepheard's at nine o'clock to present an illusion of normality. On the hour the ambassador and General Stone, commanding the British troops in Cairo and the Delta, with two armed ADCs, presented King Farouk with a demand for his abdication. He wavered a little but at the last moment, after pressure from Hassanein, he asked to be given another chance. As had been arranged beforehand with Oliver, the ambassador agreed, though rather reluctantly. Later on, assembled at the embassy with the Lytteltons, the Duff Coopers, Walter Monckton and the senior embassy staff, we awaited the result.

Though the British High Command had been uncertain about the whole operation, I am sure that the decision was correct. Otherwise I doubt whether we could have counted on the steadfast support of the government – and the people – of Egypt when five months later Rommel was knocking on the gates of Alexandria. It was with some relief that Oliver and I with Lady Moira and my Alice left to spend a quiet weekend shooting snipe in the Fayoum oasis.

14

The Rough and the Smooth

Later in the month and to our great sorrow, Oliver was at short notice removed from the scene on being appointed minister of war production. All agreed that he had done an outstanding job in those nine months. While we awaited the appointment of a successor, Walter Monckton was nominated acting minister of state and took over the Beit el Azrak. With his charm and wit and ready smile under heavy eyebrows and still heavier tortoiseshell glasses, everyone loved him. But there was one in particular – Mary Newall, the spectacular commandant of a section of the WTC ambulance drivers. She had arrived in Cairo via South Africa and Kenya the previous year, contrary to all orders from the War Office and a formal ban when she arrived in Cape Town. However she got on to Nairobi where she somehow managed to take over the command of another MTC unit who were on their way up to the Middle East. She donned a Sam Browne belt with a pistol attached over her immaculate uniform with which she wore a bright blue chiffon scarf. In Nairobi she became known as 'Pistol Mary', a nickname of her invention which followed her to Egypt, where she managed to arrive at last to the fury of Middle East Command. In Cairo, Mary with her silver-white hair and blue eyes cut a dashing figure and Walter Monckton, ever susceptible, fell deeply in love. It was not long before she moved into the Beit el Azrak where Monckton was then living. It has been said that she officially became his personal assistant at our office in the Sharia Tolumbat but that was not so, though I certainly saw her there sometimes in the mornings having driven in with him in his car. It infuriated our staff and put me in a quandary. Sir Arthur Rucker was away in Malta so I was the senior remaining official. One day I had a visit from an embarrassed brigadier at MEHQ with a formal request from General Auchinleck that I should insist that Monckton should expel Mary from the villa without delay.

Poor Walter was laid up at the Beit el Azrak at the time, so I at once drove out there. I had a preliminary talk with Mary and warned her that she must be ready to come back with me at once. I had a painful hour with Walter walking up and down the terrace during which, to my consternation, he broke into tears; but he saw that what had to be must be, and I duly transported Mary and her suitcases back to her flat in Gezira. Next morning when I arrived in the office the first thing I heard was that she was already back at the villa. Fortunately Arthur Rucker came back next day and uttered such dire threats to Walter that she once more returned to Gezira.

On 4 May the new minister of state arrived. Richard Casey had previously been Australian minister in Washington where Eden met him. No doubt his appointment was a delicate tribute to the gallant part the Australian forces were playing in the desert campaign as well as a personal compliment to the Australian prime minister, Robert Menzies. Casey was also well in with the Roosevelt administration and was, perhaps surprisingly, a close personal friend of Mr Wallace, the left wing vice-president. I had known him and his wife May in London in the early Thirties, when he was the diplomatic assistant of the Australian high commissioner, and I liked them both. He was later to become the governor of Bengal, treasurer in the Australian government and finally governor-general of Australia.

He was a tall good-looking man with dark wavy hair and a small moustache. He was something of a dandy. I never saw him when his trousers had not been immaculately pressed and he had a curious idiosyncrasy of always wearing a black knitted tie with a white silk shirt. He and his wife May, a sweet woman, were both pilots and flew their own plane in Australia until they were well over seventy. We became very fond of them and although he could not quite replace Oliver in the eyes of the military, they liked him and respected him from the start.

All summer I was engaged in an unremitting struggle with SOE to try to ensure that the policy of the Foreign Office was carried out. This chiefly referred to underground activities in Greece and Yugoslavia. I saw Terence Maxwell at least three or four times a week, as much at his wish as mine for he was always in need of support with some of his rebellious subordinates; but our meetings were also often tense. It was a matter of SOE following the official policy of support to the governments of King George II and King Peter II against the wiles and determination of strong Communist elements in Cairo. Even this policy was varied when Churchill, in the summer of 1943, determined to throw our whole weight behind Tito and leave wretched Mihailovitch to his fate. Under our arrangements I was supposed to receive copies of all important SOE telegrams from and to London and it was in 1943 that I first saw mention of Tito. We had no explanation as to who he was, just that he was operating in Slovenia. We of course guessed it was a *nom de guerre* but it was only when Bill Deakin was sent out to join him at the end of May that the position became clear. I had no quarrel with the policy to give him all possible support but I strongly opposed cutting off aid to Mihailovitch, even though he was sometimes inactive under pressure from the Germans. It was the same with ELAS in Greece where help, and particularly gold bullion, seemed to end up in the pockets of the Communist groups. This was not helped by the presence in SOE Cairo of keen sympathisers with the Communists – notably at the Yugoslav desk of one James Klugman, a known Communist – while there was a young man named Murray at the Greek desk who also made his views quite clear. It has since been said that there were phoney reports, allegedly from representatives in Yugoslavia – which I can remember – accusing Mihailovitch of collaborating with the Germans. This is not meant as any criticism of SOE representatives in the field, many of whose gallantry was unsurpassed. In the summer of 1942 Lord Glenconner took over from Maxwell and, though he also worked with me helpfully, the position did not improve.

As far as I was concerned, that whole spring of 1942 was taken up more and more by the unpredictable and often alarming behaviour of our Balkan allies who had troops in the Cairo area. I refer particularly to the Greeks and Yugoslavs whose clashing political views involved them in ever more complicated situations. There were first the small units of the regular army which had accompanied King George II or naval and military leaders during the evacuation of Greece. Then, among the vast numbers of Greek refugees now seeking shelter, there were many others, who tended to be Venizelist or republican, who passed through Turkey and the Levant seeking asylum. For the latter, now to be counted in thousands, we had already had to set up a Refugee Committee of which I was the minister of state's representative. Many of them also wanted to join up and were taken into a newly formed second brigade.

To cope with all this, King George of Greece, came out from England and established himself for several months in Egypt. He was soon followed by Mr Tsouderos, the prime minister, who had been governor of the Bank of Greece in my day. Over those months I spent hours trying to help them sort out their affairs. Among the Greek refugees arriving at the Turkish border with Syria was a young liberal politician named Canellopoulos, full of all sorts of ambitious ideas, especially in relation to himself. We had no desire for someone coming in to give a further push to the already rocky Greek apple-cart so I was determined to bring him round to the idea that all Greeks must collaborate to save the country and defeat the Germans; they could talk about politics later.

After much argument back and forth, with the King and Tsouderos eagerly playing a part, we persuaded Canellopoulos to accept a job in the existing Cabinet. He insisted on the post of minister of defence – to put him on a level with Churchill – and to represent the Greek government on the spot as a sort of minister of state. In later years, after the war, he was to become prime minister of Greece. It took a long time to sort out these affairs, with almost daily meetings with the King and Tsouderos. Even so, just as I was about to leave Egypt we had the first of several mutinies in the Greek forces.

Later, when Churchill arrived in Cairo, Canellopoulos came round to see me in a flurry, demanding to be received by his 'opposite number', our minister of defence! I was told by John Martin, the prime minister's private secretary, that it was out of the question as every moment was already taken up. I appealed to Casey, who equally failed to shake the prime minister's decision. Next day I went back to Martin's office at the embassy to try again. It was about ten in the morning and soon he came down again roaring with laughter. It appeared that Churchill was lying in his bath with an enormous sponge in his hands. He tossed it and caught it again and again; 'Can see Lopoulos, can't see Lopoulos – sorry, no, can't see Lopoulos.' In the event all we finally got was a photograph of the two shaking hands on the embassy steps.

Towards the end of April a more traumatic chain of events arose in the shape of a revolt of the small Yugoslav forces in Cairo against the government of King Peter of Yugoslavia in London. The 'boy' king had as his main advisers three brothers named Knesevitich who, with great influence over King Peter himself, were at daggers drawn with the Yugoslav military leaders in Cairo. The trouble was that this little force included the officers, senior and otherwise, headed by General Bora Mirkovitch, who had led the plot to dismiss Prince Paul the regent and thrown down the gauntlet to Hitler. They were living fully armed in a wire-enclosed camp out near Heliopolis and quite prepared to resist intrusions from any quarter – including the prime minister, General Simovitch. Emissaries were sent out from London to reason with them but all the negotiations seemed to take place through me as no one else would be listened to by the dissidents. I had constant meetings with different furious generals with unpronounceable names out from London and we had not found a solution by the time the bleak news came from the desert that Rommel had broken through and that the 8th Army had retired to the Alamein line. At that point the Yugoslav dissidents were simply told to shut up and take their positions in the defence of Cairo. But I must say I was relieved when early in 1943 British ambassadors to Yugoslavia and later to Greece were sent to Egypt to take over our functions.

About the middle of May 1942, with the temperature at Mena House over 100 in the shade, I was beginning to feel stale. I had had no holiday for over a year, apart from a rare Sunday, and Alice too had been working for much of the time seven days a week. So it was decided that we should combine an official visit to Syria and the Lebanon with a couple of weeks' leave in the mountains. Unfortunately for me it coincided with an attack of amoebic dysentery which finally landed me in the 15th Scottish Hospital in Cairo and persisted for many years. Still, we enjoyed a visit to the Spearses at the legation in Beirut and their summer house at Aley, followed by a stay at a small mountain hotel from which we could walk up to the famous cedars in the sunshine in a couple of hours. We ate Lebanese food, which was elaborate but good. The delicacy of the season turned out to be lambs' testicles, which were surprisingly appetising. On the way back we also spent a night at Baalbek with its superb Roman ruins. The Spears Mission officer, Burnet Pavitt, came to lunch with us and horrified us with an account of his enforced presence that morning with his French colleague at a 'bastinado' performed on an unhappy Lebanese by two stalwart policeman for some minor crime. The victim had to lie on his back with his hands bound and with bare feet twisted in a rifle sling while he received twenty strokes with a flat rod on the soles of the feet. Apparently this was quite a normal procedure.

We spent a few further days fishing for trout on the Orontes river which Russell Pasha had recommended and for which he had lent us his tackle. The actual source of the river is an astonishing sight for it spurts straight out from a column of rock like a modern bathroom tap. Then it runs down through a placid strip of narrow bright-green cultivation to Homs and Hama and ultimately to the sea. It had been stocked with trout a year or two before the war by a Belgian businessman. The fishing had then been good but it seemed that some New Zealand soldiers had recently been stationed nearby and had amused themselves by doing their fishing with the help of small grenades. In the circumstances we were agreeably surprised to catch a few fish of about half a pound each. I completed my trip with an official visit to Aleppo with its citadel, fortress and roofed bazaar. We returned to the legation, stopping on the way at Krak les Chevaliers, the great Crusader fortress still in superb condition, where it was said knights in columns of eight could ride up and down the central passageway.

One of our joys in Cairo was to be able to entertain our many old friends from three or four regiments which had been with us there before the war. One after another they would turn up on leave from the front or sometimes arrive in the desert hospitals off the Suez road. One day Alice and an Army wife had taken a morning off to visit a close friend who had lost a foot. Alice was driving the car and on the way came face to face with a speeding military truck on the wrong side of the road. They hit full on and both were injured, Alice badly in the leg. There was no medical help near but, through one of her curious premonitions of impending accidents, she had that morning packed a whole first-aid kit for just such an emergency and so someone was able to patch them up till they could be taken to hospital. She had even taken books to read there.

We spent many happy evenings at the house of Peter Stirling, a secretary at the embassy who, with his two brothers, entertained lavishly. Their house was always packed with guests from the desert and the corridors were full of bed-rolls and valises. Gambling was a permanent feature but often too high for our pockets. Both brothers were in the Scots Guards. It was David who formed the original SAS detachment which carried out daring feats of destruction of German aircraft in the desert and is now famous as a regiment throughout the world. Often too we played poker of a mild variety at a flat in Gezira where a lot of old Eton friends stayed when on leave. It was run by a tall and beautiful girl in the Red Cross named Sally Perry, who later married one of them and so in due time became Duchess of Westminster.

Randolph Churchill, in charge of army propaganda and a frequent and efficient guide to press correspondents at the front, was a turbulent feature of Cairo life. He spared no one and it invariably led to trouble. He was a brave man with a good heart but he had a capacity for uniquely bad manners and was inclined to take advantage of his father's position. One evening we were dining with Sir Alexander Keown-Boyd, a former senior Egyptian official, and his wife at their house in Zanalek. It was a party of ten with General Spears, now British minister to Lebanon and Syria, as the guest of honour. Randolph, rather drunk, first launched into an attack on Spears and his policy in the Levant states. Then he turned his attention to Keown-Boyd, whom he described as one of the bunch of out-of-date British officials living off the fat of the land. When the ladies got up to leave I managed to get Randolph to myself on a sofa. I told him exactly what I thought of him and explained to him the damage and pain such accusations could cause to people doing good service for Britain. After five minutes I was amazed to see him crying, with his head in his hands. I must be one of the very few to have achieved that feat.

Our routine was always the same. We rode each morning at seven o'clock round the racecourse at Gezira and were in our offices by nine. For me this included Sundays except for rare occasions. We had our siesta and were back by half past two. Occasionally we were able to take some exercise at Gezira and on Saturdays there were races which we attended if work permitted. The ambassador still kept his string of Arab horses and was a frequent winner. In amateur races Prince Aly Khan and Charlie de Zogheb – whom I still often see – distinguished themselves. In the evenings we often had a small dinner party at home and took our guests on to dance for a while at the Continental Hotel Roof or to Shepheard's garden. As well as visitors from the desert, we still had many British civilian embassy friends who asked us out, as well as a small number of Egyptian friends from days gone by. Sometimes we found ourselves invited to a formal dinner at the embassy or Abdin Palace for some grandee. Once in a while, too, we went to a cinema where on emerging into the stifling heat you found it easier to pay a few piastres to an importuning youngster for a white jasmine wreath which almost intoxicated you with its odour as it hung around your neck.

In the desert while Rommel re-formed his battle line at Agedabiya and built up his supplies, the 8th Army found themselves in increasing difficulty. Two of our armoured divisions lay facing the Germans but the remaining divisions were forced to stay where they were owing to the enormous difficulty of bringing up supplies, aggravated by torrential and hitherto unheard of rains. Raids took place intermittently until the time came in January when Rommel was able to launch a heavy attack. As so often, the fire-power of the German tanks proved decisive. Within a short time the Germans had retaken Benghazi and the 8th Army was forced back to a new line at Ghazala. We were back where we started. It was to last until mid-May.

This time a fresh strategy was worked out by Ritchie under the Auk's direction. The 8th Army was gradually re-equipped with fresh and much-improved material. There were, for example, the new American Grant tanks with their .75 guns; there were also new and more powerful all-purpose guns; and there were hundreds of new American planes. Above all there was a fresh cohesion between air and land forces which Rommel had already brought to such a high art. In numbers the two armies were nearly equal. Under the new British strategy, in the midst of vast minefields, five or six 'boxes' were established, running thirty miles down from the coast west of Tobruk to Bir Hachim. The idea may have originated with Wellington's British squares at Waterloo, with Rommel's Mark III and Mark IV tanks and guns taking the place of the cuirassiers of the Old Guard. These boxes were a mile or two square, veritable forts, bristling with guns, infantry and a few tanks. There was one known as Knightsbridge manned by the Guards, another at El Adem and so down to the Free French force at Bir Hachim to the south under General König whom I had known at General de Gaulle's headquarters in London.

In between the minefields roamed our three tank brigades, able to come to the help of any box which found itself in difficulty. The Germans first tried to turn our southern flank at Bir Hachim where the Free French fought like tigers. At first the Afrika Korps seemed to be gaining ground, until our armoured brigades opened up with the Grants, causing surprise and dismay among the Germans. Soon the whole battlefield was in action. The main offensive was against the Knightsbridge block, attacked by a whole German infantry veteran division with Italian guns and troops in support and continuous air attack. The Guards held and the Germans were thrown back again and again. So it was with the other boxes; the Germans were forced to retreat.

I am in no way qualified to comment on tactics, still less to criticise, but it has often been said that it was at this point that we lost our chance to clean up the campaign and that the proper course was for boxes to open up and to pursue the retreating Germans. At any rate, it was not done and Rommel after this respite was able to re-form and resume the attack. The battle was renewed, above all between El Adem and Knightsbridge in a place which became known as the Cauldron. This time many Grants had been knocked out, with their place being taken by smaller and often ineffective tanks. By the middle of June the boxes were forced, one by one, to break up or retire until at last only Tobruk, an island once more, was left. Then, to the horror of Churchill and Roosevelt meeting in Washington, it was reported that Tobruk had fallen. Cadogan wrote in his diary: 'I wonder what is wrong with our army?' The answer was 'Very little' but on this occasion it seemed that at least the general on the spot had missed his chance of victory.

The retreat went on; the whole British line of resistance now seemed to be in jeopardy. The Germans reached the Egyptian frontier; then the New Zealand division from Syria was flung into the line at Mersa Matruh. There, too, my friends in the 8th Hussars had been badly cut up, all to no purpose. Auchinleck immediately sacked Ritchie and took command in person. With foresight he had long before prepared a strong defensive position, against some dire emergency, at El Alamein. It was only sixty miles from Alexandria and lay at the narrowest point between the sea and the Qattara Depression, that vast hot boggy hole, way below sea level. There he made his stand, though Rommel was fast on his heels. But now it was Rommel who had come a desert too far; his men were utterly exhausted and it was he who was out of supplies, above all petrol. Much denuded of tanks and guns and utterly dejected, the 8th Army, now bereft of half its strength, dug itself in to face the Germans – who were unable to attack.

This was not how on 1 July we saw matters in Cairo. Complete evacuation was ordered to take place the next day. We had to arrange for all our employees from the German-occupied countries, who stood to be shot by the Germans, to be moved to Palestine by rail or road or by air up the Nile to Khartoum. The Middle East Supply Centre from our own office had already left for Jerusalem. So had the non-essential staff of the various secret organisations. Alice, now back in uniform, and her outfit at 'A' Force were to go to Jerusalem, as were MI5, MI6 and SOE. A smile was raised when it was learnt that fourteen Italian tarts, captured in the desert and lodged in the convent in Bulaq, were to be shipped up to Khartoum. Later we heard that they had been moved on to Kenya, where apparently they settled down happily to the satisfaction of all concerned. The embassy had decided to stay put. Waiting to hear what was in store for us, I learnt that an irregular force of British civilians equipped for operations in the Delta was being formed. I at once put my name down, hoping at last to be able to strike a blow in anger. It was not to be; the minister of state to whom I confided my intention immediately squashed my plan. He and his essential staff were moving out the next day to Bir Sheba and I was going with him.

We were instructed to destroy all our documents and files. We made a modest bonfire in the back garden which took care of the lot and a delicate wisp of smoke curled upwards to the sky. The embassy with its mass of confidential files produced a thick black cloud, as did Middle East Headquarters. 'Black Wednesday' the day was called. I had a special favourite file of 'flimsies', copies of 'in' and 'out' signals and telegrams. I asked to be allowed to keep it with me, to be destroyed at the last moment if this proved necessary. 'No,' I was told, 'all must go.' The next morning I found we had had a reprieve. I turned up at the office and asked for my telegrams. There was already a neat file laid on my desk: July 2nd. In Telegrams. Series no A(1). Top Secret telegram no.1. 'Plus ça change . . .'

The Egyptians, from the King downwards, behaved well. One could almost say that they had rallied to us in our hour of need. Possibly it had occurred to them that the newcomers might be much worse, with Mussolini sitting in Derna with a specially imported white horse waiting to make his entry into Cairo. The news from the desert improved each day. On the night of 2 July we counter-attacked. In the process one box was overrun but two others, though under heavy bombardment, stood their ground. We were still discussing demolitions with the embassy and Cairo Command but the biggest excitement was only a run on the banks. We had air-raid warnings each night but each day the news was better and both sides settled down to slog things out. For the moment the 'flap' was over. There was a lull of sorts, interspersed with raids and bombardments which lasted for nearly two months. This was the period when we all got to know 'Lily Marlene'. It came to us first from the German radio, but it was soon translated into English and played by our own services radio. Pretty soon both sides were singing it – even we civilians in our Gezira Island flats.

Meanwhile the port of Alexandria had been stripped almost naked. The Mediterranean Fleet had gone entirely. The town was empty of troops. Only the half-dozen elements of a Vichy fleet stood out stark in the harbour. At the time of the French collapse in 1940, a small yet powerful French fleet commanded by Admiral Godefroy had been operating from Alexandria in collaboration with Admiral Cunningham. Godefroy then wanted to return to France at once, but was eventually persuaded by Cunningham to remain, disarmed and neutral, in Alexandria but with generous terms of pay to his crews which they could remit to France. There were other conditions which permitted them to take their leave in Syria. The feelings of the Free French in Alexandria seeing them with their pockets full, lazing on the beach at Sidi Bishr with some of the prettiest girls, can be imagined.

After the North African landings, we decided to make a fresh effort to persuade Godefroy and his officers to change their minds, all to no avail. I was sent to make a final attempt to rally Force X, as it was called, to Free France. Admiral Harwood took me aboard the flag-ship and Godefroy and I, having several French friends in common, got on well. However, though I returned there several times, I was quite unable to move him. In February 1943 we were informed that it had been arranged for Harold Macmillan, the resident minister at Algiers, to come to call on the French to see if he could do any better; I was to accompany him. In the event Macmillan's plane crashed and caught fire on take-off at Maison Blanche aerodrome, Algiers, and he himself was badly burned in the face. Courageously, he flew over again a week or so later, swathed in bandages, and together we paid an agreeable visit to Godefroy. However, as I had warned Macmillan, he refused to budge. It was not for another six months that the fleet finally sailed slowly round Africa to Dakar for a refit, while Admiral Godefroy himself was installed in a nice house high up in Algiers with a couple of duchesses to keep him company.

Early in August 1942 the prime minister, with the CIGS, General Brooke, Alec Cadogan and others, arrived for a short visit. We went out to meet them at an aerodrome twenty miles down the desert road. The big converted bomber came to a stop and its bomb doors opened. Incongruously, the first thing to appear was a roll of toilet paper which shot out its full length across the sand like some carpet of welcome. Then followed the prime minister dressed as an air commodore with his gold-headed cane. He was driven off by the ambassador, with Casey and the rest of the retinue following him to the embassy, where he was joined by Field-Marshal Smuts and General Wavell. There were a series of conferences with the minister and the service chiefs, together and separately, at one of which I was present. Then Churchill left for the front to stay with the Auk. On their return, the changes were announced. Auchinleck was to be replaced as commander-in-chief by General Alexander. The popular General 'Strafer' Gott was to take command of the 8th Army. The Auk was offered a new Iraq-Persia command which, grief-stricken, he refused. Alas poor Gott was shot down in an unarmed transport plane before he could take up his command and so Montgomery came out to take his place. With new faces and new methods there came about a remarkable freshening of spirit in the whole 8th Army which boded well for the future.

During my whole time in Cairo I had never visited the front line. Though I followed each move with passionate interest, I had not pressed for it, feeling reluctant to burden them further with one more to add to their transport problems. So I was delighted when, towards the middle of August, the minister asked me to join him on a visit to General Alexander's headquarters just behind the main Alamein line. As we drove up the coast road through the little crenellated town of Burg el Arab, we began to see the British soldier as two years in the desert had made him. He was nut-brown in colour, clad only in a pair of ragged shorts with, if anything, on his head a steel helmet – but only to keep the sun out of his eyes. The 8th Army were not keen on them. Everyone imparted an air of supreme confidence. In the event General Alex could not be there himself for, at short notice, he had to oversee the unloading of a shipload of the new Sherman tanks which had arrived unexpectedly from America. We had an excellent dinner beneath the stars and slept well.

Next morning, accompanied by a staff officer, we visited the 2nd Armoured Division, the Free French, the 1st Australian Division under General Morshead, the 1st African Brigade under little General Dan Pienaar and the El Alamein box. During the night we learnt that a large German column was on the march between the New Zealanders towards the left of the line and the 4th Armoured Brigade, under Bill Carr, on the edge of the Qattara Depression, with the intention of turning our flank. We waited breathlessly for the dawn.

In the morning we set out again. During the night a sizeable German force had advanced right through our line beyond the New Zealand Division who were expecting to be attacked. Nothing happened. Then after some delay the Germans began to pull back and in due course turned north to attack the New Zealanders' strong position on the ridge of Alam Halfa. After visiting the 5th Indian Division under General Briggs and another South African brigade, we drove to the headquarters of General Horrocks commanding the 30th Corps. On we went to meet General Freyberg and his New Zealanders who were by now fully engaged with the Germans below us and with shells exploding all around them. It was my first and only experience of being under fire – unless, of course, you can count the Blitz. With the enemy retiring back to their lines under heavy fire we returned to Cairo properly exhilarated. This was the last time that the Germans mounted a full-scale attack on Alamein. I suspected that Ultra had given us a good account of their plans.

Dick Casey had told me of the plans for 'Torch', the impending Anglo-American landings in North Africa. Soon after the Battle of Alam Halfa he decided that he wanted me to go to Washington to meet the Americans who would be responsible for civil administration and describe to them some of the functions and problems of our own OETA (Occupied Enemy Territories Administration). I travelled via Gibraltar to England, then across to New York in a Sikorski flying boat which took some eighteen hours. After talking to people in the State and War Departments, I found that very little thought had been given to this problem, in the hope, I suppose, that the Vichy troops would not offer resistance and the countries would continue to function in French hands. Casey had also asked me to call on his friend Vice-President Wallace, and to expound the situation in the Middle East to him. I did so at some length and found him both friendly and apparently much interested. Little did I expect that he would emerge as a near-Communist in years to come.

I had to fly back the long way – through Trinidad and Recife in Brazil and, during a hurricane, across the South Atlantic by flying boat. Landing early in the morning at Fisherman's Lake, an American airbase in Liberia, after a terrible battering, we were given a full American breakfast with the first tomato juice I had ever tasted. Offered a bed to rest for an hour or two, I commented on their thoughtfulness in keeping it heated. 'Oh, the last occupant only moved out ten minutes ago,' was the reply. Stopping the next night with Lord Swinton, the resident minister in the Gold Coast, I flew on across Africa the morning of 24 October. Then over the plane's loudspeaker came the great news: after a tremendous bombardment, the 8th Army under General Montgomery had launched its attack on the Afrika Korps along the whole line. It was the end of the beginning, as the prime minister said.

It was not long before I found myself setting out on my travels again. Since June 1940 the minute colony of Djibouti at the bottom tip of the Red Sea next to Eritrea had been a thorn in our side. The main importance of the place was the Addis Ababa-Djibouti railway, Abyssinia's only rail contact with the outside world. It had also become infested by an Italian Armistice Commission, Italian spies and saboteurs and a powerful radio which reported all naval activities in the Aden area. It was well defended by Vichy French and native troops. The first territory to rally to de Gaulle under its governor, General Legentilhomme, it had been subject to a take-over by a clique of pro-Pétain officials. From time to time efforts had been made to rally it to de Gaulle, but without success. Now, with the North American landings, it was decided to make one more effort. Early in December General Platt, commanding the forces in East Africa, asked for me to be sent down urgently to help with political problems. The local commander was General Fowkes, the hero of the Battle of Gondar in the north.

I had to stop one night at Asmara, the capital of Eritrea, and found myself staying in lovely hill country at what had been the residence of the Duke of Aosta, the Italian governor-general. It was now the OETA mess run by Lord Gerald Wellesley. He told me I had been given the bedroom of the duke's mistress and it certainly looked it, with pink silk sheets and a black and white colobus monkey-skin bed-cover. There was an elegant set of lady's ivory hair brushes and comb on the dressing table and big round colobus mats on the floor. Above us in the high trees the same little piebald long-tailed monkeys jumped and chattered. Next day, on my arrival in Diredawa, I found the Emperor had come down from Addis Ababa to inspect some of the Free French troops which had just rallied and I was invited by him to attend. Driving to Harar, General Fowkes's headquarters, I was astonished to find how much the Italians had accomplished in a short period of three years – beautiful new macadam roads, shoe and clothing factories, generating stations, water supplies, hotels, and so forth.

Harar itself was a lovely and ancient Moslem walled city but I stayed up the valley with Fowkes at the former governor's palace. He had a dog, a big collie, which he adored and which went everywhere with him. He was a large man, going slightly bald, with a rather high-pitched whining voice, a sarcastic manner and a quick temper. Everyone was terrified of him except for a young oficer called John Hooson, a lawyer in peacetime, who stood up to him. The general and I got on very well from the beginning, for to my great surprise I found that he was somewhat in awe of me. He had never met a diplomat before!

I rode out every morning before breakfast in the valley below us on a sturdy Abyssinian pony. It was fresh and cool and the birds sang. I rode through woods and villages where the pretty local girls came running alongside trying to kiss my hand.

Then began a flurry of meetings, messages, air leaflet-dropping proposals and counter-proposals such as I never met before, lasting a couple of weeks. The villain of the piece was a certain Commandant Antoine, a skilful, tortuous character, who was determined to remain in effective control of the place. No solution would involve the participation of the Free French – or rather as we now learnt to call them 'La France Combattante'. An economic solution would have to keep Vichy as the nominal head. We, on the other hand, were determined to hand over control to the Free French and to embody the little territory in East Africa Command – if possible without firing a shot. As Antoine's verbal defences began to crumble, the pace grew faster. The governor, an old-fashioned French soldier named General Dupont, had little to say, though to him the name of the marshal was clearly still a talisman. At length we got so far that General Fowkes and I were invited down to the little capital for a conference. We had a long meeting and a good dinner but it got us nowhere except that Fowkes was able to remark as we drove back in the diesel train, 'A commander doesn't often get the chance of driving twice through the enemy's defences before a battle.'

Finally came the showdown. Our little invasion force was quickly assembled. On 5 December 1942 the Djibouti population were informed by leaflets dropped by air of our final demands – which itself led at once to the breakaway of a large bit of territory with a further battalion of troops to the Free French. The railway line at the frontier had been dug up for some fifteen kilometres and was now secretly put back in place by our engineers. The 28th African Brigade, consisting of some South African units and a battalion of the King's African Rifles, were deployed for action together with the now enlarged Fighting French contingent of Colonel Raynal and a few armoured cars. We also had a small air contingent consisting of eight Hurricanes and fourteen Bisleys, mainly from Aden, dropping more leaflets; also a little naval flotilla under Commodore Larcon with two light cruisers and two Greek destroyers. On the night of 27 December at Diredawa we lay listening as the battalion of Nyasas sharpened their bayonets and their pangas on a whetstone – I fear smacking their lips! The following morning in we went, the general and I and two companies of Somalis going by rail. All passed off according to plan, the RAF flew over the battlefield, our little fleet stood off at the entrance to the harbour and Colonel Raynal's Free French troops seized the vital bridges which had been prepared for demolition. One after another the Vichy positions collapsed and surrendered and finally there came a message that General Dupont was prepared to meet at six o'clock to discuss terms. Fowkes and I sat down alone with the general (Commandant Antoine was bundled off elsewhere) in the Littorata saloon, lit by a single Lilley lamp as the batteries had run down. The deed was done in the yellow glow, with just a hint, I liked to think, of Compiègne, 1918. We spent the next two days – with very little to eat – in Djibouti town, a dusty dried up place among its saltfields, to meet our Gaullist friends.

By the time I got back to Cairo, Montgomery was pursuing the retreating Afrika Korps forward to Tripoli. After their final departure from the scene, life in Cairo seemed a bit flat. I was bored by the intrigues and quarrels inside SOE, as well as among our Balkan allies. The rest of the machinery of coordination established by the minister of state almost ran itself, though new problems kept cropping up. In the early spring I accompanied the minister on a visit to Teheran, where we were much impressed with the young Shah. The stream of armaments and supplies through Iran to the Soviet Union was running well and similarly the flood of Polish refugees in the other direction.

We stayed at the British legation with the minister, Sir Reader Bullard. After nearly twenty years the gate was once more manned by an Indian guard. We visited the summer legation to the north of Teheran, with its wonderful views of the Elburz mountains, almost as far as the Caspian Sea. At the Imperial Museum we admired the jewel-encrusted Peacock throne, on which the Shah was later crowned. We also ate plenty of 'black jam', as the British troops called the caviar from the Volga sturgeon.

Our official business over, I left with Chris Fuller, the minister's GSO2, on a short but pleasurable motor tour to Isfahan. We drove back through Hamadan and across the mountains to the Iraq border town of Khanaqin. This was the headquarters of the 2nd Polish Division and we had a sumptuous dinner of caviar and gazelle with General Anders. He regaled us with stories of his imprisonment under Stalin, who had kept him standing up to his waist in water in a dungeon, and his subsequent meetings with the dictator. On our return I found a personal letter from Anthony Eden saying he wanted me to go to Lisbon at once as minister to assist the ambassador in some tricky negotiations to get the use of airfields in the Azores. Except for the anxiety of having to leave Alice behind, I could not say I would miss Cairo, from which much of the glamour seemed to have gone.

Just before I left, Alice and I were invited to the first showing of the film of Alamein, *Desert Victory*. We sat a short way down the front row from King Farouk, who was dressed in the RAF-blue uniform of an Egyptian air marshal with the inevitable tarbush. The film opened with a solitary piper of the 51st Highland Division playing on the parapet. I was not sure whether it was the advance or the charge. Or could it perhaps have been a lament? In my Sassenach ignorance I did not know.

15
The Ancient Alliance

I travelled by air to Lisbon at the end of May 1943 across North Africa, stopping a night to visit Brigadier Lush in Tripoli where our Occupied Enemy Territory officials were settling in. The next night I spent with Harold Macmillan in Algiers. It happened to be the day when General von Arnim in Tunisia finally surrendered to General Alexander with a quarter of a million men, which we duly celebrated at dinner. After another night spent in Gibraltar, I arrived in Lisbon by civilian plane. It at once conjured up typical *saudades*, the nostalgic Portuguese longing for times, people and places long gone.

I had been invited to stay at the embassy by the ambassador, Sir Ronald Campbell. He it was that I had last spoken to on a rogue telephone line to Bordeaux that dramatic night in June 1940. He was a small man, very spruce and neat with a moustache. He had a way of twisting his head to one side from time to time and a nervous trick of shooting his immaculate cuffs. But he was charm and kindness itself, with a dry sense of humour and a clear brain to meet any eventuality. Lady Campbell was grey-haired with piercing eyes and equally welcoming, even if she sometimes had a rather bossy manner towards younger people like ourselves. As they were dining out, I thought I would visit my only Portuguese friend, Alda Wright, the widow of an American judge of the Mixed Courts in Cairo, who lived some twenty miles out at Cascais.

I took a taxi which the petrol shortage had forced to carry a *gazogène*, a great oblong gas balloon wobbling on its roof. As we progressed along the Corniche road in blinding rain such as I had not seen for years, the driver and I talked intermittently in Spanish, just able to understand one another. He pointed out rather unnecessarily that I was a foreigner and asked where I came from. 'The Medio Oriente,' I said, 'you know, the 8th Army and all that.' 'Ah,' he said 'you know, senhor, whenever the 8th Army advances the whole Portuguese nation goes with it.' That was good enough for me. Having been living in places like Egypt, Syria, or Iraq, where the British were generally the subject of abuse, it came as balm to the spirit. I knew I had come to the right place. I have been in love with Portugal and the Portuguese ever since.

The friendship of England and Portugal goes back a long time. The two countries, both a little lonely stuck out in the Atlantic and each with a powerful enemy at their back, had concluded a treaty in 1373, between King Edward III and King Ferdinand and Queen Eleanor of Portugal. It has subsisted to this day and was confirmed in one way or another down 600 years by other rulers, including both Charles I and Oliver Cromwell. Under its terms, if one or other of them should be 'infested, oppressed or invaded' by an enemy the other party should if required to do so at once come to their assistance. In 1939 neither country was anxious to draw the Nazis into the Iberian peninsula, so by common consent Dr Salazar, the Portuguese prime minister, at once proclaimed his country's neutrality. This deal worked pretty well even though we were much irked from time to time by the Portuguese supplying over-large quantities of wolfram and other items to the Germans.

A few days after my arrival the embassy public relations and press officer, Michael Stewart, presented at our private cinema a well-attended showing of a film with Leslie Howard in the star role. Howard himself made a short speech and Stewart gave a small supper party on his roof to which I was invited. Leslie Howard was due to leave for England on the early morning plane but we sat long over our drinks in the most tropical night and the party only broke up shortly before two. I arrived in my offive just before nine to find a note from the air attaché on my desk. 'Regret to report that Leslie Howard's plane was shot down by a Junkers 88 over the Bay of Biscay this morning.' By common consent we and the Germans had not interfered with one another's commercial planes but from then on the KLM only flew by night with a great sweep out over the Atlantic while we shot down the German passenger planes down with no compunction.

One of the principal anxieties of Churchill and the War Cabinet throughout the whole war was the appalling losses inflicted on British and neutral shipping by the U-boats. In *The Finest Hour*, Churchill assessed the total losses at over twenty million tons, of which Britian had lost over eleven million. I recollect being told that at one point, as in the First War, we had been down to three weeks' food supplies. The submarines were everywhere – Far East, Indian Ocean and the Norwegian Sea, but eighty per cent of the sinkings occurred in the Atlantic. Seven hundred miles to the west of Portugal lay the Azores Islands. Though without any developed airports, they commanded the central Atlantic; quite early on they were also in Churchill's eye.

Then, almost at our darkest moment early in the New Year of 1941, the Portuguese government astonished us by offering to take up arms under the terms of the ancient alliance if such was our wish. Unhappily it was only liable to increase our troubles but it was accompanied by an offer to send a military mission to London to discuss possible future developments. In the event Major Humberto Delgado became the main delegate, coming to London frequently and later undertaking the supervision and construction of a full-size military airfield on the island of Terceira. He was a good friend of Great Britain. After the war he became famous – or infamous – as an extreme left-wing opponent of Dr Salazar and was responsible for the dramatic hijacking of the Portuguese cruise-liner *Santa Maria*. The British delegate, a member of the joint planning committee, was Group Captain Roland Vintras, earlier a friend and colleague of mine at Gwydyr House, who wrote an entertaining book on the subject.

By July 1942, with the U-boat attacks proliferating, a plan was finally prepared and discussed with the chiefs of staff for submission to the Portuguese government with a request for approval. Still no decision was taken and it was not until early 1943 with the sinkings worsening that the prime minister had become very restive and proposed that we should simply invade the islands and present the Portuguese with a *fait accompli*. Anthony Eden with some difficulty persuaded him to wait to invoke the terms of the ancient alliance to enable the plan for a base in the Azores to be carried out. Sir Ronald was instructed to make a formal request which (by previous agreement) was accepted the next day.

A military mision sent out to Lisbon to negotiate the details was headed by Air Vice-Marshal Charles Medhurst (our attaché when I was in Athens), Frank Roberts, a rising young star of the Foreign Office, a rear-admiral, two colonels and a number of others. The air representative and later secretary to the delegation was Roly Vintras.

They brought with them two dazzling lady secretaries. Lisbon was crawling with German agents and the German military attaché's office was one door down fron us. It had a viewing post on the roof. All arrangements had to be carried out in the utmost secrecy. Medhurst and Frank Roberts stayed at the embassy while I had Vintras stopping with me. The rest were scattered at other embassy members' homes or in hotels. All were told to arrive at the chancery for our first meeting separately and in civilian clothes. All went well and we broke up at about half past eleven. I spent some time working in my office at the back but, going out, was horrified to find them all – with their distinctive gold-stamped despatch cases – going across into the Victoria Bar directly opposite!

The Portuguese side was headed by Admiral Botelho de Sousa, the commander-in-chief with the strange title of Major-General of the Armada. Major Delgado was of course among the delegates with his air base at Terceira completed. Meeting after meeting took place, all inconclusive. The Portuguese were convinced that Germany would react aggressively and hours were spent arguing as to what we should have to supply before our landing in Terceira could be carried out. Finally, after the prime minister had laid down a target date for a settlement, it was agreed that Britain should suply six squadrons of Hurricanes and six batteries of anti-aircraft guns with ammunition, spares and instructors. On 17 August the agreement was signed and a date set for the landings.

Meanwhile those of the delegation who were not busy drawing up reports relaxed in the sunshine in the afternoons on the beach at Estoril. With the strict security measures of the Portuguese state, involving police, plain-clothes men and the dreaded PIDE secret police, the authorities were often intrigued or worried about these strange wartime visitors. One day Charles Medhurst and Vintras were arrested for loitering in Black Horse Square and only released after intervention by the embassy. On another occasion a member of the delegation had to be smuggled out of the country by our secret escape channel on account of a more serious indiscretion which landed him in gaol. We assumed that the German secret intelligence and especially the military attaché whose staff observed us all day from the house next door had a fair idea of what was going on. Soon after the signing the ambassador had to go to London to explain one or two points to the Foreign Office and I found myself in charge. I had to go down to the Foreign Ministry to sign similar agreements on behalf of Australia and South Africa with Sampaio the old permanent under-secretary for Foreign Affairs. When we had finished, I asked him how much he thought the German minister really knew of the matter. 'It's funny you should say that,' he said. 'Only just before you came in, the German minister was sitting in the same chair as you. He asked me what was this he had heard about a British air mission in Lisbon? I said "Air mission? I know of no air mission." Vous voyez, je n'ai même pas eu besoin de mentir!'

One night in September I had some friends dining out on our terrace overlooking the Tagus. As we finished our coffee, I noticed one long blacked-out shape after another creeping silently up our river. There were six of them, very low in the water. It did not take me long to realise that these were our merchant ships arriving with long-awaited weapons and men. On 8 October the British convoy of ships with the aircraft and their crews and supporting troops landed at Ingra in the island of Terceira. The Germans no doubt protested but not a bomb was dropped nor a bullet fired.

The ambassador's house was a nice eighteenth-century building in a fine position overlooking the harbour and with a beautiful garden. In pre-war days it had housed the chancery as well but in 1940 the mass of work and the enormous increase in staff made this impossible. An old palace had been bought, a classical large eighteenth-century building, in the rua São Domingo à Lapa. It had a large garden behind with a family chapel. I myself had taken a house from Jock Balfour, my old Washington friend. I also succeeded to an old Hispano-Suiza that he had acquired from some Rothschild refugee from Paris in 1940 and its nice but saturnine chauffeur, Antonio.

The house, in rua Sacramento à Lapa, was unusual. We occupied the ground floor, the basement and the garden, while the Belgian minister, with a separate entrance, occupied the floor above. It had been some sort of hostelry in the eighteenth century and both Byron and Shelley had lodged there for long periods. It had a big drawing room but above all there was a large square tiled terrace enclosed on three sides which by common consent offered one of the finest views of Lisbon harbour with the Tagus flowing beyond. It was here we took all our meals. I also took over the Balfours' staff. The cook, who was excellent, was paid the equivalent of twenty pounds a year, the little between-maid got twelve! Alice unfortunately could not join me until the autumn but as I had taken over all the Balfours' furniture and silver I settled down comfortably. With the help of Alda Wright I soon had a number of Portuguese friends.

Later in the summer I had to go to London on some matter to do with the Azores. On my return I was greeted with the news that an Italian general, General Castellano, a former chief of staff, had arrived secretly via Madrid accompanied by a first secretary from the Italian Foreign Office, the Palazzo Chigi. His mission was to ascertain the Allied terms for an armistice. Long conversations had taken place with Sir Ronald, as a result of which some 'long terms' had been put forward in detail with 'short terms' dealing with immediate arrangements. The general had been smuggled out through Gibraltar to go to General Eisenhower's headquarters at Algiers for drafting and signature of the documents.

A few days later I went to my office one morning and noticed a suitcase marked 'C de W' in the front hall of the chancery. I was told that yet another Italian general with an English companion was waiting to see the ambassador. I had them shown into my room and found that it was a General Zanussi and that the Englishman was none other than General Carton de Wiart, VC, who was notable for having lost one eye and one arm in the First War. He had been captured by the Italians earlier in the war in an air accident on his way to Yugoslavia and had just been released from the Italian prisoner-of-war camp as proof of good faith. It struck me that in a top-secret mission of this sort the Italians could not possibly have picked anyone more noticeable. However, they had come through Madrid by air unscathed. I explained to Zanussi that General Castellano had already been in Lisbon and I wondered why the Italians had sent a second mission. 'Ah,' he said, 'you see we had sent out one dove and as it had not returned we thought it wise to send another.'

After talks with the ambassador and an exchange of telegrams with the Foreign Office it was agreed that Zanussi should also be sent to Algiers. Carton de Wiart insisted on going back to England, to which the Foreign Office only agreed on condition that when he got there he should go straight to his house in the country. We had equipped them with Free French passports and after lunch sent them on their way to Gibraltar by civilian plane. I heard later that by seven o'clock that evening Carton de Wiart was in the bar at White's and full of traveller's tales!

[223]

Carton de Wiart told me that with them on the plane, to the embarrassment of General Zanussi, there had been Count Grandi who was no doubt fleeing from the furious Germans in Rome determined to punish him for his leading role in the overthrow of Mussolini. I had known and liked him when I was working for Simon. Afterwards I learnt that he was in Estoril, very short of money. He had heard that I was in Lisbon and was anxious for my help. I clearly could do nothing officially, nor could Prunas the Italian minister who was by now in the plot. Finally I sent him £100 anonymously to tide him over and soon learnt that he was making a living giving English lessons. After the war we met in London and renewed our friendship.

It is worth remembering the circumstances in which Dr Salazar took power in Portugal in 1926. The country had become a republic in 1911; the last fifty years of the monarchy, liberal and constitutional though it was, were continually disrupted by political upheavals with radical sections of Chartists, Septembrists, Progressists and other socialist elements constantly interfering in the political scene. At the same time the Great Powers, notably Germany and, I am sorry to say, Britain too, with a keen eye on Portugal's rich African possessions, were constantly intriguing in Portuguesae affairs in that continent. Under the republic things got rapidly worse; in the sixteen years after the revolution there were no less than forty-four ministries, twenty-four rebellions and over a hundred and fifty general strikes. The country was understandably on the brink of bankruptcy.

In 1926 a military coup d'état took place and Dr de Oliviera Salazar became finance minister in the new government. He was thirty-five years old, a former legal student of Coimbra University. A man of peasant origin but distinguished appearance, he emphasised repeatedly in his speeches that financial purity of purpose was the only hope for Portugal. His quiet, dynamic personality impressed itself on the nation. Though he respected democracy, he said that it had no place then in his immediate plans for Portugal. All he was fighting for was the country's survival.

I remember how many ill-informed people in England lumped him in with Fascism, which in fact had at that time only just come into prominence. He held no brief for Fascism, nor for Nazism, with the marchings and song-singing and the brutality that underlay them. As for democracy, while he admired it in Great Britain, he considered that his own countrymen were by then totally unfitted for it and must like children go through a long period of re-education before they would be fit to participate. It is true that he sought progress along corporative lines but here again his extreme caution led him to set up a skeleton system only. At the same time he insisted on private, and above all family, development and initiative. He was throughout guided by strong religious convictions, with constant emphasis on the spiritual side of national life. Admittedly he also had his Security Police.

I only met him two or three times during my service in Lisbon and it was not until twenty years later when I became chairman of 'Tanks', a British company that owned the Benguela Railway in Angola, that I came to know him well and could really appreciate the depth of his character. Physically, he was a man of distinction and charm with a fine ascetic head and keen brown eyes. When, a year or so after he died, his successor was overthrown, there can be no doubt that the mild behaviour of the revolutionaries and their rapid rejection of Communist doctrines were the result of long years of patient education by 'The Doctor' himself.

During that lovely Portuguese summer I made many friends. I lunched and dined with them and over the weekends went swimming in their pools or stayed overnight out in Cascais or Sintra. The Espirito Santo family, the leading private bankers, were specially kind to me out in their lovely home on the sea. This was the house which Ricardo Espirito Santo had lent to the Duke and Duchess of Windsor when they were fleeing in 1940 from the South of France and Franco's Spain, with their future movements still to be settled. It was also here that Schellenberg, head of the Sicherheitsdienst planned to kidnap them and had thought (quite ridiculously) that he might induce the Duke to become a Nazi puppet ruler of a conquered Britain.

There were several Espirito Santo banker brothers and, like the Swedish Wallenberg family had done in Stockholm, the elder, José, had devoted his time to the British embassy and their Allied clients while Ricardo operated the Axis side of the business. It was a sign of the times that by the time we arrived their social attentions were all directed towards their British friends. The house was of red brick, overlooking the sea in a quiet sector beyond Cascais with an exotic swimming pool. One side and both ends were covered with walls of bright blue and white seventeenth-century *azulejos*, the beautiful tiles of Portuguese craftsmen with scenes of hunting and horses or classical Greek gods and goddesses. On a Sunday we would spend the day swimming lazily, lunching on the masterpieces produced by the chef and taking our siesta in cool dark bedrooms till late afternoon. The war sometimes seemed almost guiltily remote.

Alice meanwhile was finally able to get away from Cairo but had to make the long hot trans-African journey through Khartoum, Nigeria and the Gold Coast. She had to spend one night at Bathurst in the Gambia and unfortunately managed to pick up the malignant variety of malaria known as sub-tertian fever. Within a week of her arrival in September she went down with a temperature of 105 degrees; she was delirious and often babbling wildly at night. With all the top-secret material stored in her mind after two years in 'A' Force, there was no knowing what she might divulge, so though we had nurses I tried to look after her as much as possible myself and sat up with her each night during her bad spells. Fortunately it was a variety of malaria which does not recur.

Now that we were living in a neutral country we had arranged for our son and his nanny from America to join us in October and attend the little English school near Estoril. We had booked passages in a Portuguese ship but, as it turned out, it was to sail just before the British troops were due to land in the Azores. We were extremely worried that the German reply might be an all-out U-boat attack on Portuguese shipping but I felt that to cancel the passages at this late stage might arouse German suspicions that something was up. We let them leave as arranged, but it was an anxious week.

I had been asked by Cadogan to go carefully into the whole of our secret activities in Portugal and make any recommendations I thought were needed. I found MI6 and SOE and another very active secret security body were at least on speaking terms but I had to lay down stricter rules for coordination – in particular, a requirement that any important development should be notified to me. I was also to get copies of all their signals and it was arranged that where necessary I would comment on them in personal telegrams to Cadogan. It worked well and the ambassador said that he did not mind what I did as long as he wasn't told about it. I was also asked by Colonel John Bevan, the head of the equivalent organisation in London to 'A'

Force, in the absence of any representative in Lisbon, to build up a small deception network in which Alice when she arrived would be able to give me invaluable advice. I was also to get help from the 'A' Force representative in Gibraltar. I quite enjoyed being given complete latitude in developing small schemes of deception in line with military needs. For example, I was told in advance and in a general way about the plans for landings in Anzio, south of Rome, in 1944 and asked to make plans to indicate to the Germans something quite different. I knew that our commercial counsellor at the embassy had a son who was a prisoner-of-war in a big Italian camp near Civitavecchia, just north of Rome. I also knew that the Papal nuncio had a Brazilian counsellor who was strongly pro-German. I arranged for a private interview between our counsellor and the nuncio, whom I had already met, and in the presence of the Brazilian he explained his fears. He had heard rumours, he said, of an attack and landings to take place north of Rome and was most worried because he was afraid that his son's prison camp would be overrun and involved in the fighting. Was there any chance that he could be moved elsewhere, on the grounds of health, perhaps? It was pretty crude but it brought a result in the form of a request for him to come round to be told that, alas, the Vatican could do nothing in this matter. This curious channel was to come in handy again later in the year.

Lisbon itself was crawling with German agents, not to mention Italians, Japanese and a full Vichy embassy just down the road from us. We ourselves had plenty of Portuguese agents, including one beautiful girl who became the mistress of the Japanese minister. She had great influence over him and was able to obtain the secrets we wanted by pulling a hair out of his chest every time he refused to tell her what she asked.

In Lisbon I also had my first close personal contacts in wartime with our American allies. Mr Fish, the minister, I had known from Cairo, where he had also been minister. My house in the rua Sacramento was directly opposite the American legation and I saw him frequently, though sadly he died during his term of duty in Lisbon. Down through the members of staff, career men or wartime officials, I made many other interesting American friends, some of whom performed invaluable and dangerous services for the Allied cause. Apart from the Americans, we saw few foreign diplomats – just enough to keep us in touch with what was going on among our enemy colleagues. These were everywhere and aggressive. I shall never forget a night when Alice and I went to dine and gamble a little at the casino in Estoril. We were unaware that it happened to be Hitler's birthday and we found ourselves a table next to a large German party, already rather drunk, who were ceremoniously drinking his health. They knew exactly who we were and kept turning towards us with loud guffaws.

Bullfighting went on in Portugal but in rather a tame form. Much of it was local talent but the great Spanish *espadas* of the day like Manolete or Joselito also came to the Campo Pequeno in Lisbon from time to time. They did not use swords: after playing the bull with the red cape the matador's performance ended with his placing a rosette between its horns. The the cows were driven in and the bull meekly followed them out to be despatched with a humane killer and sent to the butcher. In the opening event a bull with padded horns faced an amateur horseman dressed in full eighteenth-century costume of a long blue or red and gold coat and a three-cornered white-feathered hat. With the reins controlled from his feet, he placed the light banderillas in the bull's shoulder muscles in a superb act of horsemanship, took off his hat to bow and cantered out. Then eight men lined up one behind the other facing the bull and called him until he charged. The leading man would throw himself right between the horns and the others, wrestling with the bull or hanging on to his tail, would try to bring him to the ground. Again the cows would come in to lead him quietly away.

With Nicky safely back we had our first Christmas together for three years. Soon after the New Year Arthur Duckworth, the MP for Shrewsbury, arrived with an extraordinary tale. His wife, an American, had taken their three daughters to America in the summer. Now she had fallen in love with Benny Goodman, the clarinettist and refused to bring the children back to England. Arthur decided to kidnap them and set about it with the help of his brother, then commanding a British battleship that was refitting in Philadelphia. He got them aboard a small liner leaving from Baltimore but his father-in-law, John Henry Hammond, the head of Brown Brothers, the bankers, raised a hue and cry and by enlisting his senator was able to have the children taken off the ship. Arthur, staying with me on his return by clipper, was, I thought, lucky not to be in an American gaol.

Each day we came to like Lisbon itself more and more. There was first the formal network of superb squares and streets in the high classical style preferred by the Marques de Pombal, the prime minister, after the earthquake of 1755. This network ran from the river back into the town in a succession of government buildings and banks and shops and with a triumphal arch. Higher up was the Bairro Alto district where the writers and painters lived and which housed most of the night life of the town. At the very top was the cathedral and the castle of St George which was captured from the Moors after a long siege with the help of British Crusaders in the twelfth century when Lisbon finally fell.

In the Bairro Alto the sad but curiously moving strains of the *fado* would greet you as you wandered down the little streets. It is the national music of Portugal, said to have an African origin, with melancholy tones and always a tragic ending to the words. There was a stylised presentation with the girl singer in her black veil standing between two seated male guitar-players with her arms on their shoulders. The star in my day – and for some years to come – was the famous Amalia Rodrigues. I believe at the time she was the *namorada* of Ricardo Espirito Santo.

We often liked to spend a weekend with our son further north at Foz do Arelho where there was a safe beach and a quiet hotel. A small river ran out of a long lagoon where I tried unsuccessfully to shoot duck. We were intrigued by the fishing dogs of the local inhabitants which used to catch the fish in their mouths in the shallows where the tide met the river's current. Foz was also quite near to two other celebrated monuments of Portugal, the abbeys of Batalha and Alcobacça. The former was to commemorate the final defeat of the Spaniards at Alfabarrota in 1385. Alcobacça, built a little earlier, is equally beautiful but pure Gothic with King Pedro and his tragic little queen, Inez de Castro, buried foot to foot so that their eyes will meet when they rise on the Judgement Day.

I was invited to go hare-hunting one Sunday morning on the other side of the Tagus opposite Vila Franca de Xira. It was quite unlike anything that I had ever seen. The hares were hunted on horseback, the riders drawn up in a long line so as to cover the whole area. This consisted of open fields bordered by woods of cork-tree. In the centre a hunt servant had a pair of greyhounds on a long leash. When a hare was put up, the leash was slipped and the whole cavalcade went into action. There was a short fast hunt like a coursing match and then the procedure was repeated, sharp and short. Often the hare would get away or turn into a glade of cork trees, jinking to and fro. Sometimes he would hit a tree and be killed instantly, or else it might even be one of the greyhounds.

The hunt ended, we all proceeded to the luncheon-hut of the master, the Conde de Cabral. We sat down to a large meal washed down by plenty of *tinto*, the rough red wine of the country; then we returned to the bank of the Tagus where the little open ferry-boat took us across to our cars. There was a small wooden dock attached to the bank from which to embark. The previous ambassador, Sir Walter Selby, was seen off by his host after one of the lunches. Murmuring his thanks and shaking hands to say goodbye, he made a little step backwards and then another. He took one step too far and shot straight down into the river. He was soon rescued, suffering from a very sore chin but otherwise intact.

On one of these occasions I met a pair of twins called Palha. They were absolutely identical, tall, handsome with slim waists shown off by short-cut grey Selvilhano jackets and trousers. On their heads they wore flat round hard grey hats in the Cordoba style. We made friends and when I said I was looking for a horse to buy they invited me to visit them at their bull-breeding farm on the other side of the river near Vila Franca de Xira. I said I wanted a young gelding of the heavy Andalusian type which I wished to break in myself. I had never done this before and knew that it would tax my ability considerably. In their stables we found what I wanted, a nice-looking black two-year-old with one white sock. We settled on the price and in due course, after some setbacks but with some patient help with the lunge and saddling, I found myself achieving some modest success. Thereafter I rode every morning. I mentioned the matter to the ambassador: 'Oh my God,' he said, 'you've broken our black-list regulations – those are people who have been doing business with the Germans.' 'How can that be?' I said. The Palhas had been selling mules to the Germans for years, I was told. It was agreed that it would be too embarrassing for me to go back on my bargain and Joao, as I called him, turned into a mount which I rode rather gingerly on the racecourse in the mornings before breakfast.

Years later, after the war, Idina Haldeman, our friend from the Happy Valley in Kenya, told us that she had met the Palha twins in Portugal and fallen in love with one of them. The trouble was, which? There must have been complications when the three of them carried out a sensational desert journey by car from Morocco to Nairobi.

When I was deputed to open a new branch of the British Institute in Oporto, Alice and I were asked to stay by Max Graham, the head of the well-known port shippers. The ceremony passed off well and a luncheon was given for me next day at the Factory House, the headquarters of the port-wine industry. It is here that the serious decision is taken each year whether or not the grape harvest in the Douro Valley is good enough to declare a vintage. It was a large Regency house equipped with the furniture of an earlier period. In fact it turned out that Thomas Chippendale himself worked there for three years. The library where we drank our sherry was fully equipped with shelves of Chippendale design, as were the chairs and the wooden step ladder. The dining room was on the floor above with a long table laid for some twenty guests. I sat in the midddle next to the president of the wine-shippers and we had an excellent lunch, with a fine German Moselle followed by a superb claret. After the pudding was served I was told to pick up my napkin and move across the hall to where an identical room with an identical table and the same places were set out for us. The idea was to get away from the smell of vegetables!

After lunch Max Graham took me round to his company's wine lodge at Villa Nova de Gaia across the River Douro. There were several enormous wooden vats above us and I was asked to re-christen the Minister's Vat, a tawny, which was topped up each year. We were taken to a platform where a champagne bottle was hanging on a cord. I took my place, pulled back the bottle, pronounced the appropriate words and let it go. I failed to break it. I tried again. This time there was a welcome crash and my name went down in the old book.

In February 1944 I was summoned urgently to London to go to Norfolk House in St James's Square where the planners for Over-lord, the landings in France, including my colleagues dealing with deception, were located. I was taken to the map room and first shown the area in which the landings were *not* to take place. This was the Pas de Calais and I was informed that this was the location that with the utmost tact and discretion I must try to disseminate during the next four months. I was also told that the approximate date was the first week in June. Finally I was given a pretty clear indication of about where the landings would take place.

To say that I was shocked to be given this vital secret is an understatement. The idea of being exposed to the German agents in Lisbon when I carried such crucial knowledge seriously alarmed me. However I went ahead with my plans, discreetly working out the best ways of putting over my story. There were one or two ambitious plots but most of the seeds were sown in dinner party conversation with English as well as Portuguese friends. I went on the waggon for all those anxious four months!

Not only were there a multitude of secret agents and their bosses in Lisbon, there were also self-appointed and enthusiastic amateurs – violent anti-Nazis, enemies of the Salazar regime and many others. We got lots of little tips from unexpected quarters. They took the form of drawings, plans, snippets of information and occasional photographs. One of the most prolific sources was my barber, who would furtively push notes into my breast-pocket when I got into his chair. Throughout the winter of 1943 many of these were concerned with 'Hitler's secret weapons,' notably the V1 and V2. I sent over to Hamburger, the head of MI6 there, a representative half a dozen good drawings of what came to be known as the 'doodle-bug', the V1 flying bomb.

There were also secret and eagerly awaited reports of plots against the Hitler régime. Much of it was pure wishful thinking but one learned to distinguish the fantasy and reality. One of MI6's most effective agents was Klop Ustinov, the father of Sir Peter. He was a Balt who had been press officer to Baron Hoesch, the German ambassador in London who preceded Ribbentrop and then died in mysterious circumstances. Klop was sent to Lisbon to make contact with certain German pressmen, which he had done most successfully. In the spring when I first met him he was hot on a secret trail leading to an attack on Hitler's life and an uprising by the German High Command. In June his German contact was called back to Berlin for orders and in the process he had many details of the plan.

Klop was insistent that I should meet the man myself so that I could report to Cadogan first-hand. This was strictly against the orders given to members of the embassy staff – not to have any contact whatever with a German. However, I concluded that wearing my 'A' force hat it was permissible in the circumstances. So we met in the greatest secrecy in Klop's house in Cintra, a misty, romantic, beauty spot in the hills north of Lisbon. He told us the whole plan for the attack, with some names and places and even an approximate date in July. I let Klop make his full report and then endorsed it in one of my personal top-secret telegrams to Cadogan with a strong recommendation that it should be followed up. All that was sought was an assurance that if the coup succeeded His Majesty's Government would be willing to treat with the alternative government.

The rest is now history, with the failure of Count von Stauffenberg's bomb to explode in the right place on 20 July. As far as my telegram was concerned I received no reply from Cadogan of any kind. I suppose it was because the proposal would have been anathema to Stalin and possibly also unwelcome to President Roosevelt as incompatible with the doctrine of unconditional surrender. I always had the feeling that it was a golden opportunity missed which might have saved many lives, but I suppose it was also thought that it would not have taught Germany the proper lesson.

There was a sequel to this event. Quite soon afterwards my wife had an urgent secret call from an old 'A' Force colleague in Gibraltar via MI6 to meet a German fleeing from the counter-measures of Hitler and the Gestapo. He was arriving at three o'clock at Lisbon airport. He was a Dr Otto John and she was to take him under her charge and travel with him on the afternoon KLM flight to Gibraltar. He would be wearing a yellow buttonhole and she was asked to do likewise. After some discussion she agreed to go. They had got half way across Spain when there was serious trouble with one engine and the plane had to turn back. It was not a very agreeable prospect for either of them with the Sicherheitsdienst no doubt by now fully alerted. Still all went well and John spent the night at the office of MI6 while my wife came safely home; someone else accompanied him to Gibraltar the next morning. He came to thank Alice in London after the war and many years later was to become a controversial figure in East-West politics.

On Sunday 5 June we went to a special *corrida* at Campo Pequeno where Manolete, the famous Spanish matador of the time, was performing. During an interval we heard the news that Rome had fallen to General Mark Clark and his 5th Army. Things were looking up. The next morning I went out riding and came back just before the eight o'clock news. I turned on the radio; there followed the usual Royal Air Force march, at that time the daily introductory tune. Then the news came: 'Early this morning Allied ground forces started landing at several points on the Cotentin peninsula of Britanny.' First reports indicated that all was going well. Early as it was, we opened a small bottle of champagne.

Early in April I learnt that Sir Noel Charles, our ambassador to Brazil, whom we had known well in London, was passing through Lisbon with his wife on the way to take up the post of High Commissioner for Italy in Naples. We spent a pleasant evening dining together. Little were we to know that two months later I should receive orders that I was to leave for Naples myself at once as deputy high commissioner.

16

Co-Belligerents

The Rolls-Royce was distinctly pre-war but it had a fine high polish and the ambassadorial Union Jack was flying gaily on the front mudguard. We left Naples for Rome by the Capua road, the high commissioner and I in our gaberdine suits and green soft hats looking just as incongruous as the car itself among the mass of staff cars, jeeps and two-tonners pouring in and out of General Wilson's headquarters in the royal palace of Caserta. We had chosen the inland route, wishing to see some of the damage to each village and township in the final advance on Rome. Outstanding and heartbreaking was the Benedictine abbey of Montecassino which the Germans in spite of all their denials had in fact bitterly defended. With the non-stop bombing and gunfire over nearly six weeks, its whole front had opened up, exposing the pathetic little monks' cells. It looked like a honeycomb that had been sliced in two. The destruction was the same on a smaller scale everywhere we passed until we reached the Appia Antica road where the string of ancient Roman monuments was almost untouched.

The British embassy in the Via XX Settembre had been in the care of the Swiss minister since 1940. It had been scrupulously respected by the Germans and when we arrived there it was in perfect condition after a good cleaning. The house itself, lying right on the street adjoining the Porta Pia gate and part of the Roman walls, was a big and rather pretentious Edwardian building. Behind it there was a long stretch of lawn with flower beds leading down to the commercial department's offices. It was no great architectural loss when it was blown up by the Stern Gang, the Jewish terrorist organisation, a few years later. On the first floor it had a series of rooms for entertaining and running its full length at the back was a long gallery where we all sat after dinner parties.

Sir Noel Charles and his wife Grace, who kindly put me up at the embassy, were an attractive couple and very good company. They knew Rome well as he had been counsellor at the embassy up until the war with Italy. The chancery staff was almost non-existent. There was one highly competent second secretary, Aubrey Halford, and two honorary attachés, who in practice performed the function of ADCs. Anthony Nutting, a newly joined third secretary, arrived soon after. A year later he was to become a member of Parliament. Later, as the controversial minister of state at the Foreign Office at the time of Suez in 1956, he was to my regret to make a sensational resignation. He was a man of considerable ability and charm, but as his whole career had been so closely tied to Anthony Eden his action led to criticism which must have been extremely painful to him. We also had another young MP, Charles Mott-Radcliffe, just returned from stiff fighting with the Rifle Brigade in the region of Arezzo, who acted in a semi-military attaché capacity. Finally there was Sir Richard Nosworthy, the commercial counsellor, who was an old Rome hand who had served at the embassy before the war.

As far as I was concerned, there was only one drawback – there was almost no work. I was much puzzled at this, especially as I had been sent to join the High Commission at such short notice and had assumed that they were very busy. It was not until much later that I understood what lay behind it. Harold Macmillan had gone to Algiers in 1942 on Churchill's orders as resident minister and political adviser to General Eisenhower with Robert Murphy as his American colleague. Their particular field was the Allied relationship with the two French contenders for power, General de Gaulle and General Giraud. The focus then moved across the Mediterranean and with it both Macmillan and Murphy, while Duff Cooper was brought out to Algiers as ambassador-in-waiting to France. As events in Italy developed and the government of the country fell to the Allied Military Government organisation, the two political advisers became increasingly important. Macmillan's staff, though still small, grew larger, with Roger Makins, the most brilliant Foreign Office brain of my generation, at the head. There was much joking in Macmillan's villa at Posilippo about the 'Lord of the Med'. The foreign secretary, always suspicious of Macmillan, became anxious: something had to be done to restore Foreign Office control and so a full-fledged high commission established in the embassy in Rome became the answer.

As the battle raged across Italy from the Tyrrhenian Sea to the

Adriatic, the Germans slowly retired northwards. While the British 8th Army was advancing in the east, the American 5th Army was threatening Siena and then Florence, which finally fell on 24 August. The Germans had blown up all the bridges on the Arno except for the beautiful medieval Ponte Vecchio, and had then retired on to the semi-prepared Gothic Line running over the stiff mountainous region below Bologna. Had not Washington insisted on the withdrawal of their six crack divisions to supplement the purposeless American landings in the South of France, codenamed 'Anvil', the Germans might well have been driven right back into Austria that autumn. As it was, with the hold-up Churchill's dreams of an advance to Vienna and a total German collapse in the Balkans were swept away. We at the embassy could not help but feel that perhaps the White House was not altogether sorry that Churchill's ambitions in the 'soft underbelly of Europe' had been frustrated. Meanwhile General Alexander set up his field headquarters at Siena and prepared for a winter campaign on the Gothic Line.

A year earlier Mussolini had been overthrown. His short imprisonment ended with his brilliant rescue by air, planned personally by Hitler, from the Gran Sasso in the Abruzzi mountains, nearly 7,000 feet up. But he was never the same man again: shrunken and haggard, he had lost his nerve and from now on he did what the Germans ordered. He did not seek to stay in Milan, still less in Rome. The 'Social Italian Republic' of which he became president had its headquarters at Salo, a little town on the west side of Lake Guarda. A few army units remained loyal to him, but the main force of the *republichini*, as they were contemptuously called, was the Brigate Neri, the hated blackshirt militia.

At the same time the whole of the North was seething with underground activities, mainly Communist but also involving other partisan groups. The Communists fomented acts of violence leading deliberately to German and Fascist reprisals, which still further inflamed popular hatred. There was growing resistance organised by the Committee of Liberation of Northern Italy with branches in all the principal towns from Genoa to Trieste. It was greatly feared that when the final German collapse came, the whole North under growing Communist influence might hive itself off into a separate state with which our forces would find themselves confronted. At all costs we wished to avoid another Greek civil war on a yet grander scale.

[237]

An example of the results of such provocation occurred in a partisan bomb attack on a truckload of German troops in a street in Rome in March 1944. Thirty-three soldiers were killed and in consequence ten times that number of Italian political prisoners were taken from the gaols at random for immediate execution. This was carried out in secrecy in the Ardiatine Caves on the road to the Appian Way. Not long after my arrival it was reported that the site of the massacre had been discovered through, I believe, a goatherd who was a chance witness. The boulders at the entrance were rolled away and I, Charles Mott-Radcliffe and a few others from the Allied Commission went into the torchlit caverns to inspect. There they were, the wretched victims, lying on their faces in rows. In the dim light the scene suggested some giant box of matches that had been deliberately crushed underfoot. We went back to the Grand Hotel for a much-needed drink and ran into Virginia Cowles and Martha Gelhorn, who were members of the American Press Corps. Against our strong advice, they insisted on going in to see for themselves.

It had been arranged that Alice would join me in the autumn, having deposited Nicky at school in England. Meanwhile I had the luck to find an ideal flat in the Palazzo Capizzuchi, a late eighteenth-century building whose only defect, like so many others, was that it had no lift. It was in the Piazza Campitelli overlooking the Forum, with, in front, the great curving façade of the Teatro Marcello, mostly ruined but with a section turned into elegant apartments. It was begun by Julius Caesar and finished by the Emperor Augustus and was now known as the Palazzo Sermoneta. Our own flat belonged to a pre-war honorary attaché at our embassy and had been in the hands of the Swiss legation until Rome fell. It was full of tapestries and both Italian and English antique furniture. It had the advantage of having been occupied and carefully looked after by the major-domo, Adolfo, with his wife and family.

Adolfo was a remarkable character to whom, in those two years, I became much attached. He was not only the perfect butler and valet but a superb cook. To see him make a *fettucini verde fatto con uovo* was a revelation. He gently beat up the flour, water and a few spices with some eggs and a little spinach in a bowl and spread the paste on a clean wooden kitchen table. He then rolled it paper thin and, taking a sharp knife, ran it down by eye into dozens of even strips which went neatly into the big saucepan. I have never tasted its equal.

He greeted me with pleasure but obvious anxiety. 'How are things here in Rome?' I asked, after congratulating him on the beautiful state of the apartment. 'Ah, signore,' he said, 'bad, very bad. Non çe agua, non çe telefona, non çe lucçe, non çe niente!' Very few of what we normally call the necessities of life, let alone the little luxuries, were generally available. All food was hard to get but there was a raging black market. An Allied lira was introduced at a fixed value to the dollar, but this only appeared to be a temporary solution.

In August Churchill paid a visit to Italy for two weeks. After visiting the front he stayed a few days at the embassy where conferences took place about future policy on Italy. His son, Randolph, was working in Rome, principally, or so it seemed, busying himself in insulting all the grand Italian ladies who invited him into their homes. At one of the policy meetings, which lasted late into the afternoon, Randolph, who had been admitted out of courtesy and had helped himself to a very strong-looking glass of whisky, was continually interrupting. Suddenly the prime minister turned on him savagely. 'Randolph,' he said, 'will you shut up or get out.'

Another day Churchill received the whole Italian Cabinet, headed by Bonomi, the prime minister. There was Count Sforza, the foreign minister, anti-British and anti-royalist, for whom Churchill clearly had a special dislike. Also present were Nenni, the veteran Socialist who had shared a prison cell with Mussolini before the First World War, boastful and talkative; and Togliatti, the sinister leader of the Communist party, brought to Rome after many years of sojourn in Moscow, brooding and silent. Churchill opened the proceedings with a long address in his inimitable French. 'Obvieusement,' he said with that slight slurring of the letter 's', 'la situation d'Italie est très, très difficile.' It was putting it mildly, but it seemed to put fresh heart into the ministerial group.

There was also a visit to the troops by King George VI. He visited the 8th Army front as well as General Alexander's headquarters at the Palace of Caserta. He stayed at Admiral Cunningham's official residence in the Villa Emma on the Bay of Naples at Posilippo, where Lady Hamilton had beguiled Nelson 150 years before. It so happened that the King of Italy, Victor Emmanuel III, with his queen, the tall Montenegrin princess, had been lodged in the Villa Rosebery a little way down the sea front. Strict security was imposed on the area in which both houses lay, with a semi-circle around the bay, centring on the Villa Emma, patrolled night and day by a launch under the command of a midshipman. Soon after dawn a rowing boat was seen to pull out into the bay near the restricted area. At the oars was a small man rowing steadily. Sitting in the stern was a tall figure with a long rod. It was the King and Queen of Italy going on their usual morning fishing expedition. The midshipman hailed them and told them to keep out. On they rowed and this time there was a lot of shouting. As they drew alongside, the Queen is said to have handed the young officer her visiting card, but the shouting continued. Suddenly a window was thrown open on the first floor of the Villa Emma and a figure in pyjamas leaned out. 'What the hell is all this bloody noise?' he shouted. 'Tell them to shut up!' This was King George VI objecting to his sleep being so unceremoniously disturbed.

We had yet another distinguished visitor that month, Field-Marshal Smuts. Noel Charles was away on a few weeks' leave, so it fell to me to entertain him. I gave a small reception at the flat to which I invited the prime minister and the whole Italian Cabinet as well as a few senior Allied officers. Smuts had been speaking to several of the ministers while I stood beside him. Standing near us was the Socialist Nenni, as usual holding forth loudly. I saw Smuts listening intently; then suddenly he broke into the conversation, waving a stern finger. 'Mr Nenni,' he said, 'you must be careful. You are looking for grandeur and riches and power. You will end like Mussolini. My friend, you must be very careful.' Even Togliatti was taken aback.

My mind had long been turning towards a Parliamentary career. The end of the war was in sight and after Alice and I had long talks, I had decided to throw out some feelers in Conservative Central Office through the chairman of the party, Sir Thomas Dugdale. I had not expected to hear anything until election time and was surprised in September to get a telegram from Marjorie Maxse, the deputy chairman, asking me to come to London at once for an interview. It appeared that a candidate was to be adopted for the safe Conservative seat of Exeter. Although I had hoped for a rural constituency, Exeter, only seventeen miles from my home, would suit me very well.

I applied for some leave and duly presented myself at the Party Headquarters in Old Queen Street a couple of days before the adoption meeting. I was received most kindly by Miss Maxse who seemed optimistic about my prospects. I would have to attend a meeting of selectors together with several other candidates, answer questions and then make a short speech. If all went well, I would appear again before a full party meeting when a decision would be taken. It would then be my duty to spend as much time as possible visiting the constituency, speaking when required and in short preparing myself for the days ahead. Miss Maxse also made it quite clear that this would not be compatible with my remaining in my job in Rome. This put me in a dilemma. I was just working myself into a new and difficult assignment which would require my presence at a critical time. The whole future of Northern Italy was at stake: the Communist partisans had worked themselves into a key position which would require our most strenuous efforts if the whole of Italy were not to become engulfed in Communism, or even civil war. I told Miss Maxse that I must with reluctance abandon our plan. She understood and I arranged to take the first available plane back.

I was disappointed but decided I must try to get a seat in Parliament another time. During the few days I spent in London I had my only experience of the V1s. I read later that the total destruction was almost as heavy as that of the Blitz. It was an eerie experience. Walking down Victoria Street from Central Office, I heard what I knew was the hum of a flying bomb. I saw it through the cloud, still showing the light which when cut off meant that the engine had stopped and the bomb was on the way down. Then the light went out. I threw myself down flat, half in and half out of a tobacconist's shop door. There was a tremendous explosion somewhere behind Westminster Cathedral. Alec Cadogan recorded in his diary that at the end of July there had been 204 of these flying bombs in 24 hours.

While I had been in England there had occurred one of these events, commonplace in wartime, when one's plans were changed overnight. The position in Greece was getting more serious every day, with a full-scale Communist revolution developing. Harold Caccia had been sent at a moment's notice to Athens as political adviser to General Scobie, the British commander. Meanwhile I had been chosen to take his place as a vice-president of the Allied Control Commission (Foreign Affairs), to be combined with my present job at the embassy. I was delighted, as this would bring me right into the middle of political and military affairs with the prospect of an eventual advance up to the turbulent North early in the New Year.

On the other hand, it left me in the rather dubious position of having two masters – Anthony Eden on the one hand and the Supreme Allied Commander, General Wilson at Caserta, on the other. The Allied Control Commission, like the rest of the command, was now fully integrated with the Americans. I could see national interests might conflict but I thought I would cope. There was a further danger in that the new British high commissioner's duties also tended to overlap, with myself in the middle, with the activities of Harold Macmillan and his American colleague, Bob Murphy, both political advisers to the Supreme Commander. Fortunately we got on well together and his staff, Roger Makins and Philip Broad, were old friends.

I liked my American colleague, Bill Shott, from the word go. He was younger than I and full of bright ideas with an easy wit. Our office staff was all-American – a top-sergeant in charge and smart GIs as archivists and stenographers, and very good they were. I was amazed by the degree of cooperation and trust between the two sets of officers of the Commission. Differences of opinion were never on national lines and though there were fierce disagreements between departments, they were only on matters of substance. It was a real pleasure to be working with them.

Meanwhile the Communist newspaper *L'Unità* did its work each day with particularly vile and unjustified attacks and cartoons on the 'Luogotenente', Prince Umberto. The Allies had agreed that although Italy could not be accepted as an ally, as we were still at war, she would be welcome as a 'co-belligerent'. The result was the foundation of six so-called divisions – really only brigades – of Italian troops, many of them former prisoners of war. Under British training units known as the 'Blue', they quickly acquired considerable proficiency and when they finally reached the front line as part of the 8th Army, acquitted themselves well. The Prince took a keen interest and paid many visits to them then and later to those in hospital. He was tall, handsome and slightly bald. He went quietly about his work and was personally much respected by British and Americans alike.

The Italian government, and indeed most educated Italians, were hurt and resentful at the many controls we had to exercise over their doings, although I must say in most cases they behaved with dignity and understanding. One big problem which faced both of us was what was known by the Allies as 'defascistisation', to which the

Italians gave the less appalling name of *epuration*. Italian laws were introduced with severe penalties, including capital punishment. Special courts were set up in all the principal towns and trials were followed eagerly by the popular press. Sometimes they led to serious incidents such as the lynching of a senior Fascist official who had been seized from gaol. This incident led to the break-up of the Bonomi government in November 1944 with Nenni's Socialists and the Action Party dropping out.

In another case I found myself involved in a position where a sentence of death passed by a Roman court had to be endorsed by me on behalf of the Allied Commission. I studied the case carefully and became convinced that the death sentence was quite unjustified. I got Admiral Stone's agreement to commute the sentence. As it involved a grave decision, I also reported it to the Foreign Office in London though they had no official standing in the matter. I told them the execution was due to take place in three days; unless I heard to the contrary I proposed to commute it the day before. No reply came and the sentence was duly changed to imprisonment. I reported accordingly and got a real rocket in return – in a matter in which the Foreign Office could have no possible knowledge and had not bothered to answer in time. I was shocked by the incident where a man's life had been at stake and felt that this attempt to put their views ahead of those on the spot was yet another good reason for sticking to my decision to resign at the end of the war in favour of a career in politics.

Though I was always busy, there were occasional days of leisure. In the hot weather on a weekend we would sometimes drive to Civitavecchia for a swim in the sea and to dig for clams. Ostia, the nearest beach to Rome, was still full of German mines and barbed wire. Occasionally we went north to Lake Bracciano for a picnic and a swim but my favourite spot was Lake Nemi in the Alban hills south of Rome. It was a small, still piece of water, dark green in colour due to the steep hills around it but with an extraordinary feeling of peace. It was from the bottom of this lake that Mussolini had salvaged two ancient Roman galleys which had lain there since the days of Caligula. In remarkably good condition, they had been housed in a long museum building beside the lake. Only a few months earlier, out of pure spite, the retreating Germans had set fire to the galleys with petrol, leaving only the charred remains.

[243]

We also had within easy reach masterpieces not only of ancient Rome itself but also the medieval towns of Tivoli and the twelve Castelli Romani. Hadrian's Villa and the Villa d'Este were in striking distance and we took our occasional visitors there. In December I had the pleasure of seeing both my brothers, one an inspector of artillery down from the 8th Army front, and the other up from Foggia in the south where he became an instructor after Anzio. On Christmas Eve we all decided to attend the Christmas midnight mass at St Peter's for which our minister to the Vatican, D'Arcy Osborne, got us tickets. After we had been installed in our seats, a big crowd of American GIs, some rather drunk, pushed their way down the aisle nearby and tried to get into our row. There was a scuffle and poor Alice in her black evening dress had her mantilla pulled off her head.

After the armistice in October 1943, when the Italians had thrown open their prisoner-of-war camps in the North, numbers of British ex-POWs found their way slowly and painfully down the backbone of Italy hoping to reach British units. In some cases they got through, but many were forced to spend the autumn and winter high up in the mountains. The new Fascist government put a price of twenty-five pounds on their heads, but almost everywhere they were welcomed and fed entirely by the Italian peasants. I heard from a friend of a case where twelve POWs were looked after by the people of a small village called Gioia-ni-Marsi, seventy miles from Rome up in the Abruzzi mountains beyond Aquila. Their hosts were, it seemed, disgruntled because no one had been there to thank them. I decided to go myself. It was a strange story and I found that when the cold weather came our men had been hidden and fed in the villagers' houses even though there was a small German force in the place. They had somehow managed to pose as *contadini* and had actually played football against a team of German soldiers. They had even danced with them at the weekly hop at the village café! Unfortunately, one of them was later discovered by the Germans and the woman owning the house had been stripped to the waist and publicly flogged. She had, they told me, died of pneumonia and I was taken to see her grave. When I got back to Rome all I was able to get for the village was an elegant 'certificate of gallant conduct' signed by General Alexander, though of that they were very proud.

In our little department at the Allied Commission one of our concerns was the continued political manoeuvrings of the Italian parties. In this field we had constant conferences with the Chief Commissioner, Admiral Ellery Stone, the effective head of the Commission. In peacetime he had been a senior member of the International Telegraph and Telephone Company. In his uniform he looked like a lanky edition of Popeye but he was friendly and genial with lots of common sense. He had as his personal assistant Lieutenant Anthony Quayle, RNVR, destined to make his name as an actor, whom I liked very much. Below Stone came Brigadier Lush as deputy commissioner, whom I had known as Sudan agent in Cairo and more recently in Tripoli. There was also a big economic department headed by a vice-president.

In Italy for the first time we were invading an enemy country, even though a defeated one, and it had been necessary to set up and elaborate a scheme of military government behind the lines. There were thus three separate zones – the immediate battle area, an Allied Military Government zone run by British and American officers, and a zone which was gradually handed back to civilian Italian law. AMG moved forward like a band as we advanced up the leg of Italy. Sub-commissions from our office supervised other issues – finance, industry, agriculture, law, police, health and even fine arts.

One of the worst difficulties was keeping the Italian liberated areas supplied with food. There was near-famine in many places, for the Germans carried out a brutal scorched earth policy on top of their destruction of civilian premises and public amenities. A wet and intensely cold winter in 1944 added to the disastrous damage to the crops. To deal with this we had to draw on badly needed imports from supplies at home and elsewhere. All this had to be done by the economic section of the Control Commission.

At that time, under the armistice terms, our office was responsible for all Italy's foreign relations. They had no diplomatic bags, no cyphers and every telegram the Palazzo Chigi sent out had to pass across our desks. Fortunately my old friend Prunas from Lisbon had been appointed secretary general of the Italian Foreign Office and we were able to talk very frankly together. In these difficult and embarrassing conditions I decided that the only way to get on was to trust him completely; and it worked. Indeed, I sometimes had to say 'This is what the FO wants; the State Department are seeking something a little different. I can only tell you, speaking as man to man, that this is what I should do if I were you.' Italians have sometimes been accused of unreliability in such matters, but in eighteen months of often precarious situations, I was never let down by him or indeed any other Italian official.

In spite of his courageous dismissal of Mussolini, King Victor Emmanuel was unpopular for having accepted Fascism for over twenty years. There was continual pressure on him to abdicate. He resisted, and only on the day the Allies entered Rome did he finally appoint his son, the Prince of Piedmont, as Lieutenant General of the Realm. He was to have all the royal powers and the King was to retire to their villa near Naples. A few days later Marshal Badoglio, who had been prime minister since the fall of Mussolini, had also resigned. Signor Bonomi, an elderly pre-Fascist statesman and briefly prime minister in 1922, was asked to form a government. It was based on six parties, notably the powerful Christian Democrats and Socialists. Count Sforza, an independent and the *bête noire* of the Foreign Office, who had lived in America for twenty years, became foreign minister. He was a continual trouble-maker. The sinister Communist leader Togliatti, who had been brought into Badoglio's government after many years in Moscow, was given a minor position, no doubt waiting for his time to come.

During that autumn and the following spring I came to know Harold Macmillan very well. We were both technically on the staff of the Supreme Allied Commander and much of that work as well as that of the embassy overlapped. In addition, in an effort to soothe the ruffled feelings of the Italian government and people, a declaration was signed by Roosevelt and Churchill known as the Hyde Park Declaration, providing for transferring greater powers to the Italian government in all sorts of practical ways. Although ironically we were still technically at war with Italy, the title of 'co-belligerent' which it bore came close to that of ally. The word 'control' was dropped from the title of the Allied Commission and Noel Charles formally became the British ambassador. Italian diplomatic representatives were to be appointed to London and Washington. The political section of the Commission itself was abolished, though my own position there remained quite unchanged. Finally all the civil powers of the Supreme Commander were delegated to Harold Macmillan with the title of acting president. Thereafter I worked with him very closely.

I often stayed with him in Naples and found him a delightful host. By December 1944 he had also become deeply involved in the affairs of Greece with a Communist revolution on his hands. To the world's utter astonishment Churchill, Eden and Macmillan all spent Christmas Day 1944 together in the old legation in Athens under constant sniper fire. The prime minister could only reach the battleship where he was staying by armoured car. Eden and Macmillan travelled back by air via Rome and the Charleses gave a big dinner party at the embassy. It was all too clear that the relationship between the two ministers was far from good as I found from talking to Harold after dinner when his tongue was loosened by extreme travel-weariness and good claret. Finally he toppled over at the end of the long gallery but with our help the incident passed off without causing any attention.

Later, when the crisis was over and the Greek Communists were under control, Macmillan told me of another visit he paid to Greece. He had stopped at Mount Athos with its fourteen monasteries and its ban on all females from old ladies to cats. A special victory Te Deum service was sung at the principal monastery in his honour. As the archimandrite proceeded in the solemn procession up the aisle followed by the choristers swinging incense burners, Macmillan heard one of them, a red-haired man of about twenty-five, intoning as he passed by; 'It will do ye nae guid, it will do ye nae harm.' He was an escaped British prisoner of war who had sheltered there for three years.

The final advance to the north became our main preoccupation during that autumn and winter. We assumed that when the attack came the German forces, under pressure, would eventually swing back onto the line of the River Adige with their left wing based in Venice, and would then try to retreat north to Austria. This would leave the whole industrial plain of Lombardy, with Piedmont and Liguria, under the effective control of tens of thousands of partisans. The most numerous and far the best organised were the Communist Garibaldi brigades. The movement had been growing ever since the armistice and had been encouraged by the Allies with arms and cash. The trouble came when the Germans retreated and places like Floremce were full of armed men. There the matter had been easily handled and there was little trouble but the North was a different matter. There were said to be at least 50,000 partisans in north-west

Italy alone. If, as some military experts believed, all the German forces were to swing back intact to the east, there would be very few Allied troops available for the whole of the industrial North. An operation known as 'Tiger' was planned, under which one British battalion was to be sent in by gliders to Milan, which I was told I was to accompany. I was relieved that this was later dropped in favour of another scheme and, in the event, I and my new but elderly American colleague, Maclean, drove up north in comfort by car.

The partisan leadership of the Committee of Liberation of Northern Italy, in Milan, consisted of representatives of the six political parties which made up the government in Rome. There was no official political leader but later it passed into the hands of Ferrucio Parri of the Action Party after he had been liberated from a Fascist prison. There was also a financial section built up with funds smuggled by SOE with some local help. At the head of this was Alfredo Pizzoni, a leading member of the Credito Italiano Bank.

In practice, in both military and civilian affairs it was all a very loose arrangement, with little contact between the different parties, with the local leaders very often Communist. To strengthen it a dozen British SOE officers had been dropped by air near a string of towns fron Genoa to Trieste to act as liaison with the local partisan leaders and to help with funds and weapons. Each had his uniform with him for emergencies. At the head of this was a remarkable young SOE officer, Colonel Max Salvadori, based in Milan. He was half-Italian and bore the *nom de guerre* of 'Colonello Max'. With his tact and drive he was able to keep the difficult prima donnas of the six parties in comparative harmony.

There had been much active planning to deal with this problem of civil government in the North. The partisan movement itself had given birth to the creation of an organisation called the Committee of National Liberation. This with help and finance from SOE was active both in Rome and Florence before those cities fell. In the North there was the additional overseeing body, the CLNAI, with military and political wings. The former was under the command of a General Cadorna, the son of the Italian commander of that name.

Parri was a well-known intellectual and a member of the Action Party who had been imprisoned by Mussolini – but no one knew where. A young admirer, Count Eddie Songo, had carried out a search using the methods of Blondel looking for Richard Coeur de

Lion at the time of the Crusades. At each prison he sang one of Parri's favourite songs until he received a welcome musical response. Once found, there were immediate calls for Parri's release, but it only came about by a curious combination of quite unrelated circumstances. Allen Dulles, the brother of the future American secretary of state, was in charge of the secret OSS mission in Switzerland. Towards the end of 1944 the SS General Wolff in Northern Italy made an approach through Dulles asking for terms for a ceasefire. As a test of his credentials Dulles requested the release of Parri. This was granted at once and Parri became the leading light of the CLNAI.

Early in 1945 Admiral Stone suggested that when the time came my new American colleague and I should go forward with the American IV Corps into North Italy and Milan to help over many difficult political situations that would arise in the course of the advance and after. The idea was put to the US corps commander, General Willis D. Crittenberger, who decided not to take us with him for the time being. However, as it looked as if I should have to spend most of the summer in the North, it was suggested that I should take a short leave in England, which we accordingly did. The advance was expected to begin about the middle of April, so, for a week or two, Alice and I were able to be at Netherton with our son back on his school holidays. On 12 April we heard with sadness of the death of President Roosevelt. That same day I had a telephone message from the Foreign Office saying that the general had changed his mind and I was to return to Rome at once. The American advance was going very fast and by the end of the week I was on my way to Florence and thence straight on to the IV Corps headquarters at the front.

There was icy rain falling and a heavy mist when with other army traffic we crossed the Apennines on the narrow road over the Futa Pass on the way to Bologna which had been taken a few days earlier. We were soon down in the Po Valley, with Modena and Parma having just fallen. It was ideal tank country and on the 25th a pontoon bridge was thrown across the river at Piacenza by the American 1st Cavalry Division which had broken through the German line. Later on I met some of their officers who talked casually of having motored from there to the Swiss frontier. The pontoon itself was several hundred feet long and we bumped across quite comfortably and turned up the road to Cremona and Breschia which had fallen the previous day. By this time we were passing hundreds of German prisoners marching in line on both sides of the road on their way to the rear. At one point where we were held up, we saw a German General Wolff (not the SS commander of that name) actually surrendering to an American officer in a field on one side. Burnt out tanks and abandoned guns were everywhere. We reached Breschia as night fell and were shown to our one-man tents before a good dinner in the general's mess-tent.

General Crittenberger was a large smiling man with a round clean-shaven face and spectacles, whom I liked immediately and in a fairly short time we had overcome his distrust of diplomats. We were to spend much time together that summer. Ten years later when I was at the United Nations Assembly as minister of state for the Colonies I had the pleasure of being invited by the general to the US IV Corps reunion dinner at the Roosevelt Hotel in New York.

When I woke up next morning, I found that another tent had been set up during the night next to me on the right. As I looked out while I was shaving I saw a strange sight. There was a man in full Italian marshal's uniform walking from the new tent to a caravan with steps immediately opposite.It was Graziani. General Alexander emerged on the platform at the top. Graziani walked up the steps and saluted. Alex saluted in return but did not shake hands and they went inside. After ten minutes or so the marshal came out and the process was repeated.

There was a big American car waiting for Graziani with two American officers and a driver. The marshal sat in the middle at the back with an American on either side. There was a short delay while someone was sent to fetch an American cap for which Graziani had asked. He was apparently terrified of the Italian mob which had been howling for his death outside the prison during the night. Later in the day I found that it was my friend Colonel Fiske who about midnight had bravely gone into Milan in his jeep to fetch hin out to safety.

Alex appeared at breakfast smiling and full of his usual charm. Afterwards we were all asked to stay behind for him to address us. He told us how the German forces were on the verge of collapse and it was probable that only a few of those facing the 8th Army would be able to withdraw into Austria. After he had left, Crittenberger asked to see me and my American colleague Maclean. He explained that the main German forces had left Milan and that it had been intended to make a formal entry that afternoon. However, he had just learnt that the dead bodies of Mussolini and his mistress, with two others, had been hung up by their feet in Milan that morning. He was afraid that if we were to go in that day there was a risk that the Allies might be associated with the incident. He therefore proposed that our entry should be delayed twenty-four hours. I and my American colleague warmly agreed. Mussolini and his mistress had been executed on 27 April – directly contrary to CLNAI orders – high up on Lake Como at Dongo. Their bodies, with those of the other Fascist leaders, had been brought down to Milan in a furniture van and had been flung out in the Piazzale Loreto. It was just as well, for later that morning the newspaper *The Stars and Stripes* came out with a gruesome photograph of the scene. It was a horrible picture. They were hanging upside down with arms outstretched, Mussolini with his battered jaw half open. Poor Claretta Petacci was evidently not fully dressed and some kindly person had fastened a cord round the skirt at the knees to cover her nudity. I thanked God that we had not gone into Milan that day.

Later next morning, to everyone's surprise, the Luogotenente, Crown Prince Umberto, arrived by plane. He had heard we were to enter Milan and asked to be allowed to accompany us. The general explained that this would not be possible. He did not know whether Germans were still left in Milan or what demolitions there had been in the city. In the near future, he said, he would arrange a full public entry for the Prince.

After lunch, with a tank leading the way, we drove the general into Milan through Breschia and Bergamo. We had no idea what we should find. The sun was setting as we went through Monza when, across the railway bridge, we saw the afternoon commuters' train, filled with men and women returning from their offices. With some relief we realised that this meant that public facilities had not been destroyed. We drove into the city but there were few people in the street, though there was cheering from some of the windows.

Next day, with the corps commander and members of his staff, we met the members of the CLNAI and General Cadorena, the military commander, at their headquarters in an old monastery. We found them very pleased with themselves and, in spite of Parri's previous undertakings to the Allies, quite prepared to be obstinate about accepting the authority of the Bonomi government in Rome. It was hard to dispel their belief that it was the CLNAI alone which had liberated Italy. At our meeting I also found the banker Alfredo Pizzoni and Max Salvadori, the British SOE representative, who had been so largely responsible for keeping the CLNAI and the Partisan Military Command together and accepting Allied policy decisions. The immediate task was to get them to accept the authority of AGM in the form of a new regional commissioner, Colonel Poletti, a former lieutenant governor of New York State.

The new structure was not finally set up until the middle of May. The solution of the political problem took longer. After many meetings and consultations with Rome, on 5 May I arranged for Parri and other leaders, including Lonzo, the fanatical Communist, to visit Rome with me. After long conversations with Bonomi and his government little progress was made. On 14 May we returned to Milan with everybody bewildered and disappointed. A suggestion was made that Parri himself should be prime minister. It was not till after a whole month that this was finally adopted and a mixed Cabinet of North and South was achieved. It lasted five months.

A day or two later, wanting to see something of the outlying areas, I drove to Varese near the Swiss frontier. Some friends of mine in Rome had a large property nearby which I had promised to visit. The house with its caretaker and his wife had been quite unmolested, though on the main lawn there was now a big contingent of partisans camped with their cooking fires. In the village itself every house, including that of the priest, had a red hammer and sickle painted on the door. The village may have been in Communist hands but, as the old butler told me, this by no means represented the views of the majority of the villagers. It was a combustible situation but, with careful handling by the Allied Military Government officials, the takeover was completed. One of our problems lay in the fact that the members of the *carabinieri* had been cut to the bone under the armistice terms. We had often called for more of them but for some reason the combined chiefs of staff in Washington opposed it. In any case there were doubts whether they would be acceptable to the mainly Communist partisans in the three northern cities. To begin with it was even laid down that none were allowed into Milan at all and it was only at my insistence that the American commander finally called for them to be sent up. In the end all went well.

The German surrender came on 2 May. The next day I and my American colleague were asked by Crittenberger to fly to Turin to make contact with the CLNAI there. The German garrison had pulled out but there were still snipers in the post office and other buildings. We flew in two little Piper Cubs. Looking down on the airfield on arrival I saw an ant-like crowd swarming below us and waving madly. Apparently we were the first Allied planes to arrive. The crowd turned out to be about a thousand partisans, headed by two British ex-POWs in battledress with Union Jacks sewn on their chest and fully in charge. As we arrived in triumph at the Hotel Principe di Piemonte, we were told that the snipers never fired during lunch hour. After a brief meal, we went to the municipal building and were shown into a long room with a massive table like that in the Palazzo Venezia. Seated at it was a smiling young captain of the 9th Lancers in uniform, who had been dropped by parachute some time before. I asked where were the CLN, whom I was to visit. 'Oh, they're in there,' he said, pointing to the door. 'You'll have no trouble with them.' I gave them a short lecture in my best Italian and found they would accept all the Allied instructions. Then we flew back.

A few days later Prince Umberto arrived for a formal entry into Milan. Colonel Fiske, who had made the arrangements, and I met him at the airport. He asked to be allowed to use an open jeep. This IV Corps provided with an American GI at the wheel. As he moved out, two young Communist partisans with red scarves blowing in the wind jumped on each of the front mudguards. Off they went on a tour of the city, as good a target from the pavements or the windows as you could wish for. In spite of the enormous Socialist and Communist presence in many districts, the Prince had a friendly reception and was cheered for a courageous performance.

After the horrors of the SS torture chambers it was inevitable that there should be much violent retaliation. On the night of our arrival in Milan twenty-seven bodies were picked up in the streets and later the toll ran up to a hundred and fifty a night. In Turin the numbers were even bigger. There were so-called 'people's courts' which met in secret and after reaching their verdicts and carrying out the executions, flung the bodies out on to the streets. In many other towns Allied troops only arrived several days after the departure of the Germans had left the local Liberation Committee in charge. It also took time to set up the assize courts laid down by the law, but once done it still led to hundreds of trials and executions.

Once the new government had been formed, I went back to Milan to find myself required to make a series of expeditions to other trouble spots. The province of Bolzano with its rural German majority had actually been annexed by Hitler and had been the headquarters of the German commander-in-chief. On liberation there was urgent agitation among the German-speaking peasants for annexation to Austria. We were afraid that this movement was likely to lead to acts of violence and terrorism. The matter was not helped by the vociferous pleas in the House of Commons by a Unionist MP, Professor Savory (an Ulsterman of all people), for the province, with its neighbour Belluno, to be handed to Austria. I visited it several times to confer with the prefect and the Allied Military Government officers on the spot. I became firmly convinced that with an Italian majority in the city of Bolzano the correct decision must be to make no change. Apart from anything else, I felt that it would be intolerable to hand over territory to Austria, which was vehemently pro-Nazi up to the very end, from the Italians who had fought alongside the Allies. I gave this advice firmly to General Crittenberger and also in dispatches to the Foreign Office and hope that this had something to do with the final Allied decision to leave things as they were, with arrangements for a regional assembly.

There were also incursions by French troops into Liguria, all the way from the Mediterranean into the Val d'Aosta, where the French language was still largely spoken as part of the old principality of Savoy, the home of the Italian royal family. This occupation was openly backed by General de Gaulle, who authorised threats by his local army commander should we attempt to set up AMG. The position became critical and was only settled when General Eisenhower in turn threatened to withdraw all supplies to the French troops except rations. It was an unpleasant business, especially in the Cuneo valley where the French *maquis* were also particularly active. General Crittenberger had been asked to send someone down from Milan and to take charge. An American colonel, a Texan whom I knew in Rome, went off. He was very much a cavalryman, dressed in breeches, boots and spurs, and he carried a heavy hunting crop. Knowing that he also had a quick temper, I was a bit anxious. A few hours later I had a report that he had been addressing the local crowd at Briga, including a number of the French *maquis*, in English, standing on the bonnet of his jeep and cracking his whip. To our surprise it had the desired effect. Eventually, under the peace treaty, the French only acquired a small piece of territory, including Tenda and Briga, together with the King of Italy's extensive chamois and ibex hunting-grounds.

Finally there were the claims by Tito to large chunks of Venezia Giulia, which presented a much bigger problem. Much of the land was already occupied by Yugoslav troops, including the city of Trieste. Facing them were General Freyberg and his New Zealanders, all under the command of General John Harding of the British 13th Corps, with orders to occupy the city. The situation looked dangerous and was being dealt with at Cabinet level, so the Allied Commission was scarcely involved, However, when in the end Tito agreed to pull out of Trieste, I was asked to drive over there to talk to Harding in case we could help with the takeover. On the way I had a good lunch with Colonel McLeary, the commissioner for Venice, in his small *palazzo* on the Grand Canal. Inevitably he was known locally as 'the Doge'. I then spent a pleasant night at John Harding's splendid headquarters in Duino Castle and went into the city next morning to call on my only acquaintance, the MI6 representative, who had been there some time. 'The Jugs' had been moving out all night, he said, with their trucks loaded sky-high with loot – electric lamps, carpets and chairs, beds and bidets, even electric wiring. He showed me how they had stripped his own flat bare. This issue, which could so easily have led to fighting, dragged on for several years after the war, with Venezia Giulia being divided roughly into two, with Trieste and a narrow strip along the sea going to Italy.

During the summer events followed one another fast. On 8 May 1945 peace came to Europe and soon afterwards the Labour ministers pulled out of the government. Churchill called for an election and a stop-gap government was formed, in which Macmillan was appointed secretary for air. The election that followed with the rout of the Conservatives confirmed still further my decision to stand for Parliament. In the autumn I paid a visit to England where I was able to see Anthony Eden to tell him of my decision. He deplored my resignation and even talked to me about the possibility of my going as ambassador to Poland. When he knew my mind was made up, he offered to do all he could to help me get a seat.

From this point the Allied Commission itself began to fold up. Many technical commissions remained in the field but one section of territory after another was handed back to Italian government rule; only the disputed area of Venzia Giulia remained till the end. In July the Italian peace treaty was signed. I myself found my work much reduced and when Admiral Stone left to get back to his business life, I transferred my main activities to the embassy.

The main piece of unfinished business was the preparation of a referendum to be held on the question of the monarchy. The Labour government, unlike Churchill, were probably quite glad to see a republic, while the American government undoubtedly favoured it. Given the contrasting opinions held in Italy, with the South strongly monarchist and the North either Communist or Socialist and violently republican, Noel Charles and I had at first thought that things were better left as they were; but when the vote came in the spring of 1946 the republic was apparently officially approved by a substantial majority. However, the minister of the interior who conducted the referendum, himself a rabid Socialist, was on good authority said to have spirited bags equal to a million monarchist votes away during the night. King Umberto firmly believed this. Still it was perhaps just as well, for a royalist victory might easily have led to a Communist uprising in the northern industrial cities and perhaps wholesale civil war.

All this gave me some time for relaxation and was very agreeable. We resumed our picnics to the lakes and the sea nd often Alice and I had a game of golf. From somewhere or other Norman Fiske managed to find a dozen American remount horses, with which a few British and Americans started to play a little rudimentary polo. An Italian friend, Mario Panza, and a few other old members of the Roma Polo Club produced their polo ponies and soon we had a few chukkers going and finally even a tournament. How rudimentary it was is shown by the fact that I, with no great skill, came away with a prize for our team winning the final. Alex invited us to stay for a farewell ball at his house in Posilippo. Life was all very pleasant and relaxed.

D'Arcy Osborne had said that I ought to see the Pope, Pius XII, who had told him that he had no first-hand news of things in the North. I duly had an audience alone with him which lasted an hour and a half. Though he spoke reasonable English, we conversed in

French. He questioned me on every aspect of affairs, particularly the attitude of the council of CINAI and the attitude of the towns and villages. Milan itself was evenly divided, with the centre of the town Catholic and moderate and the outlying industrial suburbs Communist to a man. I had expected to find him stiff and secretive but on the contrary found him warm and talkative. On my leaving, he presented me with a silver medal.

The more we saw of D'Arcy the more we liked him. He had played a difficult and indeed a gallant role shut up in the Vatican for four years. He had maintained a valuable friendship with Pope Pius XII and the Curia. Later in the war he sheltered many escaping British prisoners of war, tucking them away in garages and safe houses all over Rome until they could move on.

Early the following year the first creation of cardinals since 1939 took place at St Peter's and the minister arranged for us to accompany him to the ceremony. There were thirty-six prelates involved, including our own Archbishop of Westminster and Archbishop Spellman of New York. It was a splendid scene with the whole interior of the cathedral ablaze with lights. The long scarlet-robed procession was headed by a cardinal wearing the inverted top hat of the Greek Church but scarlet in colour along with its flowing chiffon veil. He was no doubt a Uniate from the Ukraine. I felt that his prominent place was a subtle rebuke and a challenge to Stalin's anti-Christian régime. The rest of the cardinals, each wearing a red biretta, also had a twenty-foot scarlet train held by pages. As each one reached the high altar he would throw himself flat on his stomach on the marble floor while the Pope chanted the traditional words. After that His Holiness handed each cardinal his scarlet hat with its network of criss-crossed hat-strings. It was a unique occasion, a ceremony now largely abandoned.

In January 1946 I had a letter from Eden asking if I would become head of the newly formed Conservative Parliamentary Secretariat. After thirteen years of office and cosseting by the Civil Service the distinguished ex-Cabinet ministers found themselves without any outside help at all. Someone lent Churchill a small house in Wilton Terrace and the Party chairman, Ralph Assheton (later Lord Clitheroe), collected a band of enthusiastic young Parliamentary aspirants to man the new office. It included Iain MacLeod, Reggie Maudling and Enoch Powell. I have seen it claimed that these future stars were the choice of Rab Butler; in fact they were not and only came under his wing when in 1948 the Research Department and the Parliamentary Secretariat were amalgamated with the approach of the 1950 election.

My own job, with the benefit of a year in the Cabinet Office, was to organise the Secretariat as far as possible on Whitehall lines, with each man responsible for his particular subjects. We sought to provide briefs not only for ex-ministers but for all MPs and Conservative Parliamentary committees who wanted them. I myself was to take over foreign affairs (with later the help of the columnist Ursula Branston). I accepted with alacrity and was soon busy with preparations for our departure. While doing so I had a letter from Alec Cadogan begging me to reconsider my resignation and inviting me to come with him as his No. 2 to New York, where he had been appointed British representative to the United Nations. Very sadly I had to say no.

We had brought the Jaguar out of Rome six months before and decided to motor home in it. On leaving Rome we went to stay with Leonard Vitteti, an old Washington colleague, who had later been *chef de Cabinet* to Ciano. He was not yet accepted back into the Italian Foreign Office, but with his American wife had a lovely house in Perugia. With them we visited Assisi and afterwards admired the rainbow sheen of the black pigeons of the region, which I suppose St Francis must have known. The Vittetis also kept some in their forecourt. As we left I found a basket had been put into the car with a pair of these lovely birds. We took them back to England safely, no doubt in breach of all quarantine regulations and they settled down happily at Netherton. So did we.

Index